COOL CARS, HIGH ART

COOL CARS, HIGH ART

The Rise of Kustom Kulture

John DeWitt

University Press of Mississippi
Jackson

For the children
Michael, Christopher, and Deborah
and their children
Amanda, Jonathan, Emily, Jack, and Samantha

www.upress.state.ms.us

"Between Walls" by William Carlos Williams, from *Collected Poems: 1909–1939,* Volume 1, copyright © 1938 by New Directions Publishing Corp. Reprinted by permission of New Directions Publishing Corp.

Designed by Todd Lape

Figures and plates courtesy of the author unless otherwise noted
Detail of CadZZilla on page ii courtesy of Tony Thacker Collection

09 08 07 06 05 04 03 02 01   4 3 2 1
∞
Library of Congress Cataloging-in-Publication Data

DeWitt, John.
Cool cars, high art : the rise of kustom kulture / John DeWitt.
p. cm.
Includes bibliographical references and index.
ISBN 1-57806-402-3 (cloth : alk. paper) —ISBN 1-57806-403-1
(pbk. : alk. paper)
1. Hot rods—United States. 2. Automobiles—Customizing—
United States. 3. Art, American. 4. Art, Modern, 20th century—
United States. I. Title.

TL 236.3 .D48 2001
629.228'6'0973—dc 21   2001026368

British Library Cataloging-in-Publication Data available

Contents

Acknowledgments

Writing is often described as a lonely craft, but without the support and encouragement of friends and colleagues it would be an impossible one. I am fortunate to have friends like my brother Edward, my sister Linda, Merlyn Jackson, Bea and Norm Leopold, Bob Aronson, Keith Newhouse, Haj Ross and Arthur Sabatini and colleagues like Robert Ackerman and Camille Paglia, who are also friends, who buoyed me up when I was down and brought me back to earth when I needed it.

A number of students at UArts have given me insight into Kustom Kulture, but Steve McAlinn and Jonathan Stein have been especially helpful. Their openness, intelligence, and enthusiasm reminded me again and again why I am proud to be teaching here.

I would like to make special mention of the help of three individuals whose generosity was especially important to me and to this book. Each has given new meaning to the term "collegiality." Ivan Saperstein is a man I have never met, but, simply because his wife Elizabeth is a colleague, he generously gave of his time and expertise to advise me about legal matters concerning publishing, an area I had no knowledge of.

At the eleventh hour when I was desperate to finish the book and needed help with photographs, Harris Fogel, the chair of Media Arts at UArts came to my rescue. Taking time out from his busy schedule he worked tirelessly to rescue several faded negatives and poor prints.

I would like especially to thank my good friend and colleague Kent Christensen, who spent many hours reviewing several drafts of this book. His comments and suggestions have helped improve this book greatly. The only suggestion of his that I have ignored is that there should be more in the book about opera.

I am also very grateful to George Barris, Rick Dore, Sam Foose, Dean Jeffries, Gene Winfield, Larry Watson, Jim McNiel, Thom Taylor, and Richard Zocchi, who generously gave of their time to talk to me about their cars and the ideas behind those cars. On April 4, 2001 Kustom Kulture lost one of its icons, Ed "Big Daddy" Roth. His imagination and energy will be missed.

Over the last few years I have talked to many rodders and customizers who showed this unknown writer walking around car shows with a pad and a Chinon camera the greatest courtesy. Again and again I was struck by their generosity and enthusiasm. It is impossible to thank them all individually, but I would like to single out Bob Conte, the first custom car owner who agreed to talk to me at length, and Craig Hahn for the perspectives they provided on contemporary Kustom Kulture.

Thom Taylor, the designer, and Tony Thacker of So-Cal Speed Shop were particularly helpful through the long and frustrating process of locating photographs of cars I wanted to include and helping me obtain permission to use them. Every effort has been made to contact the owners of images. I would also like to thank Dave Boulé of Ford Motor Co., Car Craft, Rick Dore, Peter Eastwood, Bob Larivee Sr., Jim McNiel, Motor Trend, Jim North, Ed Roth, Greg Sharp, Larry Watson, Robert Williams, Gene Winfield, and Richard Zocchi for their help in this area. Despite the help of so many people, there are still a number of photographs that should be in the book that are not. Their appearance would have made it more comprehensive and, no doubt, better. As Kustom Kulture moves into the new millennium and, I hope, attracts the attention of more scholars, I think that it would be very helpful if rodding publishers created something akin to the "Rights and Reproductions" departments in museums.

I would also like to thank the Venture Fund of the University of the Arts which awarded me two grants that allowed me to travel to California to begin the research that led to this book and that allowed me to continue working on the book once I had a sense of its direction.

Craig W. Gill, Editor-in-Chief, of the University Press of Mississippi has been supportive from the beginning. When the book was still looking for its shape, he prodded and coaxed, but, ultimately, he let the book find its own way, even if that way included poetry, art, hot rods and rock 'n' roll. I couldn't ask for more. Debbie Self's attention to detail in her careful reading of the manuscript has saved me much embarrassment.

There is only one job more frustrating than being a writer and that is being married to a writer. My wife Judy has learned to deal with those frustrations very well. When she is telling me a life and death struggle that one of her patients (she is a nurse) just faced, and she notices that I am no longer really there, she will say, "What car are you thinking about now?" And I will say something like, "The Hirohata Merc." And she will laugh the way I couldn't. But she has given me more than tolerance. She also became my partner in this project, traveling with me to shows in Macungie, Gettysburg, and York, copying down names, talking me through ideas, helping me set up shots, and saying "Don't you have enough cars?" only once or twice along the way. I am more grateful than she can know.

INTRODUCTION

LOST IN THE FIFTIES

A recent series of commercials shot in docu-mentary black and white features groups of men in various settings: a carwash, a health club. At the carwash the men are in a waiting room as their cars are being cleaned. They are looking through magazines, staring in space, doing what men do when there is nothing to do. A station wagon emerges from the carwash. The driver's door is open. But there are no takers. There is only embarrassment. Who will claim such a car? Finally, the humiliated owner is revealed—"busted," as the voice-over tells us. The message from Mitsubishi is clear. There are cars that no self-respecting male should drive. Family cars like station wagons and minivans emasculate their drivers. If you want to regain your manhood Mitsubishi says, "Drive our SUV."

Even though the culture largely subscribes to the idea that "you are what you drive," men and women included, it is very hard to imagine a comparable ad campaign where driving any kind of car threatened a woman's sense of her femininity. Despite the obvious connection that many women have with their cars, cars are tied to issues of masculinity in unique ways. It is hard, for example, to imagine a man saying: "I wouldn't go out with her. She drives a Plymouth Reliant."

No portion of the automotive world is more tied up with stereotyped and conventional images of masculinity than the hot rodders and customizers who created a "Kustom Kulture" in the 1950s. For Charles Desmarais (1993) introducing an art exhibit at the Laguna Art Museum, Laguna, California, also called "Kustom Kulture," it is fairly simple—"it was a guy

Figure 1.
Classic highboy Deuce roadster with a typical raked stance.

Figure 2.
Chopped and channeled Deuce roadster. Notice how much lower the body is in relation to the wheels than the highboy's.

thing." But this guy thing, this culture, that grew out of deep and powerful connections to the car and what it means in America, is not so simple. When we look beyond the obvious, we find that this culture complicates and subverts our stereotyped notions of masculinity. As Temma Kramer writes in a catalog essay for the same exhibit, Kustom Kulture is more than speed and danger, or rebellion. It is not just about "Power," but "Beauty" as well:

> These young men became iron johns, small i, small j, who worshipped their Goddess, the Custom Car. This mechanical icon—the automobile—embodies both male and female principles. . . . The automobile is a synthesis of the Power and the Beauty metaphors of gender identification that post-industrial American culture has embraced. Worshipping her—the automobile—confirms manhood on the acolyte. (Kramer 1993, 44)

Cool Cars, High Art: The Rise of Kustom Kulture examines this particularly American male subculture that involves modifying stock American cars originally built between the 1920s and the mid-1960s through a complex set of strategies that transform them from mass-produced products of technology into unique pieces of art called rods and customs. These transformed, re-imagined cars do more than confirm masculinity in their builders. In their beauty, in the sophistication of their designs, and in their formal play, they parallel, in very specific ways, the ideas, techniques, and achievement of "high art" modernists. More recently, rods and customs have become decidedly postmodernist, again paralleling "high" culture.

This masculine subculture originally created largely by white working-class mechanics and bodymen, amateur and professional, has evolved over a period of more than half a century, producing thousands of significant works in a variety of styles. This body of work, largely ignored by critics, despite the longevity and the magnitude of the Kustom Kulture, raises ques-

Figure 3.
Full-fendered Deuce coupe. This coupe is chopped but not channeled.

tions not only about what we mean when we talk about art, but also about how accepted notions of gender, race, and class often prevent us from recognizing creativity in unanticipated places.

Rodding and customizing reached their high point during the period immediately following the Second World War and the assassination of John Kennedy. After a long period of decline in the sixties and seventies, the Kustom Kulture has been experiencing a surprising renaissance for almost two decades. In this reborn Kustom Kulture the same models that became rods and customs in the 1950s continue to be modified, often by the same men who built the original cars.

Kustom Kulture is not synonymous with the larger American car culture or the parallel culture with its own customizers that has grown up around the motorcycle. The car culture is made up of many subcultures, each with a particular connection to certain cars or certain types of cars. American car culture includes "low riders"—anything from a 1939 Chevy four-door sedan to a 1965 Chevy convertible to a 1992 Toyota Corolla—featuring hydraulic systems that let the driver raise and lower the car at will, allowing the car to hop, tilt, and drop down to the ground, hence the name.

The car culture also includes "street rodders" who love the "factory hot rods," the "muscle cars" built in Detroit in the 1960s. Others pursue their love of the automobile with European and Japanese sport and sporty sedans from BMW, Audi, Honda, and Toyota. The very rich lust after exotic sports cars like Ferraris. There are also off-roaders and pickup truck fanatics.

There are still many who find their automotive fantasies fulfilled with a vintage British sports car like an MG or an Austin-Healey, or by meticulously restoring a classic car from the twenties, thirties, or forties. Others concentrate on a particular car, Corvettes or Mustangs, for example. Almost every car has its loyal group of followers, including the Edsel, although probably not the Yugo.

While all segments of the car culture are interested in personalizing their cars through the addition of everything from souped-up engines to expensive mag wheels and mega-watt stereo systems, what separates the Kustom Kulture from the rest of the car culture is its passion for altering, redesigning, and, ultimately, reinventing stock automobiles, transforming them into something unique and expressive. They go far beyond mere accessorizing.

The two distinct categories of cars within Kustom Kulture—rods and customs—have their own set of practices and aesthetics, although they often overlap. Rods are generally built from pre-1936 cars, mostly Fords, but there were and are exceptions. These roadsters, sedans, and coupes are stripped-down and souped-up minimalist constructions designed for speed and to communicate a love of it. They come in three basic styles: classic highboy, chopped and channeled, and full fendered (see figures 1, 2, and 3).

Although cars have been customized since the original creations of Ford, Buick, and Olds, at the beginning of the automotive age, customizing became a cultural practice in the 1930s with prewar Fords and Mercurys. It eventually expanded to include almost every domestic production vehicle, although Fords, Chevys, and Mercurys were by far the most popular marques, built between the mid-thirties

and the early sixties. Customizers are primarily devoted to improving the looks of their cars. Although not completely indifferent to speed, they devote most of their attention to reconfiguring the look of a stock car through a process that applies individual imagination to a variety of standard modifications: chopping the top; lowering the car; removing stock components like taillights, grilles, and side trim so that they can be replaced with those from other cars after minor or major bodywork; extending and molding fenders; removing chrome insignias, door handles, even bumpers; and finishing the cars with highly reflective (and imaginative) paint schemes to show off the perfected surface of the car.

The hot rod, a quintessentially American creation, is a classic example of American ingenuity and eloquent testimony to its love of the machine. It is a cultural icon with deep roots in the psyche of American popular culture. The classic hot rod has an elemental beauty and a timeless form, and many are finished with a quality of workmanship that is a marvel, but the essentials of rod styling have remained basically the same for more than fifty years, despite some aberrations in the early sixties. Customs allow for far more expressive possibilities.

In the world of rods and customs one identifies himself as a rodder or a customizer, no matter how much respect and admiration one has for the other. (Rodders, however, have been known to sneer at the excesses of customizers. It was rodders who came up with the term *leadsled* to poke fun at slow ground-scraping customs.) Although I love rods, I find myself on the side of customizers. The wider range of options available to them and the greater risks they are willing to take in innovating makes the world of customs much more challenging and involving for me. Thus, customs play a more prominent role in this book than rods.

Kustom Kulture is more than a unique segment of the car culture which is "about" nuts and bolts and metalwork. Its history is intertwined with the invention of teen culture in the 1950s. The teen culture which emerged in a postwar California culture, already car obsessed and car dependent, embraced hot rods and customs as the perfect expression of its rapidly forming new identity. Rods and customs helped teens position themselves against the perceived conformity of the times. And, in turn, Kustom Kulture assimilated the language, the clothing, and the music that would become synonymous with youth in the fifties.

The fact that, after forty years the Kustom Kulture remains "Lost in the Fifties" as banners, plaques, and graphics declare at shows across the country where the cars from the thirties, forties, and fifties continue to be modified raises questions about the meaning of the decade in particular and the significance of nostalgia in general. These questions are an important focus of this book.

Customized cars and hot rods are often described casually in art terms; "rolling sculpture" is a common phrase repeated in articles about these cars. In most cases the term is not examined or explained. I take seriously the idea that these cars are art, not folk or popular art as might be expected, but an art which shares the same basic concerns, ideas, and techniques that high modernist artists demonstrated throughout the first half of the century. The original Kustom Kulture shared subject matter with the Futurists, techniques with the Cubists, Dadaists, Surrealists, and Abstract Expressionists and ideas with almost all the modernists inspired by the machine. They differ from high modernists only in

their medium (the car itself) and in the fact that rods and customs are created by bodymen and mechanics, not recognized artists.

When I began this study I was already aware of the striking parallels between Kustom Kulture and the practices of high modernism. What surprised me when I began to examine the contemporary scene more closely was how the Kustom Kulture mirrored the art world's shift from modernism into postmodernism. The debate surrounding the meaning of postmodernism, the so-called theory wars, with its abstract and impenetrable language, interests me less than what the debate has to say about ways of making. In all of the turbulence over locating the precise qualities of postmodern art and defining the postmodern condition, sight is often lost of the continuities between modernism and postmodernism. But, as a number of critics have pointed out, it is important to remember that postmodernism grows out of modernism, "It is a hybridization, a complexification of modern elements with other ones" (Jencks 1992, 12). To name just a few examples: Eliot's use of quotation, Cubist collage, and Dada photomontage and ready-mades lead directly to postmodern appropriation and heterogeneity; Pound's poetic method has strong connections with the postmodern love of the fragment. Precisionists such as Charles Sheeler have connections with postmodern hyperreality, and irony is as pervasive in modernism as in postmodernism, although of a slightly different sort.

Modern art offers a profusion of styles—cubism, futurism, surrealism, constructivism, abstract expressionism. Each was in competition with the others in taking the high ground as the most advanced, authentic, and innovative way of making art. In the leveled landscape of postmodernism, no style from premodern to post, from high culture to low, can claim legitimacy. For postmodernists all styles exist side by side as sets of equally valuable options in their art-making strategies. But it is the deliberate and conscious inclusion of history with all of its paradoxes, negations, and confusions, with the often contradictory social and cultural codes that it carries, that provides the uniquely post-modern frame to its use of pastiche, intertextu-ality, hyperreality, and pluralism. Postmodern art grows out of a new experience of nostalgia, often detached and ironic, not out of a commit-ment to artistic revolution. It is with this post-modernism that contemporary Kustom Kulture has so much in common.

Kustom Kulture is about making, and post-modernism offers a way of examining the con-temporary ways of modifying cars that illumi-nates the differences between cars built in the eighties and nineties and those built in the fifties and sixties. Despite being lost in the fifties contemporary rodders and customizers have not given up on their collective goals of making unique cars. There is still plenty of innovation and invention in the Kustom Kulture. It's just different now.

The book begins with a prologue—mem-ories of nights of "checking town" in Stam-ford, Connecticut—which puts me and my car on the edges of the Kustom Kulture in the 1950s. I am a solidly middle-class academic now, the first in my family, a large family made up of truck drivers, factory workers, office workers, and a "bookie," to go to college. The first artist I ever knew was Mr. DeLuca, a sign painter who lived around the corner on Vine Road. When he finished painting the signs for the High Ridge Sweet Shoppe or the Cedar Cor-ners Store, he painted for himself—pictures of surreal rooms with impossibly curved walls and

birds, dice and bottles falling from the ceiling, and women's arms rising from the floors. They were not very good paintings, but I have never forgotten them. I have done my best to look at the Kustom Kulture fairly and without preconcep-tions, but I must acknowledge that in many ways the story in this book is, at least partly, my story.

The first chapter, "The Invention of Kustom Kulture," frames the development of rodding and customizing, first in California and then across the country, in the context of the grow-ing teen culture that helped fuel its growth. While both teenagers and hot rodders existed before the end of World War II, it was in the postwar years that a number of economic, so-cial, and cultural forces accelerated the growth and influence of both worlds and quickly joined them together. The teen culture that grew ex-ponentially through the decade of the fifties drew upon the world of white working-class hot rodders for powerful symbols that helped solidify the new teen identity. The ascendancy of working-class culture and styles in middle-class teen culture is an important part of the story of the decade.

In return Kustom Kulture borrowed music, styles, and attitudes from teen culture. Borrow-ing elements of style from urban blacks, largely through rhythm and blues, the Kustom Kulture created its own version of *cool*. I examine espe-cially the close connections between the Kus-tom Kulture and rock 'n' roll. The role of media in both creating and exploiting hot rods and hot rodders is an important element as well.

The second chapter, "Making Art Out of Cars," deals with some of the issues that arise when one tries to categorize customs and hot rods: the reasons for seeing these cars as art works and determining what sort of art they might be. I discuss how attitudes toward cars and the working class often make it difficult for critics to recognize the achievement of rodders and customizers. I also consider the usefulness of such terms as *folk art, popular art,* and *high art* in defining Kustom Kulture. While there are legitimate reasons for seeing rods and customs as folk art or popular art, I believe that the most appropriate category for these creations, as works of art, is as an elite art, with no connection to any conventional elite.

Chapter 3, "Blue-Collar Modernism," traces the history of the Kustom Kulture in light of the ideas and practices of early modernists, particularly the Futurists. I detail early custom styles, inspired by the streamline and pioneered by builders like Westergard, Bertolucci, and the Barris brothers, with the Barris-built Hirohata Merc as a prime example. The connections between cubist collage techniques and the dada ready-mades and customizing practices are also explored.

The fourth chapter, "The Golden Age of Customs," deals with the full flowering of the Kustom Kulture between the mid-fifties and early sixties. Fueled by interest and money from a growing teen culture, rodders and customizers produced a profusion of new designs, techniques, and styles. In this golden era, bodywork, less dependent on the use of existing parts, became more sculptural, and paint became a more expressive medium as many builders developed their individual styles. The work of Bailon, Von Dutch, Jeffries, Roth, Winfield, and Watson appears in this chapter alongside a discussion of surrealism, dada, and the "pure sculpture" of an artist like Brancusi. The appearance of unique show cars and concept cars is also discussed. I conclude with a discussion of how Kustom Kulture almost ended in the 1960s and how it came to be revived in the late seventies and early eighties.

Chapter 5, "Back to the Future," examines the current Kustom Kulture, in light of notions of postmodernism. Beginning with the idea that we live in a mediated culture of nostalgia where history and historical references are so deeply embedded that they cannot be avoided, the chapter explores the impact of this reality in a culture that describes itself as "Lost in the Fifties." The Kustom Kulture is no longer what it was—a youth culture—yet it is bigger than ever. Still focused on cars built during the original era, it continues to innovate but in a postmodern way. The chapter shows how postmodern ideas of pluralism, intertextuality, pastiche, and hyperreality apply to contemporary rodding and customizing. The contemporary Kustom Kulture offers a profusion of styles historical and contemporary as well as blends of the two. The chapter points to CadZZilla, a 1948 Cadillac built in Boyd Coddington's shop in 1989, as the quintessential postmodern custom.

The afterword addresses the questions that arise when we consider a possible future for Kustom Kulture.

PROLOGUE

Back in the 1950s I would start getting ready for Friday nights early in the afternoon. I would pull my car into the driveway, turn on the radio, get the soap and polish ready, and turn on the hose. I attended to the hygiene of my car with an attention to detail I never applied to my room. I washed the car, polished it, and dried it with my mother's best towels. I scrubbed the wheels, the whitewalls, and even the wheel wells of my metallic blue, nosed and decked, lowered 1953 Chevy until there wasn't a spot or a streak on it. I wanted it to sparkle. I wanted it to catch the light.

I adjusted the teardrop spotlights so they were angled just right. I decided whether I wanted the Plymouth hubcaps with the bullets or to go with the red painted open wheels. When I was satisfied that the car was finally clean, I took it for a spin by the Catholic High School so that I could see what it looked like in the giant front windows. The wavy glass made it seem the car was under water or in a dream.

Saturday was date night. Friday night was for the guys—a night for "checkin' town." That's what we called cruising in Stamford, Connecticut, in 1959. On Friday nights all summer long you would see guys pull their freshly polished Fords and Chevys into the Esso Station on High Ridge and ask, "What do you want to do?" as if they didn't know that the answer was always going to be, "I dunno. Do you wanna check town?"

By eight o'clock the cars, usually with two or four guys—one was pathetic, three was awkward, and five was too crowded to be cool—would begin the circuit, checkin' town, slowly circling the downtown, up Atlantic, across Main, around City Hall, by the Plaza and the Palace theaters, to see if there were any interesting-looking girls waiting in line—girls from the west side of town with their impossible hair, their frosty pink lipstick, and their white pedal pushers so tight that they seemed more genetic than woven.

On a good night there might be forty or fifty cars making the long circuit. Most were not especially remarkable cars. They were mildly customized at best—nosed and decked, lowered in the back, spinner Olds or Dodge Lancer hubcaps flipping over slowly in the glow of streetlights and storefronts—but there was always the chance that Jerry Harold's Deuce coupe, Russell Grady's incredible black-lacquered chopped '57 Olds, Jimmy Karcher's pretty chopped '50 Ford convertible, or Jimmy Kenny's gleaming violet '55 Ford Crown Vic would show up and add some glamour to the night. One night we saw a '56 Buick convertible parked across from the drive-in. It was a candy apple blue, the first true candy color in town. We drove by it a hundred times. From car to car the word was passed: "Did you see the candy Buick?"

Sometimes the fun would be seeing Dombroski's permanently unfinished '50 Chevy, in a primer as gray as flannel with all the chrome removed, but the holes left defiantly unfilled, pull up next to a custom—he didn't like customs—and gun the Corvette mill that was shoe horned into the engine compartment as he issued a loud challenge to race. If there was any hesitation, he would yell at the nervous driver next to him, "Hey, this ain't no beauty contest, man!" Or Sonny Bennett might take the hood off his beat '48 Chevy sedan to show off the six carburetors on his GMC six. He liked to run without

air cleaners so that everyone could hear those carbs sucking in tons of air. Along with Jimmy Karcher, Roger Arnow, and Moppy Buchanan, they made up the core of the Twin Ridge Auto Club. The name wouldn't scare members of the Rotary club, but they were the outlaws of north Stamford. Much older than we were, in their twenties, they were the stuff of legends.

After checking town we would head toward the beach by cruising down Elm Street to Shippan Avenue. Cars were already lined up across from the Starlite Drive-in Theater under the bright lights that showed off new candy paint jobs and gleaming chrome. Even in the middle of the summer you could see the jackets of Cambenders, Sabres, Chancellors, Nomads, Charter Oak MC, and Twin Ridge AC on the backs of drivers slumped against their cars or bikes as we drove past. We would eye each other. Occasionally a car would leave the line and be replaced by somebody taking a break or needing a beer. But you didn't get in line unless your car was worthy.

The pace was slow—very, very slow. There were nights when drivers never shifted into high gear as they made the circuit. A driver might wave to a friend with the point of a finger, nod his approval of a newly finished car, or issue a challenge or a sneer through his dual exhausts, but there really wasn't a lot of interaction. Checkin' town was about being cool.

Along the way there might be a stop at the Tastee Freeze or Jo-Ann's Drive-in for a burger and a malted. There, the standard greeting was "What's happening?" And the answer was always the question repeated. Somebody always made a run to Port Chester or Armonk in New York where the legal drinking age was eighteen for a case of Miller's or a couple of "sixes." Church keys (can openers) were passed from back to front seat according to a number of elaborate rituals.

The next stop on the route was to check West Beach to see what was happening there. On a good night you might hear about a fight being arranged in the parking lot, maybe somebody from the Ridges against somebody from the Cove to see who was "badder." Then the circuit was repeated with minor variations again and again until deep into the night. Always with the radio on. Sometimes you could hear the same song playing on a dozen radios as cars passed each other slowly on this complicated parade route.

We were always on the lookout for something new. Some new car. Some new look. Some new direction in style. One time a bright red, almost new, raked '58 Impala with a Corvette grille was checking town, maybe accidentally, with the rear windows rolled up. It made the hardtop look like a sedan. For a whole summer

after that it was cool to leave the rear windows up no matter how hot it was. It was also cool to drive with just your parking lights on, no headlights until you got out of town.

Toward the end of the night there might be a trip up to the North Stamford Reservoir where a quarter-mile stretch of road had been marked off with painted start and finish lines and where there might be some late-night racing or just a chance to test your driving skills. This was not a place for money races. It didn't matter how fast your car really was. There was just something about being in a race that made you feel connected to the best cars in town. So Teddy Honcherik might race his father's station wagon against Peter George's father's Buick. It didn't matter if they didn't get much over fifty. It was a drag race. Just like in the movies. Just like real life.

That is the way it was in the fifties. This is the way I remember it.

COOL CARS, HIGH ART

THE INVENTION OF
KUSTOM KULTURE

When hot rodders began to appear in significant numbers on the streets of southern California in the late 1930s, the last thing on their minds was making art. They were in love with speed. They reveled in grease, garages, and gas stations. They were mechanics and bodymen, not teen rebels with or without causes. If they wore leather jackets, it was more to protect them from the biting wind whipping at them in their open cars than to look cool. The main thing on their minds was figuring out ways of going faster than the other guy. They took their rods to the dry lake beds of California—Muroc, Harper, Rosemond, El Mirage (see figure 4). They went to the lakes because the lake beds were flat and dry and wide open. You could drive all day on them. As fast as your car could take you. "All of the best and fastest rods ran at the lakes" (Montgomery 1987, 53). For Bruce Johnston, early car builder and racer, "it was a wild scene." There were "guys running in every direction. They had a few fatalities. I don't think we even had an ambulance" (Medley 1990, 108).

Besides running on the dry lake beds, rodders also were very much involved in short track racing, especially after the war. These races involved cut-down roadsters that looked a lot like midget racers, especially the nose. They ran on oval tracks up and down the West Coast. The car on the first cover of *Hot Rod* magazine in 1948 was a track roadster (see figure 5).

Figure 4.
Lakes racing in the late thirties. Courtesy of Peter Eastwood.

Rodders spent most of their waking moments figuring out how to get just a few more rpms out of high gear or how to shave a few pounds off their Model T's and A's or '32 roadsters. The look of these cars was designed to appear extremely functional—fenders and hoods removed, engines exposed, open wheels, sitting high, with cut-down windshields. It was a no-nonsense look (see figure 6). Early rods were not particularly beautiful cars. They weren't meant to be. They were rarely finished with the attention to detail that later rods received. Many were not even painted. They were just left with a patchwork of primer and original paint. Many deserved to be called jalopies.

But there was something primal and elemental about them—something that communicated a distinctly American love of the machine that couldn't be denied. There was no questioning their purpose. They were about speed. These primitive early Model T's and A's evolved into the quintessential rod of the forties and fifties, the beautifully finished Deuce "highboys" that have become synonymous with the term *hot rod.* From the beginning, however, the appearance of rods was about something more than pure function. Early rodders were laying the groundwork of an emerging aesthetic:

There was more behind these modifications than simple weight reduction and the improvement of aerodynamics. The actual weight of a chrome ornament is negligible, and the removal of certain items, such as fenders, can actually degrade aerodynamic performance (understanding of automotive aerodynamics was limited before the 1960s). What is really behind these changes is the cultivation of an image: the image of the single-minded, no nonsense pursuit of speed. (Robert Jr. 1984b, 186)

The performance they managed to wring out of flathead (or valve-in-head) V-8's and even little four-cylinder Fords and six-cylinder Chevys was remarkable. In an era when phrases like "going like sixty" and a "mile a minute" were something of an hyperbole, rodders routinely took their cars over a hundred miles an hour with engines that began life with much less than a hundred horsepower in cars that the average American considered hardly more than mere junk.

The two most effective and obvious methods that early rodders had of increasing the speed of a stock vehicle were increasing horsepower and decreasing weight. And there were generally two ways of increasing horsepower. The first was to modify the existing engine— "to soup it." Carbs were added. The size of the cylinders and the length of piston travel could also be increased. The heads and the pistons could be changed or altered for increased power. Even something as simple as switching to thinner head gaskets would add power. More efficient exhaust systems, often simple straight pipes, and modified ignition systems also increased the power of the stock engines. Engines could be perfected by smoothing every surface that might interfere with the flow of fuel or exhaust gases. Each specification could be set to the tightest tolerances, far exceeding the standards set by the factory.

Another way to increase power was to swap a more powerful engine for the original or stock engine, a V-8 for a four cylinder, for example. The rodder who "souped" a swapped engine had the ultimate rod.

The second approach, decreasing weight, was obsessively pursued by many rodders, because it didn't cost anything to remove the fenders, the bumpers, the hood, the ornaments, and even the front brakes. It cost nothing to drill metal out of the frame, unless the car was so structurally weakened that it broke apart on a particularly hard shift or tight turn.

In addition there were dozens of tricks that rodders developed to gain an edge on the

Figure 5.
Track-T roadster. The Kraft-T roadster was originally built by Dick Kraft in 1951 when it was shown at the Oakland Roadster Show. It was first restored in the seventies by Ron Weeks. Now owned by Art Bastian, who brought it back to the configuration it had in 1962 when it appeared on the cover of *Hot Rod*. One of the seminal rods.

Figure 6.
Early rod. These rods weren't all showpieces. The idea was to get the car on the street as quickly as possible. Many never were finished. Courtesy of Peter Eastwood.

competition, like rigging the rear end to lock the wheels together to prevent slippage on acceleration, or adding a mixture of kerosene, hot water, and detergent to the carburetor before a run to steam clean the jets, or drilling out stock carburetor jets to increase the flow of fuel to the cylinders. Early rodders fed on each other's creativity. If somebody got the performance of a high-cost oil pump for almost nothing by combining two cheap stock pumps, the next week there were a dozen such combo pumps at the track.

Early rodders in California were able to perfect their rods and push them to their limits because they had easy access to flat, dry lake beds in unpopulated desert areas, a relatively safe environment for high-speed runs that were almost impossible to find in the rest of the country. The weather helped too. Topless and fenderless roadsters weren't very practical in the Pacific Northwest or northern New England. Because of these wide open spaces, the early racers were more interested in top-speed performance than in rapid acceleration. But as more rodders appeared on the streets of Pasadena and Bakersfield, Bellflower and Modesto, there were inevitable challenges. Even an hour's drive to a lake bed was too far to go to settle things, so drag racing ("racing on the main drag," one of several possible etymologies for the term) became more prevalent.

Drag racing on the streets of California led to the growing public image of hot rodders as "outlaws." Almost in self-defense, communities, often with the support of the police who were tired of chasing street racers and too often not catching them, helped create places where rodders could race safely off the streets. Access roads were closed off. Old airstrips were converted to relatively safe tracks to race on—dragstrips, they were called.

According to Robert Post, the first officially sanctioned strip was a temporary one on a small section of access road near Highway 101 just north of Santa Barbara. In 1949 with the permission of the California Highway Patrol a half-mile section of road leading to a small landing field was closed off with portable fencing to allow for the Santa Barbara Acceleration Association to run drag races. A year later the first official dragstrip was opened at an airfield in Santa Ana, California. After that, strips began to open all over California as well as in scattered locations across the country organized by local timing associations (Post 1994, 1–5).

In the early fifties the National Hot Rod Association (NHRA), formed by Wally Parks and others to promote drag racing, began a campaign to make hot rodding respectable by sponsoring community-oriented projects like safety inspections and charity clothing drives. In a short time dragstrips under the guidance of the NHRA brought rules, regulations, safety measures and, through *Hot Rod,* more attention to the sport as records established for the newly created classes set standards of performance for almost every type of car. This quintessential American form of racing grew rapidly as sanctioned strips were opened across the country, although every town still seemed to have its own little outlaw dragstrip on the edge of town. To this day there is a lingering aura of the outlaw around the sport of drag racing that no amount of corporate sponsorship can dispel.

As it has evolved in the sport of drag racing, the ultimate hot rod is not really a car at all, not in the ordinary sense, but a top fuel dragster, the ultimate acceleration machine. A dragster is simply a highly modified engine sitting on incredibly long rails, between massive slicks (smooth tires) in the rear and narrow tires up front. Piloted by a driver sitting in front of a massive supercharged engine, it has one simple goal—to cover the 1,320 feet of the track as quickly as possible. Designed for straight-line runs, these vehicles have a difficult time making a simple turn (see figure 7).

The early standard for high performance was to wring one horsepower per cubic inch out of a modified flathead engine resulting in about 200 to 300 horsepower. A dragster in the early fifties could make it through the traps in about eleven seconds. At the end of the decade a top fuel dragster (running very potent nitromethane fuel instead of gasoline) could negotiate the quarter mile in under nine seconds and reach speeds in the 180s. Today, speeds in the high 290s for top fuel dragsters are simply disappointing, and since 1992 the 300 mph barrier (a speed thought theoretically impossible by some in the 1950s) has been broken routinely. In November of 1998 Gary Scelzi reached a speed of 326.44 mph at the end of the quarter mile. From a standing start dragsters can reach the end of a quarter mile in a little over four seconds. Their completely reworked Hemi-headed engines, still based on the original Chrysler Hemi engine of the 1950s, produce thousands of horsepower.

Contemporary top fuel dragsters have no more to do with the amateurs who began the sport than the average pick-up basketball game has to do with the NBA. Corporate-sponsored dragsters and funny cars—essentially front-engined dragster frames with very lightweight bodies designed to look vaguely like stock bodies—look like nothing you would see on a highway and are useless for anything but going in a straight line. Their extraordinarily long bodies are extremely light, sometimes made out of titanium. A single engine can cost $60,000, sometimes more. Builders have access to expensive wind tunnels to test a car's

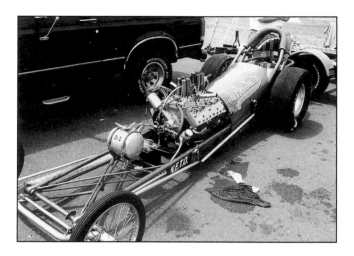

Figure 7.
Mid-fifties Slingshot dragster with a flathead engine. As drag racing has become more expensive and more professional and more remote from the ordinary driver, there has been increased interest in recent years in nostalgia drags, which brings original race cars—roadsters, altered coupes, and slingshot dragsters—back to the track.

aerodynamics. Almost every crew has a computer system, with more computing power than supports the average space mission, that can analyze everything from fuel mixture to tire adhesion. Cylinders are individually tuned for maximum efficiency. The life of engines is measured in minutes not miles. It is a multi-million-dollar sport.

The pioneers who created the sport of drag racing could not have envisaged how big it has become. They were the archetypal "grease monkeys" or "gearheads" who could turn an ordinary nothing car into a very fast something guided only by their exceptional car sense. Cars were tuned mostly by ear, not by computer or even gauges. The issue of money concerned how little the builder could spend not how much. In the midst of the Great Depression it was possible to find a working old Ford for as little as five dollars and parts for almost nothing. Junkyards were full of spare parts and, if rodders couldn't find what they needed there, they could make it in machine shop at school. Either at school or at home or at the friendly neighborhood gas station, exhaust systems could be fabricated, intake manifolds concocted, and cam shafts redesigned. This is the way that legendary names in hot rodding—Vic Edelbrock, Ed Iskenderian, and Dean Moon—whose companies still exist, supplying performance parts to contemporary rodders, got started in the 1930s.

Automobiles were his obsession and by sixteen Dean [Moon] was totally infatuated with V-8 roadsters. He loved anything that had the smell of going fast. His sense of automobiles and business led him to making fuel blocks that could deliver equal fuel pressure to multi-carburetor set-ups on flatheads. He fabricated fuel blocks in an old shed behind the Moon Cafe at night and bused tables before school—all while attending Whittier High School. (Fetherston 1992, 123–24)

These gearheads felt an almost mystical connection to their cars. They were dedicated disciples of speed. Henry Felsen's novel, *Hot Rod,* reprinted sixteen times between 1950 and 1964, celebrates, with the lurid passion of a Peyton Place, the love affair of an American high school boy and his car. It is Romeo and Juliet without the complication of Montagues and Capulets. It is about a Pygmalion who sculpts a machine image of himself to fall in love with. This archetypal American romance, man and machine, is completely fulfilling and completely safe because it is ultimately narcissistic:

No matter what his mood or his feeling, his trouble or his joy, it made everything right and good to be guiding his car, the car he had built, that belonged to him, that owed everything it was to him. Not a day passed without Bud's taking time for a spin. It was more than a ride; it was more than speeding; more than killing time. In some ways these daily sessions on the road were his hours of meditation, of true self-expression, the balm of his soul and the boast of his spirit. In those flying hours he had sought himself out, molded himself into what he was, and found his creed.

Bud's car, variously called his baby, hop-up, strip down, roadster, heap, hot rod, jalopy or set of wheels, was like Bud himself. In a way he had built a mechanical representation of his life, and its oddly-assorted parts could be likened to his patch-work past. (Felsen 1950, 17)

This quasi-religious, thoroughly romantic, sense of identification with the machine as the source of meaning in one's life was not confined to fiction. In the car enthusiast Albert Drake's memoir of the late forties and early fifties he reverently describes the many pilgrimages he made to find just one more car that had been modified in an inspiring way:

I was enormously interested in *any* car that had been modified. I walked around the city feeling the thrill of anticipation. I looked up driveways, toward garages, and in back yards. If I saw a Model A with sixteen inch wheels parked at the curb I shoved my face against the louvers to see if I could make out the shadowy configuration of a V-8, or twin carbs on a four barrel. I dropped to my knees before the front bumper as if in worship of this machine to see whether the car had hydraulic brakes. Everything was new to me, and I savored the thrill of recognition when I could identify any alterations. (Drake 1982, 14)

These early rodders had not yet achieved a level of "cool" and they didn't care. They were more like today's techno-nerds and computer geeks who might have some panache in Silicon Valley, but hardly anyplace else. Dean Batchelor, one of the pioneers of hot rodding, remembers those early days: "We were the school outcasts, always fiddling around with cars, and then taking them out to the desert to see how fast they'd go. Dirty? God, it was dirty. When the wind blew, which it did often, then alkali dust got into everything, turning us and our cars a chocolate brown" (Batchelor 1989, 70).

If rodders had been content to run the desert dry lakes or the dirt tracks, they probably would have remained just a footnote in America's long history of tinkerers. But as street racing became identified with rebellion and equated, through the hysterical attention of the media, with danger, that aphrodisiac of youth, a car culture with its own rituals and rules began to develop across California from Sacramento to Los Angeles, from Modesto to Long Beach, from Arrow Highway in the San Gabriel Valley to Baker Street in Orange County. From there it spread across the country. An image of the hot rodder emerged that fit exactly the need the exploding new population of teenagers had for role models to help shape their newly forming identities. Mixed with rock 'n' roll this image of the hot rodder was a potent combination, a cultural nitromethane.

It was a culture that shared something with the Old West, as the paintings of Robert Williams frequently suggest, often mixing cowboy with hot rod imagery. Drag racing borrows from myths of gunslingers and outcasts always on the move, coming down to two guys facing each other to see who's the fastest in town.

Two cars would line up at a light. One driver would begin to race his engine. If the other accepted the challenge, he would race his. When the light changed, they were off.

Sometimes, before there was even a race, a driver would realize that he was overmatched just from the sound of his opponent's engine. He might nod or just back off. Sometimes the word would go out to the owners of fast cars that there was a new car in town, a car that looked hot, that was cruising the strip looking for action. Sometimes the races were for reputation, sometimes for money or pink slips, titles to the cars themselves. Some drivers brought back up to races, friends, intimidating looking friends, who carried baseball bats, wrenches, or even guns, to make sure that bets were settled. Some builders went so far as to create "fake out wagons," cars that looked ordinary, even beat, but with very hot souped-up engines under the hood, to lure unsuspecting drivers into a race.

Don Montgomery, a pioneer of rodding and chronicler of its history, recounts his memories of racing on the streets of southern California in the late forties:

Each town or locality had one or more drive-ins where rods could be found. Some drive-ins had "scheduled" race nights when "everyone" would be there. Wednesday night might be at "Picadilly" (Culver City) and Larry and Carl's (Pasadena) while Thursday night was at Simon's (Five Points) and Carpenter's (Arcadia), and so on. Weekends were usually reserved for social date nights. . . .

A string of roadsters followed by a group of cars leaving a drive-in was an indication that the evenings [sic] races had been organized. Generally little used semi-rural streets were selected. The trip from the drive-in could range from 1–10 miles. Remember that with California's much smaller population then there were many roads and streets with little night traffic. (Montgomery 1987, 20–21)

Often the drive-ins were associated with a particular car club. Clubs began to proliferate in the early 1950s as more and more modified cars began to appear on the roads. No longer isolated mechanical prodigies, rodders found that together they could work on one another's cars, bench race (imaginary confrontations of the fastest cars in the area), sponsor various events, like cruises and local car shows, and support each other at the races, sanctioned or street, or just share their obsession with cars. The names of many of the burgeoning new car clubs reflected how rodders wanted to be seen. They were the new aristocracy of the road: Road Kings, El-Reys, Lords, Counts, and Dukes. They had class: Ambassadors, Diplomats, Hi-Hats, Swanx, and Aristocrats. Or they embraced rodding's rebel image when they joined the Road Rebels, Rogues, Drifters, Satan's Angels, Outlaws, El Diablos, Nomads, and Vampires. Others were content just to let the world know that they loved cars: Cambenders, Gear Grinders, Idlers, Rev Masters, L.A. Roadsters, Shifters, Torquers, and Twin Ridge Auto Club. Club members, wearing jackets like bikers and urban street gangs, were easy targets for exploitation by the media, although they were, in fact, unlikely to be involved in crimes more serious than traffic violations. But the attention they received and the outrage they spawned brought attention, even glory to being a member. Teens found that nothing was more frightening to adults than a group of them wearing the same jacket.

Teenagers certainly weren't invented in the 1950s. The term *teenager* first appears in print in 1941 in *Popular Science* magazine (Hine 1999a, 72). It was already in wide use by the mid-1940s (Palladino 1996, 93). And no doubt thirteen- to eighteen-year-olds have presented problems to parents ever since Cain and Abel. Joseph Kett (1977) has traced the unique and enduring issues of adolescence in America from the 1790s through the 1970s. Thomas Hine, who covers a similar span of time in his recent book, *The Rise and Fall of the American Teenager*, finds the origins of "this youth culture and its ability to horrify in the young urban workers of the late nineteenth century" (Hine 1999a, 76). Modern American youth culture has been traced back to the twenties and thirties by Grace Palladino (1996) in *Teenagers: An American History* and Paula S. Fass (1977) in *The Damned and the Beautiful*. Flappers, bobby-soxers, hepcats, and zoot-suiters had all left their cultural marks before 1950.

But whatever the fears, fads, and fancies that revolved around being a teenager before the 1950s, something unprecedented happened in the burgeoning postwar economy that "would revolutionize the very notion of teenagers in a few short years" (Palladino 1996, 101). Hine calls it the classic era of the teenager. It was "the golden age" when teens revived radio, created rock 'n' roll and a "whole new car culture" at the same time as they created "a lot of anxiety" in adults about juvenile delinquency (Hine 1999a, 78–82).

Because of a number of significant social, economic, and cultural changes that followed World War II, there was a growing awareness among the young that being a teenager was somehow different from what it was before and better than being anything else. For Jessie Bernard, an early investigator of teen culture, the reason the 1950s were different was simple:

"Our teen-age culture—in contradistinction to the teen-age culture of the past or of other societies—is a product of affluence" (Bernard 1961, 3). She estimated that in 1959 teens spent $10 billion on products such as records, movies, cars, magazines, clothing, and cosmetics at a time when magazines were a quarter and sneakers five dollars.

In the 1950s there were more teens than ever, and they had money and the time to enjoy their new status. The result was that teens became a major market for advertisers who reinforced teen identity by promoting unique teen fashions. In addition to being a socially constructed identity, being a teen became economically constructed as well. According to Bernard, advertisers allied with teens to form a coalition opposed to parental values and parental taste (1961, 4–5).

In the 1950s the condition of being young was no longer simply defined by the frustrations of not being treated as an adult, the central theme of so many forties shows like "Henry Aldrich" and "Meet Corliss Archer" and films like *The Bachelor and the Bobby Soxer* and every single Andy Hardy movie. The adult world had become simply "square," something to be avoided. Adults, and the lives they led, appeared frightened, frustrated, and forlorn. To teenagers conventional jobs were a "drag," growing up was meaningless (or as Paul Goodman had it "absurd"), and security was an empty value. So teenagers, wanting no part of such a world, deliberately set themselves apart from adults—in the ways they dressed, in the music they listened to, and in the cars they drove and, in the process, created a culture that celebrated their growing sense of difference. They challenged the cult of security that dominated the lives of their parents in a world made constantly insecure by thermonuclear weapons, communist conspiracies, and a cold war that kept getting hot in places like Korea at the beginning of the era and Vietnam at the end. As Joseph Margolis wrote in 1960:

The values of an adult world have to do with docility and safety and, most important, with the merits of prolonged routine work. . . . In the autonomy of the juvenile . . . we must acknowledge the existence of a subsociety . . . that, in the most fundamental manner possible, is opposed to the values of an otherwise incredibly powerful society. (Margolis 1960, 217).

Not all teens were content to stand apart from adults through their taste in cars, clothes, and music. Many, particularly among the working class, were confused, angry, and disaffected. They were the *Shook-Up Generation* profiled by Harrison Salisbury in 1958. True rebels without a cause, they defiantly challenged a society where affluence slowly trickled down. These teens took risks that frightened and/or outraged adults, thus proving their point about squares: they "rumbled," they drag raced, and they played "chicken." Some stole cars for joyrides, some experimented with drugs, and many, despite our often saccharine conceptions of the era, had a lot of sex. And many who didn't take such risks admired those who did. To the confusion and consternation of adults, teens had become juvenile delinquents who continually threatened them, often by their mere appearance.

As the media began to respond to this threat, teens were no longer portrayed as cute, awkward, naive, or ungainly proto-adults. Archie and Jughead and Betty and Veronica were replaced by Tony and Maria and the Jets and the Sharks of *West Side Story*, the bikers of *The Wild One,* and the delinquents of *Rebel without a Cause*, *The Young Savages,* and *The Blackboard Jungle*. Their problems were no longer easily dismissed as the harmless, mostly comic, excesses that resulted from adolescent afflictions like puppy love and acne.

Teens began to be seen as deeply troubled or simply dangerous. Or both. More and more the image of the teen became linked to danger, violence, and law breaking. To adults all teenagers seemed to care about was causing trouble. Teens began to appear like Johnny, the leader of the Black Rebels Motorcycle Club in *The Wild One,* who answered the question "What are you rebelling against?" with "Whaddaya got?"

Hollywood was especially quick to exploit the growing hysteria about juvenile delinquents in general and "highway outlaws" in particular. When movie producers realized that there was a distinct teenage audience, particularly at the rapidly growing number of drive-in theaters, they began to use the symbols of teen culture to reflect it back on itself while at the same time seeming to sound the alarm for the adult population. Serious films tried to explain the problem of youth to confused parents by marshaling current sociological and psychological theories: weak fathers (*Rebel without a Cause*); broken families, poverty, and absent fathers (*The Young Savages*); and poverty, unresponsive institutions, and indifferent father figures (*The Blackboard Jungle*). At the same time these films offered sexy role models of alienated and rebellious youth to the teens themselves, turning Marlon Brando and James Dean into generational icons.

The movies offered a distinctly different view of the 1950s than television did. On television the family was protected, guided, and supported by fathers who knew best. The Andersons, the Cleavers, and the Nelsons were led by gentle, understanding, and involved fathers whose lives largely revolved around their children. On the screen flawed fathers, portrayed as rigid and unloving or submissive and emasculated or simply missing, were generally seen as the source of the alienation and confusion of their sons and daughters. The movies offered substitute role models of effective masculinity—tough and compassionate—in the form of authority figures: a teacher in *The Blackboard Jungle,* a cop in *Rebel without a Cause,* and a D.A. in *The Young Savages*. It is interesting that it is the idealized view of the television family of the 1950s that has become the cultural cliché that dominates our conception of the era and not the much harsher view found in these teen movies.

As teen music became more controversial when it was linked by critics to teen violence and promiscuity, Hollywood movies began to exploit the power of rock 'n' roll as an effective lure to teen audiences. The simple use of "Rock around the Clock" over the opening credits transformed *The Blackboard Jungle* from a depressing neorealist study of alienation in urban high schools into a celebration of delinquency. Adults who wanted to ban the movie because of the music and teens who flocked to the movie all agreed on this point. Record companies also linked the music with delinquency by using provocative album covers even if the music had nothing to do with the image, producing, for instance, the cover of an album where two fighting white motorcycle types somehow represent the singing of two black R&B groups (see plate 1).

Most of the films trying to exploit this new

audience were hardly astute in their understanding of teen culture, particularly in their attempts to imitate the language of teens (much of the fun of "B" drive-in teen exploitation movies was laughing at the bizarre conceptions of teenagers that Hollywood had). Having the Black Rebels talk like urban hepcats while snapping their fingers to big band swing in *The Wild One* was particularly weird.

Hot rods offered Hollywood producers a milieu that allowed them to appeal to the growing youth market and to avoid the depressing realism of urban slum settings. Hot rods provided a formula that was perfect for suburban drive-in movies: cool characters, violence, hip slang, high-speed thrills, titillating sexual innuendo, and the cars themselves. There was a flood of hot rod movies: *Hot Rod Girl:* "She's Hell on Wheels and Fired Up for Any Thrill"; *Hot Rod Rumble:* "The Big Wheels . . . And the Slick Chicks Who Fired Them Up"; *Hot Rod Gang:* "Crazy Kids . . . Living to a Wild Rock 'n' Roll Beat!"; *Teenage Thunder:* "Young Love and Teenage Kisses. Hot Rods and Hot Tempers"; and *Wild Ones on Wheels:* "Violence Is Their Creed . . . The Law Is Their Enemy." Hot rodders offered Hollywood an additional advantage over urban delinquents: they were mostly white.

Other teen slanted movies used hot rods and customs to draw young audiences even if they weren't exclusively about rodding or racing. Teen horror movies like *The Blob* and *The Spider* gave rods to their heroes to drive. A number of George Barris customs were the true stars of *High School Confidential,* an exposé of drug dealing in high school. As far as car buffs were concerned, the black Mercury James Dean drove in *Rebel without a Cause* deserved star billing as much as Natalie Wood.

Even though it was only a mild custom, it spawned hundreds of imitations. Finally, it didn't matter to the teen audience whether these movies were anti–hot rod or even if they were just silly. In the end what really mattered about these films was the simple fact that there were real hot rods and customs in them. As Albert Drake remembers:

One night a friend and I rode the bus, then hitch hiked, and finally walked up 82nd to the Granada Theater to see a film called Hot Rod. It was a Monogram release, a real grade B production starring Myron Healy, Art Baker, and Jimmy Lyndon; the plot was worse than the acting, but what I enjoyed were the cars—real California hot rods!—and the sense of community that the rodders shared. To be part of a group, working together to build rods, shooting the breeze late at night in a cozy garage, that was what I desired. (Drake 1982, 31)

To their young audiences, even the worst of these teen exploitation films celebrated a generation that had created its own separate world with its own complex culture. These films communicated to teens that just being young had a certain seriousness. If you are able to frighten adults, you have to be serious. Teens could laugh at these movies and feel superior to their conceptions of youth at the same time they felt that their reality was being acknowledged and affirmed. Just because they aren't very good, these films can't be simply dismissed any more than sweetly sentimental teenage songs like "A Teenager in Love," "Sixteen Candles," "You're Sixteen," and "A Rose and a Baby Ruth" can be. They all validated the unique experience of being young and, in doing so, gave it a significance that helped to solidify the emerging teen culture.

Although Thomas Hine attempts to dismiss the widespread claims of increased youthful crime during the 1950s (1999a, 78–82), the concern about teen behavior wasn't all Hollywood fantasy or parental hysteria. Many teenagers were out of control. There were gangs. There were rumbles. There were riots at rock 'n' roll shows. Kids did have zipguns and switchblades. The total number of teenagers arrested in the country in 1947 was 34,376; by 1957 the number had climbed to 253,817. "We speak, accurately enough, of an upsurge in juvenile delinquency" (Margolis 1960, 211). As one Boston judge put it as early as 1953, "We have the spectacle of an entire city terrorized by one-half of one per cent of its residents. And the terrorists are children."

It is a mistake to use today's headlines to judge the social conditions of the past: zipguns, switchblades, and car aerials can't compare to nine millimeter Glocks or Uzis in killing power but, at the time, they caused just as much alarm as high-tech weapons do today. The killing that inspired Paul Simon's recent *Capeman,* as well as *The Young Savages,* can't compare to the devastation of Littleton, Colorado, or the terror of drive-by shootings, but that doesn't mean it wasn't a cause for outrage. In the context of the times fifties teens were frighteningly violent.

This threatening new teen culture was largely created by working-class kids, black and white, urban and rural, northern and southern. In fact one of the key reasons the new culture was seen as such a threat by middle-class parents was its origins in the working class—both black and white. "Class pervades all aspects of teen-age culture from clothes to taste in moving pictures to hangouts to activities" (Bernard 1961, 1). As Dr. Walter Miller, a researcher who studied middle-class youth in Roxbury, Massachusetts, in the fifties, recognized almost immediately: "Much public concern over delinquency stems not from an increase in antisocial conduct but from the fact that patterns of conduct formerly exclusive to poor, working-class or lower-middle class youngsters, have spread to the middle-class as a whole and to upper-class youth, as well" (in Salisbury 1958, 87).

This sense of threat is repeated today in the concern about gang-influenced clothes and hip-hop music in middle-class suburban high schools.

The new teen culture that emerged in the fifties was a world dominated by males, as the culture was generally, but it also had a significant, if secondary, role for teen girls, "the bad girls" that are so prominent in the whole range of teen films about the fifties from *Teenage Devil Dolls* (1952) to *Grease* (1978) and *Crybaby* (1990). These "bad girls" represented a significant break from conventional morality and signaled new attitudes about roles for girls. As the leading square says in *Crybaby*, "I'm so tired of being good."

In *Outsiders,* a novel published in the sixties but clearly locked into the social world of the fifties, a young S. E. Hinton movingly depicts the conflicts that developed between classes in Oklahoma, a conflict that was being duplicated throughout the country during the ten years from the arrival of Elvis to the arrival of the Beatles. She is obviously more in sympathy with the working-class "greasers" than the affluent "Socs" (pronounced "soshes"):

We're poorer than the Socs and the middle class. I reckon we're wilder, too. Not like the Socs, who jump greasers and wreck houses and throw beer blasts for kicks, and get editorials in the paper for being a public disgrace one day and an asset to society the next.

Greasers are almost like hoods; we steal things and drive old souped-up cars and hold up gas stations and have a gang fight once in a while. . . . I only mean that most greasers do things like that, just like we wear our hair long and dress in blue jeans and T-shirts, or leave our shirttails out and wear leather jackets and tennis shoes or boots. I'm not saying Socs or greasers are better; that's just the way things are. (Hinton 1967, 6)

This clash of classes was also a battle of taste cultures. Car enthusiasts from the middle class, for example, were more interested in the newly imported European sports cars than in American iron, modified or not. They drove newly imported MG's, Triumphs, Austin-Healeys, Porsches, and Alfa Romeos. Those who couldn't afford sports cars settled for other newly arrived foreign makes like Volkswagen, Volvo, and Renault. Other than adding badges to the grille or a nostalgic, ironic foxtail to the aerial, these cars remained essentially stock. These Collegiates or Preps or Rahs, as they were variously known, followed Grand Prix racing and were more familiar with racetracks like Watkins Glen, Sebring, and Lime Rock than they were with dragstrips. They cultivated the kind of sophistication promoted in *Playboy,* which first appeared in 1953 and which championed a lifestyle based on Hugh Hefner's fantasy of what a "swinging" college man might be interested in. According to Hefner, "The Playboy" aspired to the same sort of ersatz Eastern Ivy League *chic* that another successful outsider, from the Bronx, Ralph Lipshitz, later recreated in the preppy revival of the 1970s and 1980s under the name Ralph Lauren:

His dress is conservative and casual. He always wears loafers. . . . Brubeck, Kenton or Sinatra is usu-

ally on the turntable. . . . He is essentially an indoors man, though he discovered the pleasures of the ski slope last winter. He likes jazz, foreign films, Ivy League clothes, gin and tonic and pretty girls—the same sort of things that Playboy readers like—and his approach to life is as fresh, sophisticated, and yet admittedly sentimental as is the magazine. (in Halberstam 1993, 574–75)

Opposed to these button-down sons of the middle and upper middle classes were the blue-collar sons of the working class. Known variously as Hoods, Greasers, Bikers, Hot Rodders, or as one Rah once referred to them, "the Purple Shirts," based on their preference for brightly colored, shiny, non-ivy, non-button-down, non-oxford cloth shirts, they cultivated different tastes in cars, in clothes, and in music from "respectable" teens. They didn't see themselves striving for very much in their lives—a decent job, hopefully; a wife, probably; and kids, inevitably. Youth seemed to be the one time when they had the freedom to be something different, to be cool. That is why they clung to it so passionately and tried to make so much of it. And that passion is one of the reasons that culturally, if not socially and economically, working-class culture won the taste wars of the fifties:

The imagery of teenage rebellion was decidedly working class. The hood's costume of pomaded hair, blue jeans and T-shirt with a pack of Luckies in a rolled-up sleeve was a denial of the prevailing dream of assimilation into a suburban middle class. And it came at what was perhaps the last moment in history when factories, gas stations, and construction sites offered young people work that was a real alternative to the teenage world of high school. (Hine 1999b, 26)

There were a lot of ways the working classes could make something significant out of being young. They could choose the right clothes. They could have a cool haircut. They could learn the latest steps. If they had a little talent, or even if they didn't, they could hang out on the corners and sing the songs they heard on the radio, taking their voices high over the streets into the night. These were new songs, group harmony songs, that were about them and their lives and emotions even though they were sung by older black men with names like the Penguins, the Heartbeats, the Channels, the Cadillacs, the El Dorados, and the Jesters. Or they could sing along with the southern beat of songs by gawky white teens like Buddy Holly. In their dreams they could imagine singing with the cool of Gene Vincent or the raw sex appeal of the early Elvis or the controlled chaos of Jerry Lee Lewis. After all, Elvis had been a truck driver. If they practiced long and hard enough, they might make a record for one of the hundreds of small labels that sprang up during the decade.

Hot rodders and customizers, the source of many of the Hollywood images of the teen rebel to begin with, began to reflect back the characteristic gestures that Marlon Brando introduced in *The Wild One* and James Dean elaborated in *Rebel without a Cause*. Driving the right car—a rod or a custom—quickly became a crucial part of being cool. As Barbara Ehrenreich writes on the appeal of figures like Brando and Dean: "For despite all the developmental psychology and high school 'life adjustment' texts, maturity just wasn't sexy, and adolescent defiance—symbolized by the tough, lower-class male—was" (Ehrenreich 1983, 57).

Achieving cool meant that the rods were no longer about just going fast. Cool involved creating a style with the just right look in cars as well as in clothes, hair, and walk. Cars had a stance and so did their drivers. But cool was about much more than having the right things. Nothing was less cool than wearing the right clothes, but not knowing how to back it up— how you responded to a challenge, how you walked into a room, how you shifted gears, how you sat in your car—was even more important to being cool than the costume. If you wore a motorcycle jacket, you were wearing more than a garment. You were putting on an attitude, and you had better know how to carry it off. Being truly cool was also a bit of performative armor that could protect one from almost anything: getting hassled by the cops, being rejected by a girl, being yelled at by a teacher, being punched in the mouth. Whatever you did, you didn't want to "lose your cool." Indifference, sarcasm, skepticism were the key components of this armor.

But costume nevertheless could not be ignored. And not everyone who was cool wore black jackets, white T-shirts, blue jeans, and engineer boots. That was the biker's uniform. There were other styles. Although black teenagers were not at all prominent in rodding and customizing, they created much of the new style in clothes, in music, and in attitude on city street corners where it filtered across racial barriers and into the Kustom Kulture.

A whole class of urban dandies, "dudes" as they were called in some areas, appeared, related to the zoot-suiters and hepcats of the 1940s. They pursued a kind of high elegance that easily separated them from the gray-flanneled squares. As far as they were concerned, dungarees were for farmers and cowboys—"shitkickers." In the beginning of the decade the look was adapted from the zoot suits of the 1940s with large rolled Mr. B collars on billowing pink and yellow shirts, three-quarter-length oversized jackets in bright colors, narrow bowties, chocolate brown or bright blue pegged pants with contrasting piping or saddle stitching down the side, and blue suede or two-tone shoes, all topped off with elaborate DA haircuts and long sideburns. This was a look similar to that of the Teddy Boys of England and the early Elvis. It survives in the jump band and rockabilly revivals of the 1990s.

By the late fifties the continental style took over as the coolest look. The truly hip now preferred tightly tailored suits with narrow lapels, often in iridescent metallic fabrics. They were distinguished by cuffless pipestem trousers so short that as much as four inches of black sock showed above the preferred pointy-toed Italian-styled black shoes or demi-boots. Bright purple, blue, orange, or white on white shirts with tab collars and French cuffs were favored. Skinny ties, as narrow as three-fourths of an inch wide, looked "sharp." The ensemble was often topped off with a "Mr. Diddybop" hat, a fedora with a very narrow brim, and a raincoat regardless of the weather, often worn draped over the shoulders. The final element in the look was the perfection of the walk. It was choreographed imperturbability, the rhythm of indifference found in "The Stroll," one of the most popular of fifties dances which brought the street walk to the dance floor in a loose competition of display.

Borrowed largely from black urban culture white teen cool took on some of the same functions that it had in the black world. The major difference is that it was aimed at the adult world not at whites.

Historically, black people have used humor, shucking and jiving, "playing the dozens," and "in-

version" as ways to play it cool. These postures and poses convey power and control, alleviate anxiety, give the impression that one is suave and charming, make white people uncertain about their intentions, entertain, display pride, express anger, and hide real feelings and emotions (Majors et al. 1994, 248).

Cool always was, and is, competitive. It is also essentially a comparative exercise: what's cooler, a chopped coupe or a lowered Merc, flames or scallops, Ford or Chevy V-8's? Who's cooler? James Dean or Marlon Brando, Elvis or Gene Vincent, the Cadillacs or the Spaniels? One had to be a connoisseur of cool and yet not be too studied about it.

The largely white Kustom Kulture created its own take on cool. While there were borrowings from black culture in language, in music, and in clothes, Kustom Kulture developed its own language, its own styles, and its own rituals that grew out of the importance in their lives of the car which was not as central to the urban black experience. As the artist Robert Irwin describes it: "The car was the key, the pivotal item in the whole ballgame. Everything was wrapped around the car. The car was your home away from home. And you put months and months into getting it just right. Everything was thought out in terms of who you were, how you saw yourself, what your identity was" (in Weschler 1982, 13).

In the Kustom Kulture you could be dressed at the height of fashion, but it was impossible to be truly cool if you drove the wrong car or a badly done car. To drive daddy's station wagon to a high school dance was as damning to one's status as preferring Pat Boone's "Rip It Up" to Little Richard's or the McGuire Sisters' "Sincerely" to the Moonglows'. To own and drive a stock car simply showed a failure of

Figure 8.
Finished rods making a run on the streets of
Pasadena in 1946. Courtesy of Peter Eastwood.

nerve. To drive a custom with bad bodywork or
a poorly thought-out treatment was to make
yourself a joke. Driving the right car meant that
you could still be cool even if you were a fashion illiterate.

The code of cars was elaborate and subtle.
From makes (Fords and Chevys over Plymouths
and Dodges, American over foreign) and models (two doors over four doors, hardtops over
sedans, convertibles over everything, everything over station wagons) to accessories
(skirts, spotlights, and lakes pipes) and paint,
each choice helped formulate a statement of
identity. Simply owning a well-made custom car
became a way of achieving a significant identity
at school and on the strip. It was Hirohata's
Merc, the Matranga Merc, Larry Ernst's Chevy,
Ferranti's Ford, and the LeRoy Goulart Ford.

The car and the name became one. But it
was the car that truly mattered. Even the evolution of preferred driving positions reinforced a
shift of attention from the driver to the car. In
the beginning of the decade the cool way to
drive was the straight-up position where the
driver sat up almost leaning on the steering
wheel, keeping his back away from the seat.
This position said "look at me driving this car."
At the end of the decade the preferred
slumped-down position where the driver was
nearly invisible announced "look at my car, look
at my car."

In the prosperous postwar economy it was
no longer enough just to have "wheels." Teens
wanted to outdo the other guy not just on the
strip but in the schoolyard parking lot as well.
There was a sense of achievement and status in
having a great car. As Jack Walker, the creator
of a replica of the famous Hirohata Merc, put it,
"I wanted to be that good."

As much money and effort was put into the
appearance of the car as was spent on perform-

ance. Parts were chromed. Tops were chopped. Bodies were smoothed. Front ends were dropped. Whitewalls were added and so were spinner hubcaps. Exquisite bright paint jobs in colors never imagined by Detroit replaced the patchwork of primers that had distinguished early hot rods. Rods began to become beautiful. There were many more options for the right look. Full-fendered rods, highboys, or chopped and channeled fenderless sedans, roadsters, or coupes carved from original Model T's, A's, or Deuces (1932 Fords) were all, if done correctly, capable of looking really cool (see figure 8).

Across the country anyone who cared knew that California led the way. Albert Drake remembers when California style and attitude arrived in Oregon:

A guy named Johnny Johnson came up from California, and he was what we expected a real hot-shot, hot-shoe So-Cal hot rodder to be: red hair slicked back, a tough expression, a weight lifter given to wearing tight T-shirts. He had a red '32 Ford five window, channeled, top-chopped about four inches, and a dropped axle that gave the coupe a wicked rake. He was telling us about a ticket he received: "The screw pulled me over and I said, 'How fast?'"

"Seventy," the cop says.

"I took him across the street and told him to look back at where the coupe was parked. 'Look at it,' I said, pointing at the coupe that was angled forward like a rocket, 'that sonofabitch is going thirty-five standing still.'" (Drake 1982, 17–18)

Not everyone who initially got involved in the original California car culture in the 1930s was as devoted to speed as the rodder. From the beginning others devoted themselves almost exclusively to creating cars that had just the right look. They were the customizers, "the dudes" of the Kustom Kulture who devoted as much attention to the details of their cars as urban "cats" devoted to their clothes:

Meanwhile, a separate (slightly older) segment of Southern California car freaks weren't all that interested in speed. They wanted a better looking car. So, since they couldn't afford the coachbuilt Packards, Duesenbergs, Lincolns, or Stutzes, they took their Fords, Chevys, or Plymouths to body shops and had them customized. Most of this work, at first, was done in regular collision repair shops, where skilled craftsmen could build or repair most anything made of sheetmetal. These metalmen didn't always understand why the customizer wanted the top cut, or the fenders bobbed, or the hood louvers removed, but they did it—beautifully. (Batchelor 1989, 71)

Although there were beautiful rods and customs that were exceptionally fast, rodders and customizers had fundamentally different attitudes toward modifying cars. Philip Linhares, co-curator of the Oakland Museum show, puts it succinctly, "The hot rod's message is 'I'm fast and I'm mean.' In contrast, the custom car's message is 'I'm low and I'm cool'" (Dobrin and Linhares 1996, 15).

Customizers were the true aesthetes of the growing car culture. Nothing about the car escaped their attention. They fretted over how much to lower the car, chop the top, or extend the fenders. They studied taillights, hubcaps, and fender skirts. They obsessed over fabrics, color charts, knobs, buttons, and the placement of antennas. To fulfill their vision of perfection they often went to almost absurd lengths: upholstering wheel wells, chroming

Figure 9.
Early custom. Tommy the Greek's chopped, Carson-topped 1940 Mercury, originally built in 1941. Courtesy of the *Rodders Journal.*

Figure 10.
Early custom. Jerry Fasset's 1947 Chevy custom built by Westergard. It features a chopped top and fade-away fenders. Courtesy of the *Rodders Journal.*

the undercarriage, lowering the car to the point where even slightly steep driveways were impossible to traverse (see figures 9 and 10).

With the success of *Hot Rod*, other magazines like *Hop Up, Honk!* (later *Car Craft*), and *Rod & Custom* soon followed. These magazines had a national circulation and, for the first time, kids hanging out in the gas stations from Michi-

gan to Mississippi, from Connecticut to the Carolinas, from West Coast to East could see the exceptional rods and the customs that were at the center of California's car culture. These magazines took the imaginations of sixteen-year-olds and seventeen-year-olds to a fabled place in the sun where cars could run all year with open wheels and without tops and where every high school parking lot was a car show. California was a magic kingdom where it was rumored there were used car lots that sold finished rods and customs. For the artist Robert Williams, closely tied to the car culture both in the themes of his work and in the cars he drives, magazines introduced him to the California builders who would inspire him:

I was living in the South and mags like *Hop Up, Hot Rod, Honk, Rod and Custom*, and *Car Craft* were like my bible. I never really fit in school and mechanical things were all I understood or cared about. Von Dutch and Roth were like these gods. As soon as I saw their work I knew I had to go check them out. Von Dutch was extremely brilliant, and I can't overemphasize the influence he had on young blue-collar America. He was like a spiritual god—he seemed to add a soul to nuts and bolts, a spirit to machinery, as it were, that no mere engineer could do. Sheet metal—well, it gave the vehicle a karma all its own; it came alive. Ed Roth was to the youth of America in the nineteen sixties what P. T. Barnum was to the average farm boy in the eighteen sixties. Roth invoked the hot rod spirit of the future with over-tones of beatnik style. (in Stecyk 1993, 35)

The interest in modifying cars to improve both looks and performance grew rapidly after World War II when car-starved returning vets joined those who had endured car shortages and gas rationing on the home front. They were now free to devote themselves to creating the cars they could only dream about during the war. In fact the flowering of both rodding and customizing in the late forties and early fifties can be directly attributed to the return of these World War II vets. As Don Montgomery explains:

It is very important to realize that much of what happened in hot rodding was due to the particular circumstances of the times. World War II had disrupted the lives of thousands of young men. Up to five years had been removed from the calendars of guys who would have been working, going to college, getting married and perhaps building a hot rod. As the war wound down in 1945 the return home was an opportunity to catch up on the fun they had missed.

It was perhaps the first time in our history that such a huge group of young men in their twenties had not "settled down." The term "settled down" is considered to mean marriage, etc. Many of these young men were ready to pick up where they left off after high school graduation several years before. Most importantly many had saved some money while in the service. Some cash plus low expenses as a result of being unmarried and perhaps living at home, gave a freedom of action that young adults rarely had. . . .

The first rods to return to the streets in 1945 were the "mothballed" roadsters. Rodders fortunate enough to have a place to store or "mothball" their roadsters were back on the roads almost immediately. They joined the few rods that had remained on the streets during the war. (Montgomery 1987, 19–20)

If the returning vets kicked off the explosion of interest in modified cars, it was the rapid growth of the suburbs and their teen populations that ensured the spread of rodding and customizing across the country. Every suburb, whether in Michigan or Texas, was becoming a kind of California where owning a car was rapidly becoming a necessity even for teenagers, whose suburban jobs, schools, and homes were not often easily reached by public transportation if it was available at all. By 1960 more than a million and half cars were registered in teenagers' names (Bernard 1961, 3–4). The car was clearly at the center of life in postwar America. It was one of the most powerful symbols in American culture. It represented America's victory in the war and the essence of the good life. It also began to symbolize more than any other consumer product the new confidence Americans had in themselves as "kings of the road."

For the first time, because of the general prosperity that allowed adults to trade in their cars every two or three years, relatively new cars were widely available to youthful owners. No longer were kids forced to drive old jalopies or the family sedan; they could pick and choose from a wide variety of fairly new used cars that were available for as little as a few hundred dollars. It was important to the growth of rodding and customizing that these cars were *their* cars. They were free to do with them as they wished. As more and more teens began to drive to high school, the school parking lots became a kind of showplace (the way cars are displayed today at many shows imitates this original parking lot setting).

As the one place in the suburbs where every teen came together, high school became the laboratory of the new teen culture, where new styles could be introduced, tested, and evaluated. Teenagers in the fifties continued the pattern of staying in school that had begun in the thirties. By 1958 74 percent of seventeen-year-old males were still in school, whereas in 1930 only 47 percent of seventeen-year-olds were still in school. Because the largest increase was found in the sons and daughters of blue-collar workers, working-class taste began to have a much greater influence on teen taste in general than ever before. No longer were working-class styles automatically equated with "less popular." They had achieved a level of cool.

For car crazy kids, high school classes were often more of an inconvenience than an opportunity to learn. But car magazines like *Car Craft* and *Rod & Custom* were a convenient size, easily slipped between the pages of a textbook so that study of the latest developments in customizing could proceed unimpeded by algebra equations or the structure of a sonnet. Cars became the center of the social world of a whole segment of the teen population. In the cafeteria, in the schoolyard, cars were a constant topic of conversation. There was always something to do to your car or a friend's after school. On weekends there was the strip for cruising. Just as clothes served to identify one's place in teen culture as a "hood" or "rah" or "nerd" or "greaser," cars reinforced that identification. There was little chance you would see a guy in a black leather jacket with a perfectly coifed DA haircut driving a neat red Triumph TR3.

But the car was not merely an emblem of identity and status, like the black leather jacket or DA haircut. The car was the catalyst that allowed the rest of the new culture to flourish. Driving was the one significant privilege allowed teenagers. It gave teens freedom and mobility. They could separate themselves from adults at the same time they took their place in the adult world as drivers. In their own cars they could reinforce their own sense of being in their own world subject to their own rules. They could meet at their cruising spots, drive-in restaurants, and movies, relatively free from parental or civic authority. They could listen to legendary disc jockeys like Allen Freed, Murray the K, Cousin Brucie, Arnie "Woo Woo" Ginsberg, Jocko, Jerry Blavatt, and Harvey Holiday, who identified themselves with their teen audiences and who gave them a new culture and a new language, as well as a new music. Because of the confined space of the car the relationship between the disc jockey and the audience became more intimate, more personal, more directly involved with the kids' lives. Disc jockeys were the town criers of this new mobile village, often calling on their audiences to respond to an issue or a question by blowing their horns or flashing their lights. But the driver's seat was also an intensely private space where a teen could be truly alone. It was a place for thinking, fantasizing, and remembering.

Cars also provided tests of skill and confrontations with danger. Teen identity became tied directly to both, as the chicken race in *Rebel without a Cause* clearly shows. Nothing is more intoxicating to teenage males than playing with death. To drive fast, to drive skillfully (knowing how to double clutch and speed shift), or to win a drag race were ways of showing one's worth and courage.

The car, with front seats larger than the average sofa, was also a convenient mobile bedroom, a laboratory where the first experiments of the coming sexual revolution could take place. The fifties were not as sexless as the film *Pleasantville* suggests. In every town across the country there were dozens of secluded spots that were for "parking," a euphemism for sexual activity. At some spots it was not unusual to find three or four or more cars lined up next to each other with only steamed windows providing a semblance of privacy. Guys without dates often "bushwacked" these parkers by shining spotlights on them, hoping to catch a couple in the act and avoid being chased. On July 5 in 1960, the morning after a holiday fireworks display, the maintenance crew at Cummings Park in Stamford, Connecticut, collected twenty-seven used condoms from the parking lot and along the beach. If the motto of the sixties was "Sex, Drugs, and Rock 'n' Roll," the motto of the fifties could have been "Sex, Cars, and Rock 'n' Roll."

On a summer night in 1958 or 1959 at the local drive-in, surrounded by lowered '50 Fords and chopped '51 Mercurys, a working-class car nut could feel that whatever the future had in store for him it would be endurable because he was cool and owned a cool car.

But, as important as the car was to the development of a distinct teen culture, it can't measure up to the impact of rock 'n' roll. It is almost impossible to imagine the development of teen culture without it. Rock 'n' roll was more than the music of a generation. While every generation has its distinctive songs which furnish it with its memories, rock 'n' roll was at the center of a profound cultural shift which defined the direction that American culture would take for the next fifty years.

Rock 'n' roll created a new sense of unique identity and of opposition in youth. It not only provided "the sound track of your life," a phrase Dick Clark claims to have coined, but it served also as the creative arena for inventing a new culture that would dominate the cultural landscape for the rest of the century. No longer were teen musical idols a generation or two older than their teen audiences as was true in the forties with big band leaders like Benny

Goodman and Tommy Dorsey, for example, who looked like adults and dressed like lawyers and accountants. In the fifties songs were written and performed by their own. This was truly teen music. Frankie Lymon was only thirteen when he sang "Why Do Fools Fall in Love?" His group, The Teenagers, was just one of many that signified their identification with their audience: There were the Teenchords, Royal Teens, and The Six Teens, as well as the Teen Tones, Teen Notes, and Teen-Kings and Teen Queens. Schoolboys, Sophomores, and Students all had hits in the fifties.

Rock 'n' roll became both the bible and the encyclopedia of teen culture. It gave teens their romantic myths ("A Teenager in Love" and "So Young"), their anthems ("Roll Over Beethoven" and "Rock 'n' Roll Is Here to Stay"), their style guides ("Black Slacks" and "A White Sportcoat and a Pink Carnation"), their dances ("The Stroll" and "The Madison"), and their history ("School Days," "At the Hop," and "Summertime Blues").

A much underappreciated subgenre of rock songs is the car song. From the beginning, cars and rock 'n' roll were intimately related. As Brian Setzer, one of a growing number of contemporary rock musicians, including Jimmy Vaughn, Al Jardine, Michael Anthony, Jeff Beck, and Billy Gibbons, who also own hot rods, says, "I got into hot rods when I was about 16. It was about lookin' cool and goin' fast and the ability to do so. It was also totally connected with rock 'n' roll. Hot rods and rock 'n' roll went together. . . . There's a song on the new album called 'Switchblade 327.' It's a real '50's hot rod song" (in Breeding 1998, 26–27).

Jimmy Vaughn, who has built several significant customs in the nineties, sees little difference between his work as a musician and as a creator of customs: "These cars are exactly like my records, you know. I have the feeling in my head about how I want the car to look, how I want the body to look, how I want the curves to look" (in Asimov 1994, C4).

Mike Ness of Social Distortion, who owns a '60 Impala and a chopped '54 Chevy, is even more emphatic about the connection between the cars of the fifties and the music:

There was a certain attitude about them—it was a statement. It's like when I'm driving my sled, that black car at night looks like death. There's a certain feeling about it, you know? It's just another form of what music was. I get the same feeling driving that car as when I'm playing my guitar, because I helped design it and work on it. That's 37 years of my life being expressed. (in Pecorelli 1999, 47)

From the very beginnings of rock 'n' roll there were paeans to speed and fast cars—"Hot Rod Rag," "You Can't Catch Me," "Hot Rod," "Hot Rod Lincoln," "Rocket 88," and "Spinner Hub Caps." The catalog of recorded songs about cars, for example, for just the years 1961 to 1965, contains fifteen hundred songs. The Golden Age of the car song was certainly the early sixties when the Beach Boys, Jan and Dean, and Ronnie and the Daytonas sang about Little Deuce Coupes, GTOs, and Chevy 409's racing toward Drag City alongside the little old lady from Pasadena. Recently, Rhino records released *Hot Rod and Custom Classics,* a four-CD set containing eighty-eight songs, including "4 on the Floor" by the Shutdowns, "'41 Ford" by Grand Prix, "Draggin'" by Curtis Gordon, "Cruisin'" by Gene Vincent, and "Hot Rod Gang" by the Stray Cats. In addition, there is a continuing series of CDs from The Right Stuff, *Hot Rod Music,* that already includes seventy-seven songs on five CDs.

Rock 'n' roll also was the perfect accompaniment to cruisin' the strip. The coolest thing, in the days before cassettes and eight track, was to have a DC record player mounted under the dashboard, designed to withstand bumps and rapid acceleration without skipping, and they sometimes worked. Then you could choose just the right song to announce your arrival into the drive-in restaurant or serve as background when you tried to meet somebody. Instrumentals like "Walk Don't Run" by the Ventures, "Rumble" by Link Wray, or "Sleep Walk" by Santo & Johnny were perfect for a cool slow entrance. If you wanted to speed things up there was "Let's Go for a Ride" by the Collegians or "You Can't Catch Me" by Chuck Berry or "Rebel Rouser" by Duane Eddy. "No Particular Place to Go" by Chuck Berry was right almost all the time.

The connection between rock 'n' roll and cars is further evidenced by the proliferation of car names that singing groups adopted. There were Impalas, El Dorados, Belaires, Cadillacs, Fleetwoods, Starfires, Continentals, Bonnevilles, Rivieras, and Imperials, among a host of others, who sang in the fifties. In the early sixties the group names were even more hot rod related: Deuce Coupes, Duals, GTOs, Dragsters, Roadsters, T-Bones, and Roadrunners.

Without cars rock 'n' roll might not have become the dominant popular music so quickly. Although there were cheap record players that played only 45s available, the home was still the parents' domain. They controlled the volume and, often, the playlist. In a car teens were able to determine what they listened to and how loud it could be played. With the introduction of push-button radios, a new task was assigned to the favored "shotgun" seat next to the driver. He "played" the radio by skillfully manipulating the buttons so that there was an uninterrupted stream of music. You could lose the shotgun seat if you slipped up and allowed a Patti Page or Perry Como song on or let too many commercials slip through.

One of the brilliant touches in *American Graffiti,* the most accurate film about the California car culture yet made, is the use of Wolfman Jack's radio show and the music he plays as a choral element that links every character, every car, and every theme together. The film is almost nonstop music coming from the radios of the cars cruising Modesto. There are forty-one oldies in the movie, beginning with "Rock around the Clock," the first rock 'n' roll song that impacted the movies. As in the movie, actual cruises were choreographed and ritualized performances with accompanying music, constantly in motion and going nowhere. There was a circuit to follow at just the right pace and, if you were lucky, with just the right song on the radio.

The artist Kent Bash describes a typical night of cruising in California, the model for cruising everywhere:

When Friday night finally rolled around, my friends and I hit the roads with a vengeance! It was a wild mix of cars, girls, drive-ins, bowling alleys, racing, rock and roll music, and all of the other pastimes kids growing up in the early sixties loved. The circuit we picked out for cruising was a particular favorite: This night was the one reserved for taking in the sights and sounds found along the mother of all American cruisin' strips, California's Van Nuys Boulevard. . . . Satisfied that we had hit all of the major hot spots, we slipped down Sunset Strip and returned to the spot where it all began: the Van Nuys Bob's. By then we were pretty much inebriated with images of hot rods and cool customs dancing in our heads and we were ready to call it a night. (Witzel and Bash, 1997, 41)

With gas seldom above thirty cents a gallon for most of the decade, a car could cruise about ninety miles a night for about two dollars. Four guys, chipping in for gas, could get a lot of entertainment for about fifty cents apiece.

There was a social dimension to cruising, but for the true car nut it was always about the cars and what was being done to them. It was important to see works in progress. As the car painter Larry Watson remembers:

Everybody was trying to outdo each other. It was a big competition. If you frenched your taillights, you wanted everybody to see so you sprayed some primer on it and headed for the Bellflower Clock. Then you might nose and deck it. The same thing. Even Duane Steck's "Moonglow" was shown that way. But you never saw cars completely in primer like today. When the body work was finished, you saw it painted. Finished. There were a lot of customs out there. (Watson 1998, interview)

Henry Flood Robert Jr. reports that one leg of the cruise circuit in 1959 in San Diego involved passing by the floor-to-ceiling windows of the Convair Division plant of General Dynamics on Pacific Coast Highway again and again: "What is going on here? . . . These children of the machine age are not looking in the windows; they are looking at the windows, and what they see is the reflection of themselves and, more important, of their cars" (Robert Jr. 1984c, 178).

The creators of *Hot Rod* were correct in their prediction that the hot rod market would inevitably grow. The general prosperity of the 1950s had freed many new teens from the responsibility of helping their families meet their bills. Even at minimum wages a high school student could earn $20 to $40 a week after

Figure 11.
Newhouse catalog from 1959.

school. A number of mail-order automotive parts dealers, like J. C. Whitney and Newhouse Automotive, which had specialized in speed equipment, began to recognize the interest in customizing and began to cater to the new market. They offered "bolt on" parts that did not involve the extensive bodywork that radical customs required. For as little as $27, a "Custom Grille Conversion" which imitated the Hirohata Merc bar grille could be bought for a '49 or '50 Ford. Lowering blocks that brought the rear of a car four inches closer to the ground were only $5.95. Starfire spinners and Dodge Lancers, the most popular hubcaps of the era, were available at less than $10 a piece. Bolt-on Olds lights for '52 to '54 Fords were only $14.95 a pair. For less than $100, or about a month's part-time work, a high school student could create a look, which, while not original, at least identified the car as a custom (see figure 11).

As the car culture continued to grow cars became more radical, more creative, and more numerous. The older veterans of hot rodding who had raced flatheads on the streets before the war were available for advice and, frequently, they took pleasure in ridiculing the newcomers' youthful enthusiasms or stylistic excesses. Like the older master builders such as Barris and Winfield, whom they admired from afar, they were typically in their late twenties or early thirties; they provided teenagers with an important link to the origins of hot rodding and they taught them the importance of doing it right.

As more custom cars began to appear everywhere from Portland, Oregon, to Hummelstown, Pennsylvania, from Stamford, Connecticut, to Phoenix, Arizona, new dimensions were added to the car as a fantasy object. A customized anything was better than a stock something. While the general public went to new car showrooms to see which car they would fantasize about owning, teens now looked at them as simply raw material; what was once found only in junkyards was now located on showroom floors. Owning a new car was no longer the ultimate desire. Even if one bought a brand-new car it had to be reworked.

In 1958 fifteen-year-old Floyd DeBore wanted to buy a new car with the money he had earned working on a dairy farm. He went to Larry Watson for advice. Watson said he thought the '58 Pontiacs were different and had potential. DeBore bought a two-door hardtop and had it delivered to Watson's shop where over a year the car was given one of his most complex panel/flame paint jobs. DeBore paid for each stage of the paint work as he earned the money (see plate 2). When DeBore was old enough to drive, the car was also ready so he never had to suffer the humiliation of driving a stock car (Watson 1998, interview).

Even Elvis lost prestige among a lot of car buffs when he showed an insatiable lust for new stock Cadillacs. "Think of what he could build with his money," they said. As the sixty-year-old Frank McShane, the builder of a recently completed radical '51 Mercury, remembers: "I started looking at the new cars differently. I would wonder how could I use those taillights, what about that grille. New cars weren't that special. They were just parts" (McShane 1994, interview).

Cars were the chief topic of discussion wherever young men gathered—at the gas station, at the drive-in, in the schoolyard. Here every aspect of any car could be compared, evaluated, argued, and judged according to a highly sophisticated aesthetic that covered everything about the car, even the sound of mufflers.

There is something almost decadent in the appreciation of the nuances of exhaust systems or the perfect paint job, something too much, almost too refined. There also is something in their erudition which suggests a kind of displacement, not uncommon in subcultures—by creating a substitute world where their achievements were significant, where meaning could be created, and where real distinctions could be made, they could separate themselves from a world where others, richer and more powerful, set the standards. It suggests a significant alienation from ordinary values, a complete resistance to the common, the ordinary, and the popular. The customizer does not accept the view that the automobile is the great leveler, Marshall McLuhan's belief that "the car is a superb piece of uniform, a standardized mechanism that is of a piece with the Gutenberg technology and literacy which created the first classless society in the world" (McLuhan 1964, 223).

The car, for the rodder or the customizer, is the most significant thing that distinguishes him from everyone else. It is the only thing that protects him, and this only for a time, from a losing battle with the more privileged. It is the only thing that lets him fight back. He fights back by creating his own world, following the lead of George Barris, who called his creations *kustoms*, customizing even the word, in creating a kustom kulture.

As Erik Erikson has pointed out in *Identity: Youth and Crisis* (1968), adolescence is marked by a crisis of "identity and role confusion." Kustom Kulture offered its members a very clear context in which they could play out their own achievement of identity. One could be a hot rodder or a customizer, worship speed or beauty. One could identify oneself with the hoods or bikers. The codes of dress, language, and action were laid down, yet within these codes there was ample room for self-expression.

This new identity could be attained almost completely outside the middle-class world in a male-centered culture of the garage or at the dragstrip. In addition to these social dimensions of identity, there are psychological ones as well, that find expression in the car culture, especially for the customizers, who spent so much time thinking about "the beautiful" and working toward perfection.

In the end, however, these cars were not simply exercises in rebellion or statements about status or identity. They are not mere stereotyped symbols of an era like the motorcycle jacket or the DA haircut. In their craft, in the complexity of their designs, they also achieve a level of art. The best display extraordinary ingenuity and creativity. Tom Wolfe wrote rapturously about some of these cars in his essay "The Kandy Kolored Tangerine Flake Streamline Baby" in 1964, ironically, just as customizing was entering its "Dark Ages." The automotive symbols of that era would soon become the VW bus, the Surfer Woody, and Detroit muscle cars or "factory hot rods," as they were called. But even near the end of the golden era of rods and customs, Wolfe was able to see that they were works of art: "Barris starts taking me through Kustom City and the place looks like any other body shop at first, but pretty soon you realize you're in a gallery" (Wolfe 1963, 83).

The builders of these cars shared the same concerns that high culture attributes to the artist. To borrow just one such model, Rollo

May's in *The Courage to Create,* customizers are very much like the artists May profiles in their "encounters" with the world, in this case the world of the automobile, with a heightened awareness and a passion for form. This encounter, the key element for May that separates the true artist from the pseudo-artist, is an intense absorption that grows out of their passion and their commitment to bring "something new into being." "Forever unsatisfied with the mundane, the apathetic, the conventional, they always push on to newer worlds" (May 1973, 28). Customizers and hot rodders are not only true artists but true modern artists, that is, the art they make is based on the beauty of the machine.

It is not that unsophisticated customizers and hot rodders somehow assimilated the essential attributes of modernism by means of some sort of cultural osmosis or some sort of cultural trickle down. Rather it is that, like high modernists before them, they saw themselves entering a new world that required a new art and a new style. European artists recognized what rodders and customizers also knew, always knew in their bones, in their machine-making joy—that the car is the central symbol of the new mechanized world and, therefore, a key foundation of any legitimate modern art.

They knew also, instinctively, what John A. Kouwenhoven, a champion of the "vernacular" style in America, meant when he wrote in the late forties:

In addition to providing a sense of familiarity with and personal control over "the machine," automobiles also happen to be among the most beautiful objects which modern civilization has produced, in spite of the chromium academicism of bulbous streamlining which the professional designers have imposed upon so many of them. Along with the skyscrapers, the grain elevators, the suspension bridges, and the huge transport planes, they are among the most aesthetically satisfying products of technology—of all these objects they are the only ones which the average American can own. (Kouwenhoven 1948, 178)

Customizers go much further than the ordinary car owner. Not content merely to own and show off such an object, they must also make it better. They make it new and in their own image. As a result they have created cars that are works of art. Modern art.

MAKING ART
OUT OF CARS

The growth of the Kustom Kulture in the 1950s was part of a far-reaching postwar cultural upheaval that has dramatically shaped the rest of the century. Hot rodding and customizing parallel the development of modern jazz, the rise of rock 'n' roll, and the appearance of the Beat generation. Each was widely seen as a sign of impending cultural decline. Each was expected by critics to die a quick and unlamented death. Each was also seen as a youthful rebellion against a stagnant and repressive status quo, although the definition of youth was an extremely elastic one. And each movement developed outside and below the Establishment until it dominated or greatly influenced the cultural landscape. Primarily, rodders and customizers differ from the others in how little attention they have received.

Bebop, rock 'n' roll, and the Beats have all been designated as significant contributions to America's worldwide cultural dominance in the second half of the twentieth century. Bebop is rarely seen as "sick" music today (Sales 1992, 131–33). Rather it is almost universally understood to be the highest expression of America's classical music, jazz. The writings of Kerouac, Ginsberg, and Burroughs, once dismissed as "barbaric" and ignored by the academy, now constitute an important part of the modern literary canon. "Howl" has taken its place alongside "The Waste Land" and "The Second Coming." Never more popular than they are now, the Beats continue to inspire new generations of writers, musicians, and filmmakers. And rock 'n' roll in all its myriad forms and styles has simply become the dominant music of our time. No longer confined to the domain of the popular or restricted to a teen audience, rock 'n' roll has evolved into rock. It has its own art music and its own avant-gardes.

While rodding and customizing clearly haven't had anything close to the cultural impact of bebop, the Beats, or rock 'n' roll, the continuing growth of the practice of modifying cars over a period of more than fifty years suggests that it is a phenomenon that deserves some attention.

The question is how to see it. Bop and rock 'n' roll are music and, as Leonard Bernstein showed years ago, Charlie Parker and the Beatles can be described in the same language used to analyze Mozart and Beethoven. Despite what others said about them, the Beats never saw themselves as literary anarchists, but as heirs to a long and coherent literary tradition that includes Homer, Blake, Baudelaire, Rimbaud, de Lautréamont, Ezra Pound, and William Carlos Williams, among others. It was easy for scholars to plug in traditional literary approaches once they got over their shock.

But modifying cars presents a more difficult challenge to the interpreter. There is no readily available frame of reference to use to explain it. Is it a hobby? a fad? craft? folk art? a popular art form? a subcultural form? kitsch? The answer might seem to be only a matter of splitting hairs, but there are important implications in these labels. It is often difficult to see (and appreciate) something until it is named. And the name itself influences how we see it. Certainly one of the legacies of the modern era is challenging audiences to question their definitions of art.

Deciding to see something as art is much easier today than in the past. We have already seen bottleracks, bicycle wheels mounted on stools, Brillo boxes, and soup cans celebrated as important art. Categories are more fluid and less restrictive now. One of the universally accepted aspects of that much contested term *postmodernism* is the leveling of distinctions between high art and low, between high culture and entertainment, and tradition and innovation. Today many critics are militant about inclusiveness and are suspicious of any attempt to exclude anything from the domain of art for any reason. All forms of elitism are under attack. In addition, technologies such as audio tape, video tape, and the computer have helped create a new culture that obliterates distinctions between the present and the past, the permanent and the temporary, and the original and the copy. Culture is seen less in terms of value than of use. And everything can be used.

There is much more latitude today in what can be seriously studied. Even if they are not identified as art, blue jeans, the Spice Girls, and the Mall of America receive the same kind of serious attention from today's scholars that earlier writers invested in James Joyce's *Ulysses,* Picasso's *Guernica,* and Igor Stravinsky's *Rite of Spring*. We live in what Douglas Kellner calls a "media culture" where different media, various genres, images, and objects themselves exist primarily in terms of the meanings given to them (1995, 2–10). He advocates a method of cultural analysis "that takes culture as spectrum and applies similar critical methods to all cultural artifacts ranging from opera to popular music, from modernist literature to soap opera" (Kellner 1995, 29). The difficulty is that his theory leaves no room for quality, for art. The value of what he calls "cultural artifacts" is found in what they reveal about power relations, not in their aesthetic quality. In fact he, like a number of contemporary critics, questions the very notion of "authentic art," as being "highly problematic" because it privileges high culture at the expense of popular culture. The effect of this view is to level the field to the point where art seems to have no unique value or position at all.

Every conceivable part of the culture is understood, according to critics such as Kellner, simply as a kind of text different only in the ways that it is contextualized, not because of any intrinsic quality that it might possess. Postmodernism develops out of theories that deny essences—so it is almost impossible to find widespread agreement that anything, from Shakespeare to Picasso, possesses essential beauty, essential meaning, or essential style— much contemporary theory recognizes only shifting indeterminate contexts. Everything exists in a complex network of contested signs whose meanings are determined through the struggle between the producers of these signs and their consumer/interpreters. Cultural analysis, in contemporary terms, reveals "both the way the dominant ideology is structured into the text and into the reading subject, and those textual features that enable negotiated, resisting, or oppositional readings to be made" (Fiske 1989a, 98).

On the other hand, among those critics who hold on to notions of quality and excellence, the tendency has been to widen the privileged category of art by including works that have been excluded, ignored, or devalued by a traditional cultural establishment because they were created by members of marginalized groups, such as rap music, graffiti, and quilting. In the context of the breakdown of cultural hierarchies, contested cultural terrain, and the postmodern accent on pluralism, it is not difficult to make a case for the inclusion of custom cars and hot rods as works of art.

But this tendency to include more and different kinds of creative activity under the mantle of the fine arts, in fact, has been a general trend in critical circles since the beginnings of the modern era. The traditional fine arts— painting, sculpture, architecture, music, and poetry—were joined by the serious novel in the nineteenth century and photography, film, and jazz in the first decades of the twentieth century. Even television shows have been recognized as worthy of serious investigation as texts and entitled to respect as art forms. What contemporary critic would not recognize the significance of John Ford? Television shows like *Homicide* and *The Sopranos* are praised as important art works equal to the best that Hollywood has produced, something inconceivable as recently as thirty years ago. It is no longer possible to question seriously whether Charlie Parker is one of the most important figures in modern music. Composers like John Zorn and Frank Zappa, who have one foot in rock 'n' roll and the other in the modernist avant-garde, tend to make the whole question of high versus low culture absurd.

It is not just the more inclusive spirit of the current era that accounts for the wider range of art forms that is studied. The early modernist assaults on what had been generally understood as the essential qualities that made something a work of art, like tonality in music or representation in painting, or rhyme and meter in poetry, as well as the general assaults that modernists made on traditional values of skill, beauty, and aesthetic pleasure, have weakened our confidence in defining art or even locating it. Duchamp's ready-mades, dada sound poems, and futurist performances, to name just a few examples, prepared the way for making it almost impossible to say what disqualifies something from being art.

Not all modern art, however, is "anti-art." In fact much work that appears to be anti-art is quite the opposite. For many modern artists the challenge was to develop new conceptions of skill, form, beauty, and aesthetic pleasure as they broke away from art based on representation, traditional subject matter, and materials, and from the very idea that art was an imitation of something and not a thing-in-itself. The challenge, for example, that Georges Braque, one of the founders of Cubism, faced was to "create a new form of beauty, the beauty that appears to me in terms of volume, of mass, of weight" (Braque 1908–1909, 259–60). For a dada artist such as Kurt Schwitters modern art still requires skill and discipline, "I have taken a step in advance of mere oil painting, for in addition to playing off color against color, line against line, form against form, etc. I play off material against material. . . . Freedom is not lack of restraint, but the product of strict artistic discipline" (Schwitters 1921, 383–84). For an abstract artist like Robert Motherwell modern art satisfies a basic human need that art has addressed for centuries: "The need is for felt experience—intense, immediate, direct, subtle, unified, warm, vivid, rhythmic" (Motherwell 1951, 564). It is this strain of modernism that rodders and customizers have a deep connection with.

Even though modern art has made it more difficult for critics to identify the common characteristics that link together disparate objects under the single term art, it is hard to find one who suggests that art is a meaningless category. On the contrary most recognize that it is still a term loaded with cultural prestige and power. Anything given the label of art by the ever-present (and ever-elusive) cultural establishment becomes more valuable, culturally and economically, and more potent politically.

Art represents and sanctifies what is valued in modern society; it imparts both cultural authority and importance to particular ideas and images. The authority attaches not only to the objects designated as art, but also to those who create and appreciate such objects, giving them social status and honor. (Metcalf Jr. and Weatherford 1988, 142)

Whatever is named "art" also gets a voice. People respond to scratches on a piece of metal, strewn bits of paper, and cut-up books differently when they are acknowledged by some authority as art. These works are placed in special cultural spaces and described in specialized languages. They are given meaning. The struggles that have taken place in recent years, the so-called culture wars, over NEA-funded exhibitions, pornography, and the literary canon demonstrate how meaningful the term remains even if it can't be adequately defined.

In recent years the focus of postmodernist criticism has shifted from deconstructions of meaning to issues of race, class, and gender and how their representations in various media are constructed and contested. Contemporary theory champions diversity and seeks to foreground work of marginalized groups in the arena of public discourse. For American cultural critics the focus has been much more on race and gender than on class, especially the white working class. This is not the case in England, especially in the contemporary field of cultural studies, where much attention has been paid to the cultural practices and politics of the white working class, perhaps because class struggle is still so much more a part of the political debate there than in this country.

The voices of the American white working class have tended to be represented in the political arena by conservative figures such as Patrick Buchanan. Because conservatives have also focused much of their efforts on preserving categories like the Western canon of "great" books, arguing for the value of tradition and resisting "weakening of standards," it is unlikely that they would champion hot rodders as serious modern artists. With a few widely scattered exceptions, the work of almost exclusively white working-class car builders has been invisible to cultural critics, just as the whole class has generally been:

Whether the blue-collar male is actually as benighted as he seems, or perhaps has some good reason for his belligerence, is not a question that has consumed sex-role theorists. He was assigned, in the scheme of things, to the lowest level of consciousness, the dumping ground for all the vestigial masculine traits discarded by the middle-class life. His association with a prior stage of the middle-class life cycle—boyish "physical striving"—only confirmed his diagnosis as a psychic retard; and, in keeping with American egalitarianism, this diagnosis substituted for more overt and now outmoded forms of class prejudice. (Ehrenreich 1983, 136)

The prevalence of such a prejudiced view of working-class culture makes it difficult to conceive of working-class car builders as sensitive, intelligent, innovative, and imaginative, as well as very skilled, creators of art works.

Sometimes it is not a matter of class *per se* that makes it difficult for critics to "see" Kus-

tom Kulture, but the very ideas they have about cars in terms of class:

Pop psychology tells us that Americans cherish the car as status symbol or sex symbol or symbol of power. That is a middle-class point of view. It suggests that most of us drive only passenger cars or sports cars. But most blue-collar Americans think of their automobile in economic terms: it is either a work tool, essential for their livelihood, or a form of capital. This is particularly true of young, low-income Americans: they acquire an old car in bad condition, or a van or a pickup, replace its engine, modify its chassis, paint it, show it off—and then sell it at a profit. . . . All in all, for one who is unskilled, and poorly educated and young, there is no better way of making money than having a car. (Jackson 1994, 167)

No doubt there are working-class individuals who see cars in purely economic terms. But not in the Kustom Kulture. The idea that a rodder or customizer chooses an "old" car to "fix up" for economic gain is absurd. John Brinckerhoff Jackson simply doesn't understand or can't appreciate the potency of the car in the working-class world. He doesn't recognize how the symbolic meanings of rods and customs differ from the cars of the middle class where meaning *is* derived largely from marketing and advertising. In the Kustom Kulture, especially, cars—modified old cars like Deuce coupes and '57 Chevys—are not only symbols of status, sex, and power but also of individual identity and group allegiance. More important, they are expressions of a sophisticated aesthetic. With rare exceptions these cars are built with the full knowledge that the builder will lose money in the process. They are a labor of love. They are built to be perfect. They are cars like Bill Hirth's understated 1950 Ford coupe,

Figure 12.
"Black Thunder." Bill Hirth's Ford coupe has been chopped, sectioned, and mounted on a Monte Carlo chassis so that it rides like a modern production car.

"Black Thunder" (see figure 12), which was chopped, sectioned, shortened, and channeled in his own garage, not so he could sell it, but because "I had the time to build the car I always dreamt about" (Hirth 1999, interview).

The attitudes that academics have toward cars in general also makes it difficult for them to see rods and customs as art. Academics are responsible for a good portion of the anti-car sentiment prominent since the mid-sixties when John Keats's *Insolent Chariots* and Ralph Nader's *Unsafe at Any Speed* appeared and made hating cars fashionable. For them the car

is at best a necessary evil, a basic form of transportation, at worst a destroyer of the environment and a threat to the very idea of community. Academics seldom equate cars with dreams. They are more a social and cultural nightmare. As Stanley Fish satirizes his colleagues' taste in cars:

On a day in the mid-seventies—it may have varied in different parts of the country and at different universities—American academics stopped buying ugly Volkswagens and started buying ugly Volvos, with a few nonconformists opting for ugly Saabs. . . . Why Volvos; why not Oldsmobiles, or Chryslers, or Mercury station wagons? The answer I think is that Volvos provided a solution to a new dilemma facing many academics—how to enjoy the benefits of increasing affluence while at the same time maintaining the proper attitude of disdain toward the goods affluence brings. . . . The ugliness of the Volvo becomes its most attractive feature for it allows those who own one to plead innocent of the charge of really wanting it. . . . We don't buy these big expensive luxurious cars because we want to be comfortable or (God forbid) ostentatious; we buy them because we want to be safe. (Fish 1993, 102)

It is not enough for academics simply to buy an ugly car in order to escape the harmful effects of Madison Avenue and Detroit. They emphasize how unimportant the car is, and should be, by cultivating a kind of benign neglect of their cars. Their cars are often unwashed, letting their typical gray or blue paint fade into an indeterminate color somewhere in between. Minor dents become signs of moral rectitude. They make a fetish out of indifference. What joy they find in owning a car is found only in beating planned obsolescence by keeping their cars for many years. In such a world the idea that someone might spend thousands of dollars chroming engine parts, slamming a car to the ground (lowering it drastically), rounding hood corners, chopping its top, or souping its engine would be incomprehensible or simply bizarre. For the most part, though, those who do such things to cars are merely invisible to the academic community.

At the same time, these car builders have not been exactly clamoring for the prestige of the label of *artist*. The term, while it is seen to have some value, seems remote and essentially irrelevant to many of these builders. When I asked Frank McShane, for example, if he thought his gleaming chopped red '51 Mercury was a work of art or if he thought of himself as an artist, he shook his head, "No, not really. I like to build cars. That's not really art, is

it?" (McShane 1994, interview). Being seen as artists brings as many problems as it does advantages. Other builders nodded politely when I said I thought their work deserved to be seen as art. As far as they are concerned, there is not much benefit in the label.

These builders have also not really articulated their own positions in any great depth. Although they acknowledge their passion for building and their interest in design, they are often content to explain what they do simply in terms of making their cars look better and enumerating the changes they have made. They are less comfortable with the larger meanings of what they do.

It is not just the builders who are suspicious of the label artist and examining the practice more critically. Noted rodding historian Pat Ganahl, former editor of *Rod & Custom* and current editor of the new, high-end *Rodder's Journal,* is very skeptical of the art world's ability to understand car culture and dubious about the label. In the catalog for the show "Kustom Kulture" at the Laguna Art Museum in 1993 he distances himself not only from the museum world ("Museums and galleries usually get this wrong"), but also from the very idea that these cars might be art:

There is nothing artistic about automobiles. They are functional machines skinned with bodies designed to promote their salability on show room floors. Sure, some buyers literally love these designs, but that doesn't make them art.

A hot rodder strips this mass-produced vehicle to its bare essentials, pumps the engine full of horsepower, and possibly adds a few innovative embellishments to mark it unmistakably as his hot rod—immediately identifiable as such at first sighting on the street. The customizer smooths and sleekens the factory body, removes excess ornamentation—especially brand emblems (again, to personalize and mystify the car)—lowers it as much as possible, and coats it in luscious, custom-mixed paint. Neither the hot rodder nor the customizer is an artist; what they do is a craft. (Ganahl 1993, 8)

In the end he is not even sure if the show he introduces "gets it right."

Part of Kustom Kulture's reluctance to embrace the term *art* comes from the general conception that Americans have of artists. Even in the nineties, it is hard for them to see artists as other than odd, even exotic creatures. The media have reinforced characterizations of artists as self-absorbed eccentrics, frauds, sissies, hypocrites, parasites, and pretenders. Ned Rorem, the accomplished composer, reported in a recent radio interview that he suffered more in his life for being an artist than for being a homosexual. Excluded from public discourse on almost everything but their own lives and celebrated too often more for the scandal of their lives than the accomplishment of their work, American artists remain somewhat alien creatures, a situation the Beats took great advantage of, celebrating their difference rather than lamenting it. For working-class males, the idea of being an artist often seems to be something to be avoided rather than sought after, despite the fact that what is clearly visible in their work is artistic achievement. It's safer to shrug it off, not to have it matter.

But it does matter.

It is not difficult to appreciate these cars simply on the level of craft. Certainly one can't deny the difficulty of the work that goes into making a radical custom. It is one thing to decide that the roof line of a '49 Mercury is wrong, and should be lowered and tapered, or

that the fenders on a '55 Chevy should be extended seven inches to accommodate huge Packard taillights, and another to bring it off seamlessly without the aid of manuals and guidebooks. But there is much more going on in making a custom than solving difficult technical challenges. These modifications must also work together if the car is not to become simply an oddity.

Despite what is often said by their builders, these cars were and are intended to have aesthetic value, that is, they were built to demonstrate advances in style and move their audiences emotionally even if they were not consciously intended to be art as such. They exhibit most of the well-known and generally accepted attributes of art objects—they are well made, imaginatively designed, and expressively painted. The cars also often demonstrate an awareness of historical style, and the best achieve uniqueness of style. They are not "anti-art" in the way that the Duchamp ready-mades are. Like Braque's paintings they are about beauty. In line, rhythm, balance, harmony, tension, and form they fit the traditional aesthetic vocabulary. They easily conform to the definition of a modernist aesthetician like Clive Bell, who emphasized in 1914 the importance of "significant form," that is, a form which is intended to produce an emotional response as the quintessential quality of art (Bell 1914, 15–23).

But there are social dimensions to art as well as formal. If only one person chops a car's top, it is merely eccentric. But when thousands do it, it becomes a cultural practice, one that is rooted in a powerful identification with the car and the desire to express the meanings of that identification. Modifying cars, like all art, is both self-expressive and social.

The first hot rods were meant to be raced. Those who watched were participants and spectators, fans at a sporting event not art lovers. But the first customs were built to be viewed. They were intended for an audience, on display or in performance, whether sitting in a parking lot, slowly cruising the strip, or rapidly accelerating from a stoplight. Even today they are presented in artfully designed settings or carefully orchestrated performances. As it is in art galleries and museums, the best cars present to a knowledgeable audience new designs, new strategies, and new combinations that continually revise and extend current practices. There is an art history here, not so different from the succession of styles one finds in modern art. From the very beginning of customizing, styles, both individual and regional, evolved, became passé, and then were revived. A Barris custom is clearly different from a Winfield. An early fifties custom is very different from a late fifties custom. And each custom radically re-imagines the original (see figures 13, 14, and 15).

Even hot rods have become more artifacts than race cars, more a statement about the perfection of the idea of hot rod than useful as a racer. As early as the late forties hot rods were being built for looks, not just for the track. Since 1948 the one judged best of all has been awarded the America's Most Beautiful Roadster (AMBR) award in Oakland or San Francisco.

For the critic and aesthetician Morse Peckham, a historic evolution of styles, what he calls "stylistic dynamism," is essential in identifying what can be fruitfully recognized as art: "Any object (or perceptual field) from any culture may, then, be properly categorized as having been the occasion for artistic percep-

tion if a chronologically arranged sequence of such objects shows both a functional identity and a non-functional stylistic dynamism" (Peckham 1965, 71). For evidence of the stylistic dynamism of Kustom Kulture refer to plate 60 which traces the evolution of styles of bathtub '49 to '51 Mercs from the early fifties to the late nineties.

In addition a work of art is, according to Peckham, distinguished from everything else not because of any particular characteristics that it has as "a something" that has been identified as art, but through the role that perceivers play in the presence of these somethings that exhibit stylistic dynamism. As he says, "A work of art is what the perceiver observes in what has been culturally established as a perceiver's space" (Peckham 1965, 65).

And so, according to this view, there *is* a real difference between Duchamp's shovel and one that you or I might buy in the hardware store. It hangs in a gallery to be gazed at, not in a garage to be used. Duchamp's is art because we look at it as art in spaces that are reserved for art, and so it immediately takes its place in a long history of disparate objects called "art" and it changes as we understand that history. Even Duchamp didn't understand entirely how powerful the role of the art viewer is in changing our perceptions of an object:

Readymades were intended by Duchamp to be devoid of aesthetic interest. Their selection, he has said, took place in a moment of total visual anesthesia. But though Robert Motherwell exaggerates when he says that the *Bottlerack* of 1914 appears in retrospect to have a more beautiful form than almost any deliberate sculpture made that year, there is no question that after years of assimilation of real

Figure 13.
Stock 1951 Mercury Club coupe. Courtesy of Ford Motor Co.

objects into sculptures of all sorts, many of the Readymades have taken on an inescapable "arty" look. (Rubin 1968, 19)

Stylistic dynamism in the custom car world is fueled by the same forces that fuel it in the world of art galleries—the vision of a handful of masters responding to a cultural moment. While thousands of customizers practiced their art in garages and driveways across the country, they generally followed the lead of important builders such as George and Sam Barris, the Ayala brothers, Gene Winfield, Joe Wilhelm, Joe Bailon, Bill Cushenberry, Darryl Starbird, the Alexander brothers, and Larry Watson. Each developed a unique style and, like Ezra Pound at the beginning of the century, saw that the obligation of the artist was to "make it new." Like more traditional artists, these builders were commissioned by patrons; there is no other way to describe them even if the pa-

trons were only fifteen years old as Floyd De-Bore was when he brought his '58 Pontiac to Watson a year before he even had a driver's license. Their bodyshops produced thousands of works often without more specific directions than "give me something new."

This model of dissemination of stylistic innovations conforms almost exactly to the one Ezra Pound proposed at the beginning of the modern era in the 1920s when he divided artists into the following categories: Inventors ("men who found a new process"), Masters ("men who combined a number of such processes and used them better than the inventors"), Diluters ("men who followed after" and who produced "something flabbier") (Pound 1929, 23–24). Customizing has its inventors (Westergard and Bertolucci), its masters (the Barris brothers, Winfield, Bailon, Watson, Jeffries, Roth, and Von Dutch), and its diluters (in bodyshops and backyards across the country) who validated the innovations of the masters.

Artworks are not valued by audiences just for their appearance or construction, but also because of the meanings that can be extracted from them. As Social Distortion's Mike Ness recognizes, rods and customs "make a statement." They are interpreted as well as perceived. Hot rods and customs are rich in meaning—aesthetic, social, and political. They raise interesting and important questions about the car and its place in the culture, about the builders and their personalities, about the expressive power of form and color, about cultural styles and identity.

A major source of the power that these cars have to move their audiences emotionally comes from the fact that their subject matter is also their medium. The car was and is a potent cultural symbol. Its meanings are embedded in

Figure 14.
Barris '51 Mercury convertible. One of the original custom Mercs built by Barris. Made a significant appearance in the movie *Running Wild* in 1955. Restored by Bill Layton.

America's understanding of itself. The car functions as a sign of power, prosperity, status, and accomplishment. Despite pollution, gas shortages, and traffic jams, the car continues to represent, perhaps more than any other commodity, ideas of freedom, progress, and hope. We continue to believe, as we buy more SUVs, Ford's optimistic version of the myth of the open road that was presented first in one of its 1951 ads:

Today the American Road has no end: The road that went nowhere now goes everywhere. . . . The

Figure 15.
Winfield '51 Merc. Built for Bill Wolfe. One of the few significant bathtub Mercs built in the late fifties. It is not chopped because Wolfe didn't want to pay the extra money (about $150) for the chop job. Courtesy of Gene Winfield.

wheels move endlessly, always moving, always for-ward—and always lengthening the American Road. On that road the nation is steadily traveling beyond the troubles of this century, constantly heading to-ward finer tomorrows. The American Road is paved with hope. (in Lewis and Goldstein 1983, 289)

Modified cars are not easily seen in ways that would produce complex "readings," be-cause they are positioned within this myth and outside of it at the same time. In fact, the very reason for their widespread success, their connections to the teen culture of the 1950s, is, at least partly, responsible for their invisibil-ity. Rods and customs are often so entangled in the clichés and the sentimentality of the fifties—the jukeboxes, the sock hops, the soda fountains, and gas stations—that it is difficult to separate them from the cultural white noise that surrounds them and to look at them on their own terms. Too often they have become mere anonymous accessories, like leather jackets and tight sweaters, to nos-talgia for teen rebellion, teen heroes, and all the teen fads that have come to represent the fifties. They are hard to see as unique works of art created by individual artists. Today even the builders themselves often have a hard time separating their cars from their rosy memories of the era.

Even in the first few tentative steps to rec-ognize these cars as aesthetic objects, such as the 1993 show at the Laguna Art Museum, there is still some hesitancy in describing the cars completely in aesthetic terms. In the pref-ace to the catalog, for example, Charles Des-marais, the museum director, seems more com-fortable presenting customizing as some sort of anthropological phenomenon than as an art movement: "With floods of cultural hormones pulsing through Southern California's veins, the region became a focal point for American youth—a metaphor for post-pubescent energy and anxiousness and creativity. And so, a craze became something else, with its own language, mores, traditions and art—a culture, cus-tomized for its age and geography" (Desmarais 1993, 7).

In *Seeing Is Forgetting the Name of the Thing One Sees,* the artist Robert Irwin tells a very illuminating story, worth quoting at length, about the art community's resistance to recog-nizing these cars as art:

Of course, what's going on in such situations [modifying cars] is precisely an artistic activity. A lot of art critics, especially New York *Artforum* types, have a lot of trouble seeing the validity of such a contention. I once had a run-in with one of them about this—this was years later, in the middle of the Ferus period. This guy was out here, one of the head honchos, and he was upset—what was it?—oh, yeah—because Billy Al Bengston was racing motorcy-cles at the time. The critic just dismissed that out of hand as superficial self-indulgence. And I said you can't do that. We got going and ended up arguing about folk art. He was one of those Marxist critics who like to think they're real involved with the peo-ple, making great gestures and so forth, but they're hardly in the world at all. Anyway, he was talking about pot-making and weaving and everything, and my feeling was that that all was historical art but not folk art. As far as I'm concerned, a folk art is when you take a utilitarian object, something you use everyday, and you give it overlays of your own per-sonality, what it is you feel and so forth. You enhance it with your life. And a folk art in the current period of time would more appropriately be in the area of something like a motorcycle. I mean a motorcycle can be a lot more than just a machine that runs along; it can be a whole description of a personality and an aesthetic.

Anyway, so I looked in the paper, and found this ad of a guy who was selling a hot rod and a motorcycle. And I took the critic out to this place. It was really fortunate, because it was exactly what I wanted. We arrived at this place in the Valley, in the middle of nowhere, and here's this kid: he's selling a hot rod and he's got another he's working on. He's selling a '32 coupe, and he's got a '29 roadster in the garage. The '32 he was getting rid of was an absolute cherry. But what was more interesting, and which I was able to show this critic, was that here was the '29, absolutely dismantled, I mean completely apart, and the kid was making basic decisions about the frame, whether or not he was going to cad plate certain bolts or whether he was going to buff grind them, whether he was just going to leave them raw as they were. He was insulating and soundproofing the doors, all kinds of things that no one would ever know or see unless they were truly a sophisticate in this area. But, I mean, real aesthetic decisions, truly aesthetic decisions. Here was a fifteen-year-old who wouldn't know art from schmart, but you couldn't talk about a more real aesthetic activity than what he was doing, how he was carefully weighing: what was the attitude of this whole thing? What exactly? How should it look? What was the relationship in terms of its machinery, its social bearing, everything? I mean all these things were being weighed in terms of the aesthetics of how the thing should *look*. It was a perfect example.

The critic simply denied it. Simply denied it: not important, unreal, untrue, doesn't happen, doesn't exist. See, he comes from a world in New York where the automobile. . . . I mean, automobiles are "What? Automobile? Nothing." Right? I mean, no awareness, no sensitivity, no involvement. So he simply denied it. (Weschler 1982, 17–18)

There are a number of labels that critics might accept before they would see these cars as examples of modernist art. They might be more comfortable with Irwin's notion of folk art or some category of popular art. But even these categories present problems.

Certainly a case can be made that modifying cars is a popular art form. The criteria are certainly loose enough. If it is anything, building rods and customs is popular. It is practiced by tens of thousands of people from coast to coast, enough to support a multi-million-dollar industry specializing in a wide assortment of parts, ranging from engine modifications like add-on superchargers to complete replicas of classic bodies like the Deuce and the '40 Ford. It is possible to construct a complete car from parts in catalogs. Each year there are hundreds of car shows across the country that draw hundreds of thousands of visitors to see as many as seven or eight thousand cars in a single show. In their origins customizing and hot rodding certainly began "with the people" in the garages, gas stations, and driveways across America.

But the history of the terms *popular art* and *popular culture* is, like *art* and *postmodernism*, a contested one. Early in its use popular culture was a term loaded with negative value judgments. The popular was equated, by such critics as Dwight Macdonald, with a debased form of culture, "a cancerous growth on High Culture" (1953, 59) that leads to a kind of mind-numbing groupthink. For another critic it marked a "corruption of past high culture" through "mutilation and condensation" (van den Haag 1957, 524). Critics on both the left and the right have condemned popular art as homogenized, formulaic, simplistic, and sentimental. On the left, particularly in the Frankfurt School, much has been made of popular culture as an important tool of capitalist exploitation, creating false consciousness and pseudo-values.

Others like William Gass, a literary critic, devalue the popular from a purely aesthetic point of view:

> The products of popular culture, by and large, have no more esthetic quality than a brick in the street. . . . Any esthetic intention is entirely absent, and because it is desired to manipulate consciousness directly, achieve one's effect there, no mind is paid to the intrinsic nature of its objects; they lack finish, complexity, stasis, individuality, coherence, depth, and endurance. (in Browne 1970, 15)

Customs certainly do possess "finish, complexity," as well as the rest of Gass's criteria for aesthetic value. It is difficult to see how these negative characterizations of popular art can be applied to hot rodding and customizing.

Another difficulty with the term *popular art* is that it has often been used synonymously with *mass culture* and therefore identified with the production of the large culture industries: television networks, recording companies, and Hollywood studios, rather than with individual artists or independent creators. One of the most widely used early anthologies published in 1957, for example, is titled *Mass Culture: The Popular Arts in America* and divides its sections by these large media: mass literature, television and radio, motion pictures, and advertising.

Even critics who are more sympathetic toward popular culture often damn it with faint praise. Abraham Kaplan writes in "The Aesthetics of the Popular Arts":

> My thesis is this: that popular art is not the degradation of taste but its immaturity, not the product of external social forces but produced by a dynamic intrinsic to the aesthetic itself. . . . Popular art is thus doubly derivative: art first becomes academic and then it becomes popular; as art achieves style it provides the seeds of its own destruction. (Kaplan 1967, 321–22)

Still others like Herbert Gans defend popular art as just adequate for its particular audience: "Because taste cultures reflect the class and particularly educational attributes of their publics, low culture is as valid for poorly educated Americans as high culture is for well-educated ones, even if the high cultures are, in the abstract, better or more comprehensive than the lower cultures" (in Alland Jr. 1977, 132). Hardly a ringing endorsement of the quality of American popular culture.

More contemporary and theory-oriented critics like John Fiske have drawn useful distinctions between mass culture and popular culture: mass culture represents the productions of the mass-culture industry—its films, television shows, recordings, blue jeans, soft drinks, and so forth, while popular culture represents the resistance that consumers of these products have to being dominated by them. Thus, when Timberland products became popular among rappers several years ago (to the confusion and consternation of Timberland executives who spent millions of dollars a year constructing woodsy meanings for their products that had nothing to do with the urban ghetto), we have an example of what Fiske means by popular culture—creating new meanings for mass-cultural objects by "resisting" meanings imposed from above. The same sort of thing seems to be happening today to Abercrombie & Fitch, although its corporate management has learned the lesson and isn't resisting the change of its products' meanings as it counts the profits.

Fiske's concept of "resistance" as key to understanding the popular is very relevant to the original hot rodders and customizers who, at the height of American corporate power, "undid" the meanings assigned to cars by Detroit and Madison Avenue and created new ones by demonstrating that an old Chevy, covered in primer, could be more desirable than a more expensive brand-new DeSoto; that a chopped and channeled twenty-year-old Deuce coupe could turn heads much faster than a new Cadillac, supposedly the ultimate object of automotive desire. But what Fiske's distinction does not allow for is an adequate consideration of the workmanship, the devotion to craft, the sophisticated sense of form, and the imagination that goes into these cars. Just the kind of material creativity his theory seems to deny:

> With very few and marginal exceptions, people cannot and do not produce their own commodities, material or cultural, as they might have done in tribal or folk societies. . . . The creativity of popular culture lies not in the production of commodities so much as in the productive use of industrial commodities. The art of the people is the art of "making do." (Fiske 1989b, 27–28)

But customizing is more about "making" than "making do." It is about more than just using commodities to construct "meanings of self, of social identity and social relations" (Fiske 1989b, 11), although it often does that as well.

If Robert Irwin's definition of folk art, "a utilitarian object" given "overlays of your own personality, what it is you feel and so forth," were universal, I would have less of a problem seeing these cars as folk art even without an identifiable "folk," because he recognizes the crucial questions that these cars raise. He understands the process that the builders of these

cars go through. He appreciates the similarities between what he does as an established artist and what that "kid" was doing, making the essential decisions, the "real aesthetic decisions, truly aesthetic decisions," that have to do with the act of creation. But too many critics are like the one in Irwin's story, unable to see these cars as folk art because they share a much different set of assumptions about such art. The view of folk art out of cultural studies is likely to echo John Fiske: in "capitalist societies there is no so-called authentic folk culture" (1989b, 27). Or a definition of folk art might follow the views of more conventional critics like Edmund Feldman, in *The Artist: A Social History,* who believes that it has fairly easily recognized characteristics: "the typical qualities of the age-old folk art tradition: frontality, semiabstract form, realistic detail, careful finish. Consistency of form or technique does not especially worry the folk artist" (Feldman 1995, 34).

These are not qualities that are easily applied to hot rods and customs. Here the term is also clearly associated with a "folk" historically, geographically or culturally removed from highly complex industrial cultures. These folk, according to Feldman, seem to be primarily interested in decoration. That puts them at the opposite end of the aesthetic spectrum from customizers and rodders:

> Today we speak of the "gaily decorated" character of folk art—the embroidery of a peasant skirt, the flowers painted around the edges of an earthenware bowl, the cheerful designs carved into the plain surface of a piece of furniture. From the standpoint of the folk artist this ornamentation enlivens the object, makes it bright and attractive. It is a concession to aesthetics. From another standpoint the artist's wish is to cover vacant surfaces—the result,

perhaps, of *horror vacui*, the fear of emptiness. The same motive may impel urban youngsters to cover the walls of a building or all the surfaces of a subway train with spray-can graffiti. Plain, undecorated objects make the folk uneasy. . . . Folk art is almost always utilitarian art. . . . We are dealing with works of genuine artistic worth created outside the norms of art-historical development and high-art tradition. But folk art does belong to a tradition—the Neolithic tradition, which is the oldest continuous tradition we have. (Feldman 1995, 36–39)

Closer to this notion of folk art are so-called art cars—cars decorated with literally anything or everything: thousands of marbles or hundreds of clocks or toy soldiers, Elvis memorabilia, and television sets—which are transformed into "a personal totem, a shrine on wheels" (Kannapell 1999, 18). But Kustom Kulture is a product of an industrial culture not a neolithic one.

Other folklorists are more sympathetic to a wider range of folk art. Henry Glassie has effectively argued that folk art should not be limited to traditional notions of the "folk." His work emphasizing the aesthetic qualities of everyday life has led to studies of a whole new range of folk works from modifying tract homes to creating gardens, from storytelling to tattooing. He has also convincingly made the case that pejorative terms like "naive, provincial, crude, primitive and unsophisticated" do not define folk art and that it is a mistake to consider folk art condescendingly as "substandard but charming." He even recognizes the creativity in car customizing:

In my day, no self-respecting teenage boy would drive his parents' car. The kid who bought a Ford used the profit from his paper route to buy an old one. Then with the help from Manny, Moe and Jack, he reinvented it, removing the opulent chrome ornaments of the adult, filling holes with lead, painting the body with splotches of barn-red primer, and almost never giving it the lacquered finish of his dreams. Thus, recreated, the Ford became an expression of a second culture. The culture of the Ford Motor Company and the culture of the teenager came to coexist fitfully in automotive fabric. . . . The customized car (that is what we called them) like the old house modified over the centuries, like the whole vast landscape, embodies creative layering. It expresses simultaneously the wills of many makers. . . . The user's will endures in the act of alteration. . . . Use becomes creation when objects become parts of objects, when the physical context becomes a creative composition. (Glassie 1999, 81)

Glassie's idea of "creative layering" is very useful in understanding the art of customizing, but his example of a typical backyard teen customizer who creates a conservative mild custom ignores the achievements of master builders like Barris and Winfield. Thus, the distinction Glassie makes between folk art (conservative) and elite art (progressive) seems to lift the masterpieces of Kustom Kulture out of the realm of folk art: "While the elite artist may be willing to risk his standing to appear ahead of his times, it is only the rare folk artist who strives for innovation; his replication is an affirmation of a tradition" (Glassie 1982, 130).

Dick Hebdige's conception of a subculture that emerges from his examination of English style communities, from teddy boys to skinheads and punks, also has some important application to a consideration of car culture even though he resists seeing style in subcultures as artistic in a conventional sense. Hebdige, for example, criticizes J. Nuttal's view that "decorated rocker jackets . . . show the creative impulse at its purest and most inventive":

> Subcultures are not cultural in this sense, and the styles with which they are identified cannot be adequately or usefully described as "art of a high degree." Rather they manifest culture in the broader sense, as systems of communication, forms of expression and representation. They conform to the structural anthropologists' definition of culture as "coded exchanges of reciprocal messages." In the same way, subcultural styles do indeed qualify as art but as art in (and out of) particular contexts; not as timeless objects, judged by the immutable criteria of traditional aesthetics, but as "appropriations," "thefts," subversive transformations, as *movement*. (Hebdige 1979, 129)

Hebdige is excellent at locating the oppositional elements in the styles that subcultures adopt and which in turn frame the class struggles that originally impelled the development of these styles. "Each subculture," he says, "moves through a cycle of resistance and defusion" (Hebdige 1979, 130). As he sees it, commodity capitalism ransacks subcultures in search of new styles, thus forcing subcultures continually to invent alternatives in order to preserve their sense of identity outside the system. For Hebdige, subcultures are expressive forms that reveal "a fundamental tension between those in power and those condemned to subordinate positions and second-class lives" (Hebdige 1979, 132).

The issue of class is clearly central to an understanding of the place (or lack of it) of hot rodding and customizing in American culture.

The origin of hot rodding as an "outlaw" movement of white working-class males, embodying conceptions of style and cool, as well as risk and rebellion, is crucial to understanding how it spread through the culture.

The hot rodder as icon is part of the same paradigm of masculinity that helped form teen identity in early rock 'n' roll through various outlaw images of Elvis, Gene Vincent, Eddie Cochran, and Jerry Lee Lewis. The subculture that emerged from the marriage of rodding and rock 'n' roll was certainly oppositional. From the beginning it defined itself against middle-class values and conventions by celebrating speed, danger, and kicks.

Hebdige has much to offer on the complexity of these subcultural styles, but his late-Marxist analysis, in addition to missing the "creation of timeless objects," ignores the celebratory elements, the carnival spirit of popular culture, that one finds especially in the car culture—the joyous Americanness of this subculture that produced anthems like the Beach Boys' "Little Deuce Coupe" and Ronnie and the Daytonas' "GTO," rituals like the cruise, and notable cars like the Hirohata Merc, Moonglow, and the Beatnik Bandit.

What critics, from Glassie to Hebdige, miss is the "stylistic dynamism" that characterizes Kustom Kulture where the pursuit of new styles, new techniques, and new forms continually renews the practice in ways much closer to the art world than to the folk or popular.

Kustom Kulture is not just defusion and opposition, it is celebration of beauty, form, rhythm, and, ultimately, perfection. The car is not just a symbol of opposition, it is also a symbol of identity and connection. The car represents mastery of the key symbol of modern technological society. It is power and it is about power and being empowered. America's love of the car is consistent with what David E. Nye calls the "American Technological Sublime":

The sublime underlies the enthusiasm for technology. One of the most powerful human emotions, when experienced by large groups the sublime can weld society together. In moments of sublimity human beings temporarily disregard divisions among elements of the community. The sublime taps into fundamental hopes and fears. . . . It is an essentially religious feeling, aroused by the confrontation with impressive objects, such as Niagara Falls, the Grand Canyon, the New York skyline, the Golden Gate Bridge, or the earth-shaking launch of the space shuttle. (Nye 1994, xiii)

And for the members of the Kustom Kulture, this feeling was sparked by channeled Deuce coupes, chopped Mercurys, and the earth-shaking launch of AA fuel dragsters.

As absurd as it might seem to think about cars, any cars, in these terms, their impact can be profound, even life changing. In 1971 Rick Dore was in Phoenix and happened to see a chopped Merc on the road. He followed it for blocks before losing it. "I wasn't even into cars. My wife knew more about customs than I did" (Dore 2000, interview). But Dore, a native of New York City, had found his life's mission and a new career. He is now one of the most important builders of contemporary customs. A decade earlier Ray Soff saw Jimmy Karcher's chopped '50 Ford convertible in a show at the New York Coliseum. Still in his teens he vowed that one day he would own that car. He spent almost two decades tracking it down, eventu-

ally finding it wrecked in a field on Long Island. After much research—he has meticulously reconstructed the entire history of the car—he has restored it to its original condition. He has turned down many offers to buy the car. "Why should I sell my dream?" (Soff 2000, interview). Countless others have been similarly inspired by cars such as the Matranga Merc, the Hirohata Merc, the Watson '50 Chevy, the Doane Spencer Deuce, and the Grabowski T-Bucket.

In the end the most useful book that I have encountered as I have sorted through these questions is one of the older examinations of modern American culture. In *The Arts in Modern American Civilization,* published in 1948, John A. Kouwenhoven identifies a cultural tradition that he calls the "vernacular," which began to develop as the country itself took shape. It is a "democratic/technological" tradition which produced a host of simply designed tools in the eighteenth and nineteenth centuries. The design of useful things like rifles, furniture, jigs, and gins allowed a practical people, breaking away from another tradition, the ornate European cultural tradition, to express their "repressed artistic impulses." A unique aesthetic developed out of the isolation of America and from its deep Puritan roots: "American people had developed skills and knowledge which enabled them to create patterns of clean, organic and indigenous beauty out of the crude materials of the technological environment" (Kouwenhoven 1948, 25).

It is an aesthetic that led Americans to refuse to let the completion of the George Washington Bridge take place, the encasing of its towers in decorative stone as the original design called for, preferring the simple and raw quality of its naked steel. It is also the aesthetic that led to the architecture of Louis Sullivan, "the first flowering of an architecture indigenous to modern civilization" (Kouwenhoven 1948, 74). It produced the powerful forms of the grain elevators and factories which inspired Walter Gropius and the Bauhaus. It is also found in the values that Kouwenhoven sees at the heart of jazz: valuing the creativity of the individual performer, reworking the standard materials of the mainstream culture, and flouting prescriptive authority. It is this distinctly American view of the arts that enabled Buckminster Fuller, another vernacular artist, to write: "When there is time perspective on Ford equivalent to the 400 year interval between ourselves and Leonardo da Vinci, which enables us to appraise da Vinci as the greatest artist of the Middle Ages, Ford will undoubtedly be acclaimed by the people of that later day as certainly the greatest artist of the 20th century" (Fuller 1963, 211).

Although he doesn't state it directly, Kouwenhoven implies that American culture has been a modernist, if not a modern, culture almost from its beginnings because of its immediate affinity with the machine. Hot rodders and customizers instinctively participate in this vernacular tradition at a high level. The fact that their machine-based aesthetic is so close to that of the high modernists is not some strange synchronicity but simply the result of the fact that modernism, without realizing it, began by imitating the basic values of this American vernacular tradition that has always worshiped the machine.

The resistance to recognizing the artistic value of custom cars that Robert Irwin describes, reflects a struggle that has been going on in America for hundreds of years between the indigenous vernacular tradition and what Kouwenhoven calls "the cultivated" tradition that follows European models of beauty. Tom Wolfe immediately and correctly saw that these cars were not just about art but about the tensions within modernism, when he wrote his essay "The Kandy Kolored Tangerine Flake Streamline Baby":

If you study the work of Barris or Cushenberry, the aforementioned Silhouette, or Ed Roth or Darryl Starbird, can you beat that name? I think you come up with a fragment of art history. Somewhere back in the thirties, designers, automobile designers among them, came up with the idea of the streamline. It sounded "functional," and on an airplane it is functional, but on a car it's not, unless you're making a Bonneville speed run. Actually, it's baroque. The streamline is baroque abstract or baroque modern or whatever you want to call it. Well about the time the streamline got going—in the thirties, you may recall, we had curved buildings, like the showpieces later, at the World's Fair—in came the Bauhaus movement which was blown-up Mondrian, really. Before you knew it, everything was Mondrian—the Kleenex box: Mondrian; the format for the cover of *Life* magazine: Mondrian; those bled-to-the-edge photograph layouts in *Paris-Match*: Mondrian. Even automobiles: Mondrian. They call Detroit automobiles streamlined, but they're not. If you don't believe it, look down from an airplane at all the cars parked on a shopping-center apron, and except that all the colors are pastel instead of primary, what have you got? A Mondrian painting. The Mondrian principle, those straight edges, is very tight, very Apollonian. The streamline principle, which really has no function, which curves around and swoops and flows just for the thrill of it, is very

Figure 16.
XPAC 400. Show car built by George Barris about 1961. It was an air car that hovered above ground. It could be operated by remote control. Courtesy of Greg Sharp Collection.

free Dionysian. For reasons I don't have to labor over, the kids preferred the Dionysian. And since Detroit blew the thing, the Dionysian principle in cars was left to people in the teen-age netherworld, like George Barris. (Wolfe 1963, 85–86)

Wolfe, unfortunately, sets up a misleading dichotomy between two types of modernism (Apollonian and Dionysian) that is the result of choosing atypical cars to pin his argument to. The XPAC 400 and Silhouette were show cars built in the early sixties to impress model car companies who were paying a lot of money for wild "concept" cars (see figures 16 and 17). This was at a time when the traditional practice of customizing street cars was beginning a steep decline. These show cars have no more to do with the actual practice of customizing than the creation of such monstrosities as the Munster car (looking like a hearse) or the racing coffin known as "Drag-u-la," built about the same time. There are just as many Mondrian-based customs as there are streamlined customs, in fact the streamlined look was largely out of fashion by the late fifties. Larry Watson's "Kandy Kane" Buick painted in 1960 is much closer to Mondrian, especially the Mondrian who believed the future of painting was to be found in "the use of pure color and straight lines in rectangular opposition" (Mondrian 1943, 362), than it is to any conception of the streamline (see plate 3). Wolfe misses the full variety of customs in his rush to knock what he sees as a sterile form of modernism, an attack he would continue in *From Bauhaus to Our House.* But Wolfe's basic insights about the artistic and expressive qualities of these cars and their connection to issues of modernism are still accurate.

Given the options, perhaps the best way to categorize rods and customs is to see them as elite art with no connection to any elite. Finally, however, it matters less to me whether rodding and customizing are categorized as folk or fine art. What interests me more is recognizing the remarkable correspondence between the ideas of pioneer modernists, especially those influenced by a machine aesthetic, and those of customizers. There are numerous connections—from their emphasis on pure form to their use of found elements and collage, from

Figure 17.
Silhouette. Built by Bill Cushenberry. It won the Grand Sweepstakes Custom Award at the Winternationals in 1963. Courtesy of Greg Sharp Collection.

their celebration of pure color to a fascination with abstraction, from challenging traditional notions of beauty to creating new realities through new styles. Customizing is not a degradation of modernism or its pale imitation. Modernist culture and Kustom Kulture exist in parallel universes. Modern art owes as much to the car as customizing owes to modern art.

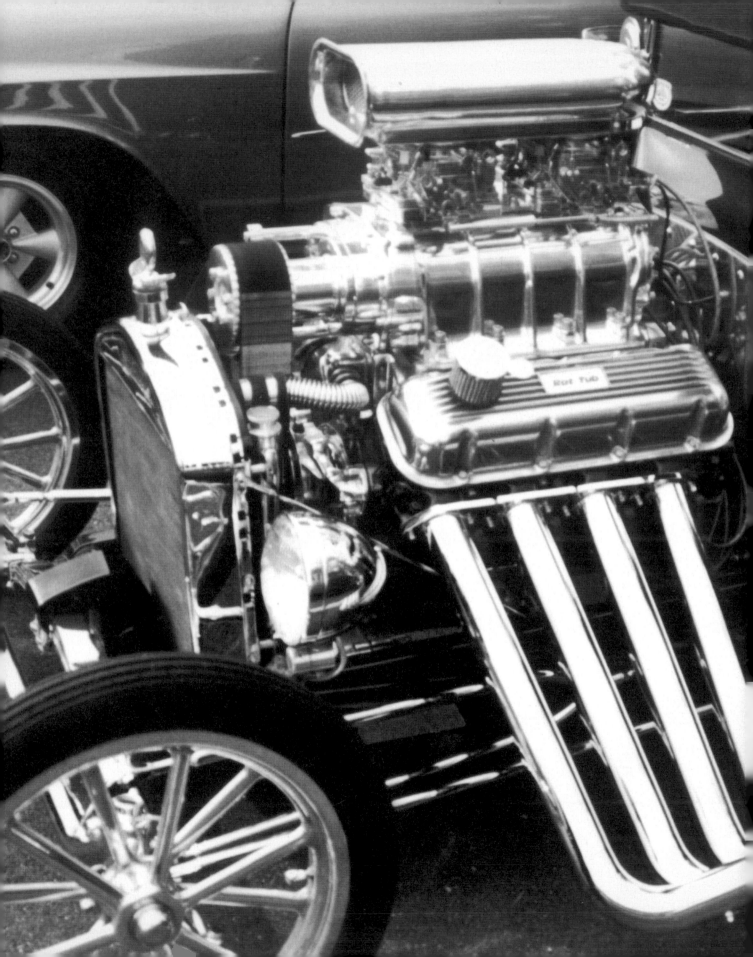

BLUE-COLLAR MODERNISM

What begins as an ordinary night in 1908 for a group of excited young writers and artists and ends with a wild ride through the streets of Milan almost immediately becomes celebrated in "The Foundation and Manifesto of Futurism" as the exciting birth of the modern age—the mechanized world of the Future—the inspiration for truly modern art. Fillippo Tommaso Marinetti and several unnamed friends also transform this joyride into the myth of their own rebirth as they terrorize the sleeping citizens of Milan. "The furious sweep of madness took us out of ourselves and hurled us through streets as rough and deep as stream beds. . . . and we sped on, squashing the watchdogs on their doorsteps who curled up under our scorching tires like starched collars under a flat-iron" (Marinetti 1909, 284–85).

This was not merely a car ride but a ride in a new "snorting beast"—a "Pegasus"—a hound, "hardly tamed"—spinning like "a dog trying to bite his tail"—"a fine shark"—in Marinetti's jumble of overheated metaphors. How else can he communicate the absolute exaltation of racing into "the immense distorted mouth of the wind"?

Anticipating the hot rodders of *Hell on Wheels* and *Running Wild,* Marinetti proclaims the intoxication of danger, the thrill of speed, and the great excitement of disrupting a boring, sleeping world. The ride also offers those who are willing to risk it a chance to enter the world of the future, a new world created by technology that obliterates the tired old civilization of the West.

As he heads into this unknown but exciting future, Marinetti barely misses two bicyclists and veers off the road into a muddy ditch filled with industrial waste which becomes his baptismal font. Hardly discouraged or even chastened by his accident he is rather inspired by it—reborn, in fact, as the car itself is revived.

When I got out from under the upturned car— torn, filthy and stinking—I felt the red hot iron of joy pass over my heart. . . . The machine emerged slowly, shedding at the bottom like scales its heavy body so sound, and its soft upholstery so comfortable. They thought it was dead, my fine shark, but the stroke of my hand was enough to restore it to life, and there it was living again, speeding along once more on its powerful fins. (Marinetti 1909, 285)

This ride, this accident, signals the dawn of new age which offers the promise of leading Italy out of its obsession with the past, out of its stagnant decadence and its "inherited sloth" into the energetic, seemingly indestructible, new world of the machine. Marinetti insists that the car changes everything for the artist. The past is dead. No longer is the artist confined to the drawing room or the studio or to a single vantage point in nature. The old world is a world of lethargy, of *ennui*. It is the *fin de siècle* world where boredom and detachment masquerade as sophistication. This world is finished for Marinetti and his friends who now identify themselves with "the stokers working before the infernal fires of the great ships" and the "black phantoms that poke the red-hot bellies of locomotives launched at mad speed." Like Paul, thrown from *his* horse, they have become disciples, disciples of speed and energy.

In the name of the future, Futurists are willing to discard everything from the past. Tradition no longer matters except as an impediment to progress. Museums are cemeteries. Libraries have become mausoleums. In their place are the advances of modern technology: street lamps and the power plants that supply them and the bridges and airplanes and the factories that build them which have become the new source of inspiration for the truly modern artist. The automobile is the new muse.

Futurism is a youthful revolution: "the oldest among us are thirty; we have thus at least ten years to accomplish our task." Futurist art is not about beauty and the sublime, about refinement and taste or about anything that connects art to the "useless admiration of the past." In the eyes of the futurists "art can only be violence, cruelty and injustice."

Like a modern Martin Luther, Marinetti shakes the old world to its foundation by proclaiming deliberately shocking ideas about beauty, art, and the uselessness of the past in a manifesto for an art movement that does not yet exist, that is itself in the future:

1. We intend to glorify the love of danger, the custom of energy, the strength of daring. . . .
4. We declare that the splendor of the world has been enriched with a new form of beauty, the beauty of speed. A race-automobile adorned with great pipes like serpents with explosive breath . . . a race-automobile which seems to rush over exploding powder is more beautiful than the *Victory of Samothrace.* . . .
5. We will sing the praises of man holding the flywheel of which the ideal steering-post traverses the earth impelled itself around the circuit of its own orbit. . . .

10. We will destroy museums, libraries, and fight against moralism, feminism, and all utilitarian cowardice. (Marinetti 1909, 286)

The experience of seeing a countryside speed by, to be able to see what's ahead, behind, and to the side in an instant, of being simultaneously in both an interior space and the passing landscape inspired the Futurists to invest the same "dynamism" or energy in all their work. They also wanted to create the same simultaneity of colliding experiences that a car ride provides in their painting, sculpture, theater, even in their food. Art, to be relevant, had to present the same total experience, involving all the senses, including that of time, they experienced behind the wheel.

As they worked out their new aesthetic in an avalanche of manifestos, they began to apply their ideas in poetry, sculpture, performances, and in swirling paintings like Russolo's *Dynamism of an Automobile*, Balla's *Automobile+Speed* and *Abstract Speed* (see plate 4). Ironically, in their attempts to paint abstract speed, they were limited by the very technology they celebrated. The machines that would have allowed them to produce works which matched their ideas were themselves in the future. With traditional media like paint, metal, and paper they merely opened a window to a future that would be made possible only with the invention of video, computers, digital imaging, and synthesizers.

Recently, after years of neglect, Futurists have been seen to have anticipated everything from kinetic art to performance art, from multi-media rock shows to MTV, from postmodern restaurants as theater to channel surfing. According to Marjorie Perloff's groundbreaking study *The Futurist Moment,* the revival of interest in Futurism and Futurist-inspired art forms like "performance art, visual poetry and intermedia works" reflects a contemporary recognition of cultural origins: "After decades in which artists and poets decried technology as the brutalization of the landscape and the machine as the enemy of the human spirit, in what we might call the 'science-fiction' world of the early century, which contains so many of the seeds of our own mythologies" (Perloff 1986, 195).

From the simplest mechanical device, like the screw or a gear, to the most complex machine like the dynamo, the machine inspired the first two generations of modern artists to create art that was devoid of ornament, that was reduced to its simplest form, and in which form followed function. Artists found an elemental beauty in the products of industrialization. Only the conventions of the past, they said, prevented us from seeing that beauty.

As the cubist Fernand Léger put it, "Many individuals would be sensitive to the beauty of common objects, *without artistic intention,* if the preconceived notion of the *objet d'art* were not a bandage over their eyes" (Léger 1924, 277). Rather than decorate ordinary objects with filigree to make them "finer," as had been done in the nineteenth century with everything from furniture to sewing machines, the modernist conception was to recognize the simple beauty of the essential form of machines and machine-made objects and apply the principles of simplicity and utility to works of fine art. Screws didn't need Greek columns and neither did homes. Dynamos could do without elaborate friezes, so could office buildings. As the architect W. R. Lethaby wrote so confidently as early as 1911, "Now that ornament is no longer organically integrated into our culture, it has ceased to be a valid expression of that culture" (in Banham 1960, 94).

The perceived perfection of machine form offered a threat to artists whose labored hand-crafted works began to look quaint and obsolete in comparison to the elegant perfection of the machine. The dadaist Marcel Duchamp, who changed the face of twentieth-century art with his ready-made sculptures of mass-produced shovels and urinals, understood early how challenging the example of industrial forms would be for the modern artist. At the *Salon d'Aviation* in 1911 he confronted the sculptor Brancusi, "Painting is finished. Who can do anything better than this propeller? Can you?" (in Wilson 1986, 261). Or as the architect Le Corbusier put it, the challenge facing architects was to be able to build "a house like a car" (in Banham 1960, 243). The Russian Futurists, Constructivists, and Suprematists, as well as the Bauhaus, DeStijl, Dada, and Surrealism, all took up, in differing ways, the gauntlet that mechanization had thrown down to the modern artist.

In response to this challenge artists began to undermine the hierarchy of the arts that had existed in the West since the Renaissance. No longer were utilitarian objects inferior to painting and sculpture just because of their usefulness. As Léger put it, "The more the machine perfects its utilitarian functions, the more beautiful it becomes" (Léger 1924, 278).

It was not only how they functioned and looked but also how they affected viewers that made machines so inspiring. The products of factories began to take on the spiritual power and meaning that had formally been found only in nature or the greatest works of traditional art:

When automobiles, railway cars, steamships or other objects of an industrial nature stimulate you in the same way that you are stimulated when you look at the Parthenon, at the windows of Chartres, at the Moses of Michelangelo, or at the frescoes of Giotto, you will have every right to speak of them as works of art. (Bel Geddes in Woodham 1997, 67)

The presence of monumental constructions like the Eiffel Tower, the Brooklyn Bridge, the George Washington Bridge, the Hoover Dam, and the Pennsylvania Turnpike seemed to dwarf the work of the individual artist. At times artists simply paid homage to the massive achievements of an industrial society as Charles Demuth did in his 1927 painting *My Egypt*, which equates the large grain elevators of Lancaster County, Pennsylvania, to the pyramids. Likewise in the twenties and thirties the painters Joseph Stella and Georgia O'Keeffe celebrate the Brooklyn Bridge as a sign of the modern, while the precisionist Ralston Crawford creates the new landscape, a visually dominating roadway that obliterates nature in his painting *Overseas Highway*. For the sculptor Morton Shamberg a plumbing trap combined with a miter box becomes an image of "God."

This new art is an art that abandons nature, as well as tradition, as the ultimate source of form and beauty and replaces them with the forms, finish, and materials of man-made objects. Chromed steel supplants fine woods, bakelite takes the place of marble, and concrete succeeds quarried granite. The modern church, office building, and house would derive their shapes from factories, grain elevators, and power stations not ancient temples or Gothic cathedrals.

This is the art that became the International Style that produced the modern skyline full of skyscrapers that dominates the modern city from Tokyo to Manhattan. The ideas behind this art affected more than just architecture and painting. William Carlos Williams wanted his poems to be "machines made out of words." His "Between Walls," for example, presents a simple shape built out of pieces of lines and patterns of syllables as it plays the geometry of its verticality against the natural horizontal movement of English on the page. Written in the late thirties it is as devoid of decoration as a Richard Neutra house or a Winfield custom, eliminating even the flourish of capital letters and the clutter of punctuation marks. This poem is designed and assembled as much as it is written.

Between Walls

the back wings
of the

hospital where
nothing

will grow lie
cinders

in which shine
the broken

pieces of a green
bottle

(Williams 1986, 453)

Like a Calder mobile "Between Walls" is more about the complex movement of the eye than it is a description of heightened experience of the kind that one might expect to find in a poem. It is an almost impossible poem to read aloud with anything like ordinary speech. The poem is not so much a voice we hear in our heads as it is an object which hangs in space. The eye follows the ordinary, deliberately nonpoetic words, as they turn, hang, collide and, finally, stop, suspended in space. There is little here but the pure form: the mathematics of a precise division of words into an order—ten lines divided into twos, each pair having a similar shape and length. No traditional music, no metaphors, no personalized point of view, not even what might be called a complete thought. It is poem as pure form—a verbal sculpture—a machine. All you have to do is rearrange the lines to see how crucial the shape is to the success of the poem. Any change and it falls apart. Shaped as it is it is a beautiful fragment of a poem, a simple shape, that forces us to look for the connections and supply the missing pieces that will turn it into a sentence, that will complete it. In the end it is a "customized" poem.

Ezra Pound's famous tenets of the Imagist movement, first publicized in 1912, also matches the principles of the emerging machine aesthetic of the first part of the century:

1. Direct treatment of the "thing" whether subjective or objective.
2. To use absolutely no word that does not contribute to the presentation.
3. As regarding rhythm: to compose in the sequence of the musical phrase, not in the sequence of the metronome. (Pound 1929, 3)

Works created under the influence of the machine often struck audiences as being impersonal, cold, distant, lacking in the emotion that one expected from art. Mass-produced objects made anonymously in factories or monumental public works or massive factory buildings, while inspiring to artists, often seemed disconnected from the emotional life of the ordinary individual. Modern society has resisted much modern art and design. The automobile is the exception. Although it is just as much a product of mass production as the telephone, the light bulb, and the washing machine, from its very beginnings it has represented something different—a deep personal and emotional connection that often becomes a kind of romance.

Here is the writer Octave Mirbeau in *La 628-E8*, titled after his auto registration number, in 1908: "I love my automobile . . . she is my life, my artistic and spiritual life . . . full of riches . . . she is more dear, more useful, more full of education than my library, where the closed books sleep on their spines, than my paintings, which hang dead on my walls all around me, with their immobile sky, tree, water and figures" (in Silk 1984, 35).

Rather than an impersonal object, displaying a rational ordering of materials translated into a perfect form, the car seemed to be a machine which also lived and breathed. Consider a few of the animal metaphors in Marinetti's manifesto: car and man combined are a "centaur" about to be born; the overturned car is a beached "shark," and exhaust pipes are "serpents with explosive breath." Here is Mirbeau again:

Machines appear to me, more than books, statues, paintings, to be works of imagination. When I look at, when I hear the life of the admirable organism that is the motor of my automobile, with its steel lungs and heart, its rubber and copper and vascular system, its electrical nervous system, don't I have a more moving idea of the imaginative and creative human genius than when I consider the banal,

infinitely useless books of M. Paul Bourget, the statues, if one can call them that, of M. Denys Puech, the paintings—a euphemism—of M. Detaille? (in Silk 1984, 66)

Unlike bridges and grain elevators, the car is a personal possession. You can appreciate the beauty of a Raymond Loewy pencil sharpener, but you fall in love with his '53 Studebaker. There is a relationship with the car that is a kind of intimacy. Even outside the Kustom Kulture it is maintained, accessorized, displayed as an extension of one's self. It is named. It is loved. It is one form of industrial culture that creates and extends identity rather than diminishes it.

As Pontus Hulten suggests, possession of a car is the fulfillment of an old dream: "What then is a car? It is, I think, the flesh given to that old phantom: personal freedom, individual liberty. It is the twentieth-century realization of that great nineteenth-century dream: personal independence" (in Silk 1984, 13). (For a more comprehensive treatment of the influence of the car on modern art, see Gerald Silk's "The Automobile in Art" in *Automobile and Culture* [1984]).

Not only were automobiles a model for the new art, but the men who created them and worked on them became the models of the new artist. They seemed to have a deeper connection to the new forms of machine art than classically trained artists. The mechanic, who had an innate affinity for the machine, already understood what traditional artists had to struggle to grasp: "One finds today, with increasing ease, men of the people without culture or education, who are nevertheless endowed already with what I call the gift of mechanical prophecy, or flair for metals. They are workmen who have already undergone the education of the machine, and in some way are affiliated to machinery" (Marinetti in Banham 1960, 123).

Hot rodders and customizers certainly have a "flair for metals." But they want to do more with the car than appreciate its beauty or enjoy the freedom it offers. They want to make it completely their own. By modifying, altering, transforming, and improving the existing car, they also combine a nineteenth-century dream with a twentieth-century reality. They are master craftsmen imaginatively transforming the most symbol-laden industrial product. The Romantic Self meets the assembly line. Rodders and customizers want nothing to do with the uniformity, standardization, multiplicity of the mass-produced object. At root they have a deep connection with the ideals of the Bauhaus, whose mission it also was to marry the tradition of individual craftsmanship with the reality of industrial production. According to its founder Walter Gropius, it is only "class-distinctions that raise an arrogant barrier between craftsman and artist!" As he writes in the "Manifesto of the Bauhaus" in 1919: "*Architects, painters, sculptors, we must all return to crafts*. . . . There is no essential difference between the artist and the craftsman. *The artist is an exalted craftsman . . . a foundation of handicraft is essential for every artist. It is there that the primary source of creativity lies*" (in Whitford 1984, 202).

To the rodder and customizer a stock car, looking and running just as it did out of the factory, is only potentially a work of art. To leave it that way is understood as a failure of nerve and a lack of imagination. They see the car as their medium of expression and not just as an object of desire. It is a medium that allows them to construct something that has

never existed before—a unique object, that began as one of thousands of identical versions of itself—that comes to embody the values of imagination, craftsmanship, and self-expression. Using the same aesthetic ideas and techniques as other modern artists, they transform what is already a symbol of modern life into something more surprising, challenging, and complicated than the original. Something new. They are blue-collar modernists creating a machine that lives up to the Futurist manifesto's call for "a new form of beauty, the beauty of speed."

Machine art in the Kustom Kulture is at its purest when rodders and customizers focus their attention on the automobile engine itself. Rodders and customizers, like modernist sculptors before them, find beauty in pistons, turbines, camshafts, spark plugs, gears, and connecting rods: all the parts that make up any machine. Artist and mechanic alike love the engine both for its beauty and dynamism. For a Futurist like Boccioni, it is sculpture which moves in more ways than one:

> The in-and-out of a piston in a cylinder, the opening and closing of two cogwheels with the continual appearance and disappearance of their square steel cogs, the fury of a flywheel or the turbine of a propeller, are all plastic and pictorial elements of which a Futurist work in sculpture must take account. The opening and closing of a valve creates a rhythm just as beautiful but infinitely newer than the blinking of an animal eyelid. (Boccioni 1912, 303)

Rodders want ultimate performance and dedicate themselves to extracting the most power from any given engine. But they are not indifferent to the look of their engines. In fact most want the engine to look as good as it

Figure 18.
Classic flathead engine. Despite many limitations, the flathead V-8 remains the iconic hot rod engine primarily because it was the original. "Flatheads Forever" is inscribed on a lot of T-shirts.

Figure 19.
Chromed overhead engine. By the mid-fifties newer overhead valve engines, particularly Chevy small blocks and Chrysler Hemi engines, dominated Kustom Kulture. This blown (supercharged) V-8 shows how an engine can become the center of attention in a rod and dominate its design almost to the point of absurdity.

runs, like a jewel, to show the world what their power looks like and how much they care. The classic roadster, running without a hood, makes the engine compartment into a pedestal and transforms the engine into an object of beauty (see figure 18).

Each engine has its own distinctive shape: the almost horizontal heads of the Buick, the sleek lines of the small block Chevy, and the massiveness of the Chrysler Hemi, each communicating a different idea of power. Because rodders are in love with the parts that make up the whole—the shapes of carburetors, the curves of exhaust pipes, and the mass of a supercharger—they spend a lot of time choosing the parts that not only make the car go faster, but also look just right. When all the pieces are in place every part that can be chromed is usually chromed. Chrome is the universal alchemy for transforming the engine from a dull utilitarian object into a gleaming art object. The irony is that rodders remove almost all the chrome from the body of their cars, where chrome is expected, while in the hidden engine compartment they dip everything from air cleaners to radiators in the gleaming metal. Like the design of the Pompidou Center (Beaubourg) in Paris the inside of the rod becomes the outside, the invisible becomes visible, and the smooth becomes muscular and contorted (see figure 19).

For most drivers the engine compartment is a *terra incognita*. Tucked away under a seldom-opened hood and, usually, a thin veneer of grease and oil, the engine is a mystery when it works, and when it doesn't, it produces only confusion and despair. Engine compartments are like the boiler room in O'Neill's *Hairy Ape*, a hidden, degraded, but necessary place where the dirty work gets done. Rodders see the world much differently. The engine is not only familiar, but an intimate. Drag racers routinely tear down engines and rebuild them between races. In the early days of drag racing when all the racers were amateurs, a call might go out between races that a racer had blown his rear end and needed one that would fit a '56 Chevy, for example. Almost without exception somebody in the crowd would offer his own car for parts. What would have been a major repair at most shops was, with the help of a few friends, just a minor inconvenience. A rodder who knew engines could pretty much tell you what was happening inside by just listening or holding his hand over the exhaust. The engine was not just a means to an end for them. It was the end. They knew and loved their favorite engines' quirks and idiosyncrasies. The engine was anything but dirty and neglected. Abused often, but never neglected. And never dirty.

Rodders want their engines to look, sound, and perform in a way that communicates a single message: this is a hot engine in a hot car. Not only is every part which can be, chromed, but every other part of the engine is also given lavish attention as well: everything is clean, perfectly clean and ordered; wires are wrapped in colorful braid or colored to match the body and routed directly with hose guides to eliminate disorder; hoses are transformed from ordinary black rubber into silver threaded snakes; and air cleaners take on a myriad of evocative shapes. Exhaust systems are altered not only to allow for unrestricted passage of gases, but also to create complex sculptures of tubing. Some hug the side of the engine or wildly reach for the air like the legs of an angry insect. Some are exuberantly, comically rococo. Pipes curve, twist, or simply go straight to the rear. Pipes run alongside the bottom edge of the body, others emerge through the fenders, most often the pipes end their path to the rear

of the car with two simple chrome extensions on the dual exhausts that announce to the world with a deep rumble: this is a car to worry about (see figure 20).

Combining beauty and speed in ways that the Futurists never imagined, the rodder reintroduces us to the familiar which is one of the most basic functions of art. It is through an act of imagination, as defined by William Carlos Williams, that ordinary things are detached from ordinary experience so that we might see them anew. The transformation of these utilitarian and humble parts in the most neglected (as far as design goes) space of the automobile into the locus of attention is not unlike the work of the Russian avant gardist Vladimir Tatlin, who placed his assemblages in the neglected corners of rooms as he urged artists to work with "real materials in real space" to create new perceptions.

By working on, improving, and trying to perfect the product of the engineering departments of the largest industry in the country, largely self-taught rodders and customizers demonstrated that the products of mass production do not necessarily produce "mass man" at the mercy of the machine. They put the lie to the notion that industrial culture inevitably threatens human freedom and ultimately reduces humanity to the condition of oppressed victims—a persistent theme in critiques of modern culture from Franz Kafka and Walter Benjamin to Charlie Chaplin and Terry Gilliam. The car is a medium for expression for rodders rather than a tool for oppression. Rodders and customizers use the engine, a symbol of power, to take power for themselves, literally and figuratively. There is power in performance and power in the knowledge of exactly how to create and handle that performance. Rodders and customizers don't

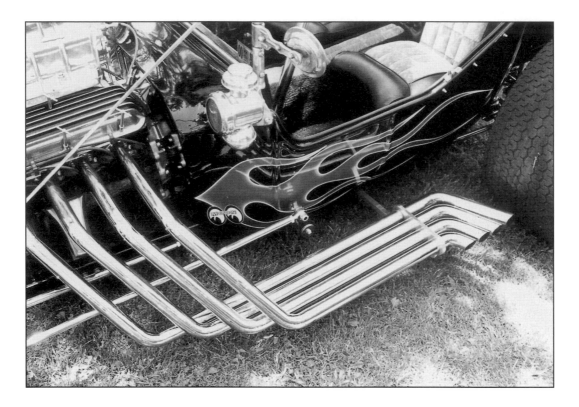

Figure 20.
Headers. The exhaust system lends itself to sculptural treatments because it is the one part of the engine where there is almost no practical restriction on expressive possibilities. Pipes can be straight, curved, twisted, short, long, raised, or lowered.

accept the car as created by industry. Despite their love of the car and their loyalty to a particular marque, they know that every car can be improved and be made to stand out from the masses. They are close in spirit to Theo Van Doesburg, a dadaist in the 1920s before moving to the DeStijl group in Holland:

The machine is, par excellence, a phenomenon of spiritual discipline. Materialism as a way of life and art took handicraft as its direct psychological expression. The new spiritual artistic sensibility of the twentieth century has not only felt the beauty of the machine, but has also taken cognizance of its unlimited expressive possibilities for the arts. . . . Under the supremacy of materialism, handicraft reduced men to the level of machines; the proper tendency for the machine (in the sense of cultural development) is as the unique medium of the very opposite, social liberation. (in Banham 1960, 151)

The expressive possibilities of the engine are not limited to its looks or performance. For the rodder the car is a musical instrument that produces true "industrial" music. An engine that doesn't sound just right isn't finished. There is a distinct sound to speed and a distinct sound to the modifications that produce that speed—the whoosh of air being sucked into multiple car-buretors, the distinct rump rump of a 3/4 race cam at idle, and the whine of a blower. Each engine has its own distinct sound as well. A flathead V-8 sounds very different from a Chrysler Hemi. A GMC six will always sound different from a small block Chevy V-8. And those sounds can be enhanced, amplified, or modified. An auto parts company hawks its "Turbo-Tone Mufflers" with the line, "our cus-tomers tell us that it's the perfect tone." An-other ad for "The Original" brags that "the sound never changes. . . . A true hot rod sound."

Half the appeal of going to a dragstrip is to experience sheer decibels of blown Hemi en-gines at full throttle shooting flaming nitro-methane exhaust through straight headers. One can buy recordings of drag-race sounds—the greatest hits from the strips. The sounds can make even heavy metal seem like elevator music.

The sounds of these engines are orches-trated to create just the right mix of noise and harmony. Steelpac mufflers are loud. Glasspacs are mellow. Straight pipes assault the ears. Un-tuned engine noise is just ugly. Any engine will make lots of noise as anyone who has blown a muffler knows. But only a carefully tuned, per-fectly balanced, correctly modified engine pro-duces true music.

Car builders want the world to know there is something "under the hood" even when they are idling at a traffic light. Part of the fun of a cruise is to compare the different sounds of the cars passing by and to guess what it is running just from the pulse of exhaust and the whine and clatter of engine sounds. In the fifties there were certain rituals that revealed through sound alone that a car was special:

coming down a hill and backing off in second gear to produce a deep popping in the ex-haust, idling real low at a stoplight so the smoothness could be admired, driving by cer-tain buildings that reinforced exhaust sounds, adding a little screech of rubber by popping the clutch on every shift—all these demon-strated knowledge and power. Revving at lights was also a way of getting rid of wanna-bes. If someone took your challenge to race, you could tell in a minute what you were up against as soon as he hit the gas. In *American Graffiti*, John Milner immediately knows that his Deuce coupe's days as top dog are num-bered when he hears John Falfa's very hot '55 Chevy drown him out at a stoplight as they cruise Modesto.

In 1913 Luigi Russolo's Futurist manifesto "The Art of Noises" demanded a new source for music in the twentieth century. No longer would simple harmonies satisfy the musical ear. Everywhere from the "noisy atmosphere of large cities," to isolated country roads si-lence was disappearing while a dissonance produced by machines was evolving into a new sonic universe, a world of "noise-sound":

We will get enjoyment from . . . the eddying of water, air and gas in metal pipes, the grumbling of noises that breathe and pulse with indisputable ani-mality, the palpitation of valves, the coming and go-ing of pistons. . . . We enjoy creating mental orches-trations of the crashing down of metal shop blinds, slammed doors. . . .

WE WANT TO ATTUNE AND REGULATE THIS TREMENDOUS VARIETY OF NOISES HARMONI-CALLY AND RHYTHMICALLY. (Russolo 1913, 85)

Russolo invented his own instruments, *in-tonarumori* or music/noise makers, to imitate the machine sounds he heard all around him. In his piece *Meeting of Airplanes and Automobile,* he also used backfires, droning engines, and other actual machine noises. In the twenties George Antheil used an airplane propeller in his *Ballet Mechanique.* Contemporary composers have used synthesizers, digital processors, and tape machines as well as chainsaws and motorcycles to create and recreate the music of machines. Car builders use the machines themselves, as themselves, to create another sort of modern music. They tune their noises "Harmonically and Rhythmically," fulfilling Russolo's prediction that one day "motors and machines . . . will be consciously attuned . . . into an intoxicating orchestra of noises." And rodders are not only artists but music critics as well, as Albert Drake recalls:

> When I was a student at Franklin High, I spent lunch hours hanging around with other guys at a place called The Doghouse where we listened to each passing car's exhaust and thereby judged the driver's "acceptable qualities." And we listened to the tonal pitches and subtle sound variations of dual pipes the way teenagers today listen to the subtle acoustics of a thousand dollar stereo system. Some exhausts were too harsh, some too tinny, some too quiet. Mellow was the "correct" sound, and if there was a slight backing off, a slight crackling, when the driver shifted, that was a bonus. . . . Tonal qualities were difficult to predict. One method of obtaining that mellow sound was to pour oil in a new muffler and set it on fire; a break-in method called "burning it out." (Drake 1982, 7–8)

Customizers seldom lavished as much attention on their engines as rodders. If the original engine wasn't souped up, usually a mildly re-worked later engine, often from a wreck, was substituted for the original. In the beginning it was mostly a question of replacing one flathead with another. Early fifties customs favored overhead valve Oldsmobile and Cadillac V-8's. Later, Chrysler Hemis and Buick "nailheads" became popular. The appearance of the Chevy V-8 in 1955 changed everything. While there are still Ford and Chrysler loyalists, the almost universal choice for customizers today is the Chevy V-8, for which there are literally thousands of after-market parts available both for looks and performance. There are dozens of options, for example, just in the choice of air cleaners. Since the goal of the customizers was more often "low and slow" than "show and go," wringing ultimate performance out of their mills was unnecessary. In many cases, if it looked right, sounded right, and ran okay, all they had to do was add chrome and paint and the engine was fine. Customizers were obsessed with how the skin of their cars looked.

In the late 1930s, when customizers began to define the aesthetic that would soon be embodied in the California custom, their designs were greatly influenced by the contemporary craze for streamlining. Following the flowing lines of rare and exotic cars like the 1932 Pierce Arrow Silver Arrow, the 1938 Bentley 41/4 Litre Embiricos, the 1938 Bugatti 57 Atlantic, the 1938 Dubonnet Xenia, and the 1938 Talbot-Lago T150 SS, they transformed the conservative, timid designs of Detroit, mostly by Ford, into expressions of the most advanced style of the day. (One of few attempts to mass market a streamlined design in the thirties, the Chrysler Airflow was a commercial failure, perhaps because it wasn't streamlined enough.)

In the 1930s, especially in America, streamlining was generally seen as the most modern of styles, a popular expression of machine art. It signified a continuing belief in the beauty and function of the machine. Streamlining was also a sign of faith in science and technology and a sign of confidence in the idea of progress at the height of the Great Depression. According to Sheldon and Martha Cheney, writing in 1936, there was enormous, almost religious, power in the streamline form even when it was absurdly applied to everything from oil burners and vacuum cleaners to pencil sharpeners and water pitchers: "The machine conscious mind begins to relate all such products of scientist-artist design back to the most conspicuous symbol and inspiration of the age, as the reverent medieval mind related everything to the symbol of the cross" (Cheney 1936, 102).

Itself influenced by the smooth designs of contemporary airplanes like the Douglas DC-3 as well as by studies of the swimming efficiency of sharks and porpoises, streamlining was generally characterized by an ovoid gliding form, the much admired teardrop shape, and by smooth continuous surfaces. It represented a shift in the machine aesthetic from an emphasis on machine parts—gears, turbines, screws, and pistons—to a focus on the skin of the machine. Except when applied to airplanes, dirigibles, and some racing cars, streamlining provided an essentially nonfunctional surface, merely symbolizing function rather than aiding it.

Harry Westergard, one of the most influential early customizers, applied his incredible facility with metal to lowering roof lines, smoothing contours, and stretching the body of Fords and Mercurys into a shape closer to the ideal teardrop. He set the standard not only for design but for workmanship as well. According to his partner, Dick Bertolucci, he could "take a piece of metal and do *anything* with it" (Ganahl 1989, 70).

The cars Westergard worked on, late thirties and early forties Fords and Mercurys, all began with essentially the same basic design: narrow and tapered three-piece hoods, narrow vertical grilles, bulbous fenders attached to the body, full wheel openings in the fenders, bumpers consisting of a simple straight metal bar, external running boards, a high roof line and, until the early forties, taillights and headlights mounted on the body.

Typically Westergard would chop the top, immediately changing the basic lines of the car by reconstructing the roof. He would also lower the car, usually by channeling it, that is, dropping the body over the frame. Cars could also be lowered by adding blocks between the rear springs and the axle and by cutting coils out of the front springs. Other modifications included substituting a La Salle or Packard grille for the original, filling the sides of the hood, bobbing the fenders, dropping the headlights down between the hood and the fender, frenching taillights into the rear fenders, adding teardrop fender skirts, and sometimes removing the running boards. Fenders were often molded into the body, and sometimes the front fenders were extended into the doors in what was known as a "fade away." Door handles were shaved (replaced by electric solenoid buttons) as was most of the chrome trim. Cars were topped with rigid padded convertible tops from the Carson Top Shop in Los Angeles. "Carson Top" has since become a generic term like kleenex. The cars

Figure 21.
Westergard custom. Owned by Bruce Glenn, this convertible features a steel lift-off top, molded fenders, ribbed bumpers, and solenoids to open the doors instead of handles. Courtesy of the *Rodder's Journal*.

Figure 22.
Ohanesian Merc. Generally considered one of the best Westergard/Bertolucci customs, it features typical modifications—lowering, chopped top, Chevy grille, steel lift-off top, molded fenders, removal of all trim, including door handles, all painted a Bertolucci maroon—on an atypical four-door convertible sedan. Bertolucci continues, to this day, to turn out beautifully crafted automobiles in his shop in Sacramento. Courtesy of the *Rodder's Journal*.

were usually finished in dark colors, black or dark blue, although there were a number of two-tone and lighter-colored cars. In the late forties Bertolucci developed his own maroon by adding gold powder to '48 Chevy Oxford Maroon; it became so popular it was known as "Sacramento or Bertolucci Maroon" (see figures 21 and 22).

The result was a car that not only looked like coach-built European and American cars but also shared its shape with streamlined locomotives like the *Commodore Vanderbilt* and *The Mercury*. In fact one can see the same basic lines—swept back, the dynamic arching up of the front, with the back hugging the ground like an animal ready to pounce—in chairs designed by Alvar Aalto or Paul T. Frankl. Even though these cars were often built in driveways and backyards (Westergard's studio was a chicken coop in back of his house), they express the same love for the machine that produced the most advanced designs by the most prominent companies.

One of the most imitated cars in this early style that helped defined this first stage of customizing in California was built by George and

Sam Barris in 1949 when they completed a '40 Mercury for Nick Matranga (see figure 23). The Barris brothers, more than a decade younger than Westergard, had informally apprenticed themselves to him in Sacramento, observing what Westergard did and then trying to imitate him. During the war George left Sacramento for Los Angeles where he heard there was a very active rodding and customizing scene. Sam joined him in 1945 after leaving the service, and they opened a new shop on Compton Avenue in Los Angeles. Here they began to create the customs that made the brothers famous.

The Matranga Merc, picked by *Rod & Custom* magazine as one of the "20 Best Rods and Customs in History," is one of the most imitated early customs. Its nose tilted up aggressively, its rear hugging the ground, it is one of the smoothest designs of the era. Chopped more in the rear than in the front with curved quarter windows that give the car the appear-

ance of being a hardtop rather than a standard coupe, its roof line flows into the trunk lid seamlessly, cleverly echoing the lines of the rear fenders. Instrumental in the reconstruction of the basic line of the car was Barris's decision to raise the windshield space into the roof line and to use a '41 Merc rear window which had a slightly different slope from the original; '41 Buick fender skirts repeat the lines of the roof and fender; '49 Caddy Sombrero hubcaps, the standard choice of late forties and early fifties customs, replaced the stock caps in the front, their mass effectively counterbalancing the rearward tilt of the car. The fenders themselves were molded into the body as were the running boards. It was painted in the Barris version of the classic maroon metallic paint developed by Bertolucci. The door handles were shaved. The interior was finished in a combination of maroon mohair and pearl-white naugahyde. Under the hood was a chromed 255 cubic-inch flathead with polished Offenhauser heads, and three Stromberg 97 carbs finished the project. The Matranga Merc has become one of the most recognizable customs ever built, inspiring dozens of copies.

In 1949, four years after the war, Detroit finally introduced its first genuine postwar designs to an eagerly awaiting public. The Fords and Chevys and Mercurys and Cadillacs that had preceded them were for the most part simply retooled versions of prewar cars. Although disappointing as far as technical innovation was concerned, the '49 to '51 designs did offer customizers a significantly different palette to work with. Some were more advanced than others. The design of the '49 Ford was, for example, more original than the '49 Mercury. And GM cars offered more modern design elements than Ford cars did.

The design of the 1949 Mercury was already dated when it appeared on showroom floors. Characterized by a short, slumping deck, a two-piece V-shaped windshield, small windows, thick, bulbous lower body proportions, and rounded prewar back end styling with fenders that did not extend beyond the decklid, the car was anything but sleek and low. But Sam Barris saw the potential for the car as a custom almost as soon as it appeared. He bought one and studied it for weeks. The changes he made were not especially radical in terms of the practice of customizing, but the combination of traditional customizing techniques and the new Mercury design resulted in

the classic postwar custom—the 1949 through 1951 "bathtub" Mercs.

As he had done with the Matranga Merc, Sam Barris chopped the top, shaved the hood and deck, added Caddy hubcaps and fender skirts, lowered it more in the rear than the front. It was painted a brilliant dark green. Between 1950 and 1955 the Barris brothers built a half dozen significant bathtub Mercurys, all variations of the same general design. George Barris emphasizes that these early customs were "redesigns": "We were not designing a car from the ground up. We were working with the basic design of the car as we found it. What we tried to do was to make it better than the original by making all the elements work together better" (Barris 1998, interview).

Other builders, notably Gil and Al Ayala, also saw the potential in the new Mercurys, despite their design flaws. They recognized that the new Mercury, as well as other postwar designs, offered fresh options to customizers who craved a distinctive new look. The wider, flatter hood, the more integrated fenders which created larger expanses of metal on the sides of the car, the wide grille opening, the wheel openings integrated into the lines of the fenders, and the bumpers which were not merely tacked on but were more connected to the front and rear end design allowed for far more customizing possibilities than those offered by prewar designs.

No car benefits as much from a top chop as the '49 to '51 Mercury. Dropping the roof line down four to five inches transforms a naturally round, dowdy shape into a massive, low menacing cruiser. The long expanse along the sides of the car allowed for a variety of chrome strips from Buicks, Pontiacs, and DeSotos, among others, to be used to add accents or to separate two-tone paint jobs. The wide horizontal grille opening was almost infinitely flexible. It could accommodate a floating bar, multiple bars, egg crate designs, various grille teeth, or a variety of combinations.

By 1953, the Barris brothers, George and Sam, were already well-known customizers in California. In addition to a number of '49 to '50 Mercs, they had customized postwar Buicks, Chevys, and Fords. A number of their cars had already appeared on the covers of magazines. But when their '51 Mercury Club Coupe, built for Bob Hirohata, appeared on the cover of the March 1953 issue of *Motor Trend,* a mainstream auto magazine that featured road tests of current production cars as well as features on the occasional rod and custom, they became figures of national interest and a growing legend. That same month there were articles on the Hirohata Merc, as it came to be known, in *Hop Up* and *Hot Rod* as well. Later in the year *Rod & Custom,* in its first year of publication, featured an article in which Hirohata described his journey across the country along Route 66 from California to Indianapolis. The appearance of this one car in 1953 crystallized the new direction that customizing was taking. The impact of this chopped Mercury was the equivalent in the car world to Elvis's first recordings for Sun records. Elvis didn't invent rock 'n' roll, he just took the shifts in teen musical taste that had been evolving slowly across the country from Lubbock to Memphis, from Harlem to Cleveland, and accelerated the process until the whole country was rocking just months after "Heartbreak Hotel" (see plate 5).

While not close to the arrival of Elvis on the cultural Richter scale, the appearance of the Hirohata Merc did have a monumental effect in the world of young car buffs, particularly white and working class, who were just recognizing that they were different and somehow new just for being teenagers. Here was a car that projected a sense of style that spoke directly to them. It was beautiful, rebellious, and nothing like what their parents drove or what the Preps or Squares drove.

The pictures of the Mercury in *Rod & Custom* reveal much more about its impact than Hirohata's rather innocuous text. The "Mercillac," Hirohata's own name for his car with its newly installed Cadillac engine, is shown in front of stores, in a schoolyard, being stopped by an Oklahoma state policeman (who pulled the car over to get "a better look"), and being barely able to negotiate a slight rise in a New Mexico road because the car had only about two inches of clearance. Unlike the typical artfully posed magazine pictures in attractive surroundings, usually including a beautiful young woman in a bathing suit, even if there was no beach in sight, the Hirohata Merc was shown on real streets in real towns. The effect of the car in these settings is disorienting, like finding a piece of great sculpture in a supermarket.

In these settings the car is hard to read, to make sense of. It is clearly an American car, but its identity is obscured. There are no insignias or logos or badges. It is too low to be an ordinary car. The rear wheels are barely visible. The chopped top obscures the driver's view and our view of the driver, providing only what seems like a slit to see through, like a medieval helmet. The roof line seems to have been pushed into the body, yet the effect is anything but grotesque. The car is beautiful and somehow threatening at the same time. It is no accident that the Pharaohs, the only mildly menacing figures in the very car-astute

American Graffiti, also drive a chopped '51 Merc, although not a very good one.

Whatever its setting, the car drew spectators like a movie star sitting in a local restaurant. Wherever Hirohata stops the car becomes a source of wonder. In the schoolyard picture, the car is almost invisible as the students surround it, clearly amazed at its appearance. At one gas station, the attendant approaches the car assuming that the car has flat tires in need of repair. He keeps circling the car wondering how Hirohata could drive it to the station. In front of a Zales Jewelry store, the pedestrians ignore the displays in the window and turn their eyes toward the exotic green jewel of a Mercury on the street.

The effect of the articles about Hirohata's Merc was profound. They signified that something new and exciting was happening, and it was happening in California. Just as the New York Armory Show of 1912 had shown America the most advanced art in the world, the appearance of the car on the streets of New Mexico, Oklahoma, Missouri, and Indiana introduced the most advanced custom work to American car enthusiasts. It also clearly located the source of these innovative ideas in the West. The customizing that had been done in the East, transforming humble American models into sports cars or into imitation luxury cars, suddenly seemed very old-fashioned or wrong-headed. California seemed to be a place where such cars as the Hirohata Merc could actually be seen on the streets, where they were believed to be as common as station wagons in the rest of the country.

California soon became the car Mecca, envisioned as a paradise by car-struck teens across the country. Although California had clearly been leading the way in rodding since the thir-

ties, it wasn't until the 1950s that the rest of the country generally became aware of how advanced the cars there were. When Hirohata's Merc took first place at the Indianapolis show, the conquest of the East was complete. First using a *k* in "kustom" in Sacramento, Barris helped found the "Kustoms of Los Angeles" after his move south. Soon each of his cars bore a "Barris Kustom" crest. "Kalifornia Kustom" entered the nation's car lexicon just as "Cubism" and "Fauvism" had for a different generation in a different medium in a different time.

The general consensus has been that the Hirohata Merc is probably not even the best work produced by Barris. (It received only an honorable mention in *Rod & Custom*'s "Twenty Best of All Time" list in 1991.) But the reaction to Hirohata's two-toned coupe was so great that whether or not it was the best is ultimately irrelevant. Compared to what was seen in the rest of the country, it was good enough. Doug Thompson of Kansas City, who was sixteen when the car appeared in *Motor Trend* and who recently completed an exact replica of the Hirohata Merc, remembers what it meant to him, "You have to understand, Sam and George Barris were really why I had become a customizer. When I saw the original Hirohata Merc in the magazines in 1953, I swore that someday I would be that good—good enough to build a car like that" (in Remus 1990, 38).

What the Barris brothers had done was not only to modify an existing car (that had been going on for years) but to capture in metal a kind of Platonic ideal of what a contemporary American car could be. It did not look to Europe for its ideas. It did not follow Detroit's lead in deciding what makes a luxury car. The Hirohata Merc became an immediately recognizable icon defining an era, a style, and an attitude.

The most significant and noticeable change made in the Merc body is the chopped top. This one modification is an enormously complex operation. Imagine cutting a section from the middle of a cone, discarding the middle, and then reattaching the top of the cone to the bottom. In order to do so, a series of complicated cuts must be made in the top and the gaps filled with sheet metal so that the fit is perfect. New windows must be fabricated or repositioned and pillars moved or removed. Even mundane details like new windshield wipers for the smaller windshield must be accounted for. Each weld, each seam, must be smooth so that it looks like it might have come from the factory. To be successful, the final result, according to Barris, must be designed to integrate the lines of the roof into the lines of the body and fenders. As he says, "You can't have one line going one way and one in another. And it shouldn't look as if the top had just been squashed" (Barris 1998, interview).

Sam Barris, generally considered the real genius of the two brothers with the torch, cut four inches from the front of the Mercury's roof and seven from the rear. The stock rear window was reinstalled at a rakish new angle in order to fit the lines of the new roof. As was done with the Matranga Merc, the coupe was transformed into a faux hardtop by cutting away the window post and replacing it with a chrome channel (see plate 6).

The rear fenders were extended to accept '52 Lincoln taillights which were frenched, that is, molded neatly into the fenders without chrome, while the front fenders were extended four inches for balance; '52 Ford headlight rims were frenched into the front fenders. The stock chrome was removed from the hood, trunk, and sides; the hood was extended into

the grille; the trunk corners were rounded; and '52 Buick side trim flowed into functional scoops carved into the rear panels to assist in brake cooling. The scoops were punctuated by trim from a '52 Chevy grille (see plate 7). The Merc's grille was constructed from a '51 Ford grille from which the bullets had been removed. It was mounted so that it appeared to be floating in the grille shell. Exhaust ports were added to the rear bumpers.

In order to accommodate the drive shaft in the radically lowered body, a new drive tunnel was fabricated. A new interior of rolled and pleated white and green naugahyde covered the seats, headliner and kick panels. The stock dash was enlivened with custom plastic knobs fabricated by Bob Hirohata himself.

Before the trip east, the stock engine had been replaced by a brand-new '53 Cadillac overhead valve V-8 which doubled the horsepower of the original valve-in-head engine. The clutch was taken from a Ford and the flywheel from an Oldsmobile. It is important to remember that all these parts were not simply interchangeable. They had to be modified to fit. And there were no manuals to show how to do it.

If one had just the parts list alone, it is easy to imagine just a hodge podge, a car looking like one of those eccentric vehicles that used to grace the back pages of *Life* magazine, cars with forty or fifty taillights or covered with household appliances. This Barris-built Merc is not like that at all. Even to the uneducated eye everything works together in one seamless design. The lines are smooth and flowing. The curved motif of the side chrome is repeated in the scoop and in the shape of the chrome window channel. The feeling of movement in the very stance of the car is enhanced by the hand-formed rear fender skirts and the lowering of the rear more than the front. By lowering the car, adding the sweeping side chrome and extending the fenders, a series of graceful lines replace the boxiness of the original. The design takes full advantage of the new Mercury's long lines and its width which add to the drama of the radically chopped roof line. These are not modifications for modification's sake. As Barris describes the process, "I'd see something I liked, make a series of sketches and then try it out. Sometimes I wouldn't like it. And I'd do it again. Finally, it all had to work with a design" (Barris 1998, interview).

If there is one thing that sets the Hirohata Merc apart from previous customs, it is its colors. It is not monochromatic black, dark blue, or maroon like other customs, or the innocuous beiges, pale greens, and grays of stock cars, rather it is a strikingly rich two tone—Sea Foam Green with Organic Green side panels, exquisitely sprayed by Junior Conway. From the vantage point of the 1990s these colors fit exactly our technicolor memories of the decade. Today they are a cliché, but in 1952, when the car was built by Barris, this palette was dramatically new.

Throughout the decade almost every major customizer took his shot at this model of Mercury. The evolution in style from early Westergard to the Barris and the Ayala Mercs, from Bailon to Gene Winfield, demonstrate a growing confidence and a variety of styles available to the customizer. More radically altered, more brightly colored than the first customs, these Mercs communicate a sense of their weight in every detail, from their massive grilles to their huge skirts. Yet the heaviness is nicely balanced by the lightness of its many curved lines. These modified Mercs, never sleek or trim, represent a specifically American notion of beauty that has to do with a feeling of mass and an aggressive stance. Just as the '32 Ford Roadster is the quintessential rod, the '49 to '51 Merc is the quintessential custom car—infinitely malleable and prodigiously expressive. A new car was being created by customizers—a new kind of car.

But this new aesthetic, embodied in the Hirohata Merc, that came to define the "Kalifornia Kustom" was not as dominant in the beginning as it is in retrospect. As late as 1952, the year before the Hirohata Merc was completed, when George Barris and Gil Ayala had already created a number of substantial customs, the editors of *Motor Trend* in a paperback book, *Restyle Your Car,* presented a much more varied and confused picture of the state of customizing. In addition to California customs their book includes a chapter on exotic foreign sports cars, featuring designs from Farina, Zagato, and Ghia as well as a long section on Detroit experimental designs. Of the "Ten Best Customs" selected by the editors, six are conversions of standard American sedans and convertibles into cars that resemble foreign two-seater roadsters or Detroit experimental roadster/convertibles like the Harley Earl Buick Y-Job. One featured car, although not picked as one of the best, built by Charles Martz in Aurora, Missouri, is a remarkable conversion of a dull late thirties Hudson four-door sedan into a sleek two-seater runabout. In an era when there were no American-made sports cars it is not surprising that handy metal men might decide to make their own (see figure 24).

Out of the ten best only one Barris creation was selected, the important Larry Ernst Chevy. None by the Ayala brothers, or any other major California customizer, was included in the list, although a smooth Ayala '49 Merc and several

Barris customs are featured elsewhere in the style sampler section. Significantly nine of the top-ten cars originate on the East Coast or in the Midwest.

Acknowledging that customizing was driven by the quest for individual style, the editors offered advice on how to achieve that goal through "proper planning." The problem is that *Restyle Your Car* offers no consistent framework to the potential customizer. Almost anything goes. Taste is not a real factor. Nor is there any coherent sense of what might be called art.

Dividing customs into four categories: (1) Simple Style, Conservative Techniques; (2) Simple Style, Radical Techniques; (3) Complicated Style, Conservative Techniques; and (4) Complicated Style, Radical Techniques, the editors attempt to organize the myriad possible choices that face the prospective customizer. The problem is that the system they devise isn't very helpful.

Although not explicitly connected to a region, the Simple Style is essentially the West Coast look pioneered by Westergard and extended by the Barris and the Ayala brothers: "dechromed, lowered and smooth." Here the object of the styling is "to make the car a whole; the eye sees no one part of the car but instead is forced to take in the entire line of the basic automobile structure at once."

The Complicated Style, although also not identified as such, seems to be more of an East Coast style. It attracts attention to the car by "ornamenting it profusely with chrome and other attachments and also—this is a recent development—by distorting the shapes of basic components of the car such as fenders, windows, the hood, etc."

"Radical" in *Restyle Your Car* means build-

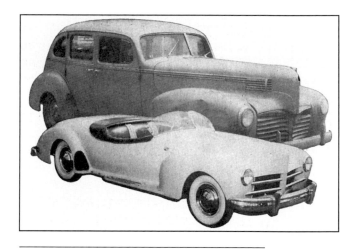

Figure 24.
Martz Hudson. The contrast between the original homely Hudson and the resulting convertible is remarkable. Also remarkable is the amount of work that was required to make such a transformation. Courtesy of *Motor Trend* magazine.

ing a car from the ground up, typically a sports car, the Martz Hudson conversion, for example. Confusingly, the editors write: "Radical and Conservative have no relations to the looks of the car." Thus, according to this system, Barris customs are basically conservative because he works on perfecting a stock form rather than creating a completely new one no matter how extensive the modifications to the existing car are.

The greatest divergence from what became the dominant aesthetic in the fifties is to be found in the idea of "complicated style." Nothing would have made a true Kalifornia Kustomizer cringe more than to read "add everything to the stock car you can, and let the eyeballs fall where they may." The complicated look allowed for jokes: "A car that has been really loaded with everything ever made,

Figure 25.
Complicated style. The folk art characteristics of the complicated style are evident in this fin-happy Buick convertible with its affection for taillights, exhaust pipes, and bumper guards. Courtesy of *Motor Trend* magazine.

chrome and otherwise, with the intent of amusing its owner and those who will see it, is a perfectly legitimate approach to the problem of individualizing one's car" (see figure 25).

Cool and humor don't often go together. This is not to say that California practitioners of the simple style didn't have a sense of humor. When joke cars, however, became a show-car trend in the sixties, with cars in the shape of outhouses, bathtubs, and coffins, the jokes weren't particularly funny. Nevertheless, there is much play in early fifties custom cars. Clever visual puns and subtle plays on objects and materials, in the spirit of Picasso, like removing decorative chrome and adding pin striping in its place, are more their bent than the mockery of Duchamp's painting a mustache on the Mona Lisa. The Kalifornia Kustomizer might want to make you smile, but he didn't want his car to *be* a joke.

The complicated stylists, as shown in *Restyle Your Car,* didn't seem to mind getting laughs. They were creating conscious or unconscious parodies of Detroit excess. The results are cars that pile grilles on top of grilles, a Mercedes above a Lincoln above a Cadillac, that add exhaust pipes, portholes, taillights, and fins in profusion. There are cars that look exactly like a Lincoln in front and a Cadillac in the rear. These are cars that never met a piece of chrome they didn't like. This so-called complicated style survives in heavily accessorized Harley Davidson "Full Dresser" motorcycles.

In 1953, the year that followed *Restyle Your Car,* the world of car customizing underwent a sea change. By the end of the year the Hirohata Merc had made its trek across country. Kalifornia Kustom became synonymous with customizing. A Kustom Kulture began to develop that supported this approach to modifying cars. No longer was the best custom a conversion of an American car into an ersatz European roadster. No longer did editors urge their readers to "study the lines of an MG roadster." The roadster to admire was now a Model T or A or Deuce. While there were still cars covered in chrome trim and accessories or in imitation of European designs, they were seldom featured in custom car magazines. Under the influence of the Hirohata Merc the East Coast style more and more imitated what was coming out of California. (In 1958 the *Custom Cars Annual,* from the same publisher as *Restyle Your Car,* relegates a few sports car conversions and complicated customs to a chapter titled "Weird Customs" at the back of the book.)

Growing out of the California practice of perfecting stock automobiles, a new way of categorizing custom cars became the clear standard. It was grounded simply in the amount of work involved in creating the finished product:

(1) Mild customs have very minor changes: removal of chrome and ornaments, lowering the body, changing hubcaps, adding spotlights, lakes pipes, new paint, and so forth.
(2) Semi-customs, in addition to the above modifications, include frenched and often tunneled headlights and taillights, rounded hood corners, reworked grille shells with new grilles, different side trim, extended fenders with new taillights, and so forth, while maintaining the basic lines of the original.
(3) Full radical customs add complicated and complex body work like chopping, sectioning, and channeling to the mix.

To a large extent the dominance of what *Motor Trend* originally called the simple, conservative style marks a triumph of the ideas of high modernism over the essentially folk art aesthetic of the complicated style.

The first principle of this modernist "simple" style is the focus on the most basic form of an object by removing ornament. Thus, hoods and trunks were dechromed—nosed and decked—and headlight and taillight rims were frenched. Bumper guards, chrome strips, and door handles were often removed to enhance the basic line of the car. This first strategy of customizers is right in line with the principles of Adolf Loos, who had advocated "elimination of ornament from useful objects." Customizers also have an affinity with Hendrikus Peter Belage, the modernist architectural theorist, who believed that "in architecture, decoration and ornament are quite

inessential while space-creation and the relationships of masses are its true essentials" (in Banham 1960, 141).

This emphasis on mass in customs was usually achieved through relatively simple methods. Just lowering a car, for example, gives it an appearance of weightiness. The key, as Barris points out, "is to give it weight without looking heavy." The stance of the custom—that is, its relationship to the ground—is one of the most important elements in the final design of a custom. How the car sits, how low it is, how the stance relates to other modifications (for example, a "rake," a car lower in the front than in the rear, seldom works well with fender skirts), are all crucial decisions that affect the final look of the car. An almost stock car with the right stance, as Larry Watson showed, can look much better than a heavily modified car with the wrong stance. Paradoxically, removing metal through more radical bodywork like chopping the top also helps create a more massive appearance by bringing the whole car even closer to the ground.

The overall result of these modifications is a look that more and more emphasizes horizontal lines over the more vertically oriented designs of thirties and forties cars. Like much of the modern architecture of Le Corbusier, Neutra, and Gropius, the typical early fifties car becomes a construction which emphasizes layers of overlapping and parallel horizontal planes. Modified wide grille openings, the reworked grilles themselves, flat wide hoods, chopped tops, and even the humble bumper all work together to create this lower, wider, more massive look.

One of the most striking connections between California customizers and modernist artists is to be found in their approach to found materials that Pablo Picasso and George Braque originated with their groundbreaking experiments with newspapers, wallpaper, printed paper, rope, and other materials in their cubist collages and *papiers collés*. These collages also have their analogues to the folk arts. Creating images of trees, birds, houses, and other common objects out of collected materials like cigar bands, orange crate images, and postage stamps had been a relatively common practice since the availability of cheap printed material in the mid-nineteenth century. But Picasso and Braque are doing something much more complicated than mere representation. Neither representational nor abstract, their works oscillate between focus on the materials themselves and image making. They are engaged in a complex exploration of the nature of representation, the confusions of meaning we assign to things we recognize, and the intersections of high art and commercial art.

In *Le Suze (Glass and Bottle of Suze),* for example, Picasso uses the label from a bottle of a popular aperitif as the focal point; surrounding it are irregularly shaped pieces of cut colored paper, which in turn are surrounded by cut-out pieces of newspapers and a small piece of ordinary wallpaper. In addition there are marks made by the artist with charcoal. With the help of the title it is fairly easy to see shapes which correspond to the glass and a bottle sitting on something that can be construed as a table. But the objects here don't quite cohere in ways that they do in ordinary paintings. The heterogeneous materials force us to focus on the parts of the whole. Because of the gaps between pieces of paper, confusions of perspective, and the absence of conventional visual cues, our eyes are drawn to shapes that exist as

shapes themselves—the rhyming curves of newspaper and black construction paper, the rhythm of the edges of newspaper, the overlapping of planes, as well as to the contrast between the materials pasted by the artist and the black marks made by his own hand. The materials also draw us away from the painting—what is the significance of using this label and this particular newspaper? What is special about Suze? Are you supposed to read the paper? To find what? Scholars have connected the use of Suze to Balkan politics and the November 18 edition of *Le Journal* used in *Le Suze* to war and pacifism and to collage itself (the front page of a newspaper typically "collages" many stories or realities). Yet *Le Suze* is anything but disordered. As much as the discordant materials seem to strain the unity of the piece, threatening to dissolve it into fragments, it never loses its powerful form, its gestalt. It is always a still life (see plate 8).

Collage is more than a way of making images. It has become a way of seeing and understanding the modern world. Photographers from Eugene Atget to Paul Strand, architects like Robert Venturi, and writers like William Carlos Williams and William Burroughs have also made use of a vision which finds significance in the arrangement of heterogeneous materials whether they are found in storefront windows, on commercial strips, or swiftly passing by along the road. Composers have combined taped sounds in collaged *musique concrète*. Over the past eighty years, film, theater, and dance have all incorporated collage elements into significant works. Even channel surfing the television has its connections to a collaged reality.

Sculpture, in particular, has taken advantage of the breakthroughs of Picasso and Braque to reenvision the world of three-dimensional objects. These *assemblages*—Picasso's own three-dimensional still lifes; Marcel Duchamp's "assisted ready-mades" such as mounting an actual bicycle wheel on an ordinary stool; dada pieces like Hausmann's *Mechanical Head* and Kurt Schwitters's *Merz* constructions, made from the discarded materials he found in the street; Vladimir Tatlin's assembled corner pieces; Joseph Cornell's many boxes; Robert Rauschenberg's "combine-paintings"; and surrealist "poetic objects" and mannequins—all play with the same sort of juxtapositions of preexisting materials that cubist collages depend on. The artist in the twentieth century no longer has to create a work out of nothing or from an elemental piece of rock or metal. It is already there, in pieces, in the environment. The artist just has to find them and put them together in an interesting way. The result, according to William Seitz, is more "poetic than realistic, for each constituent element can be transformed. Physical materials and their auras are transmuted into a new amalgam that both transcends and includes its parts" (Seitz 1961, 83).

Car customizers do not approach modifying cars exactly like a Picasso contemplating the nature of painting in works like *Le Suze* or creating a new kind of sculpture in an assemblage made out of painted wood and upholstery fringe. They are simply interested in making their cars look different and better, yet their work as collage has more in common with Picasso than it does with folk art creations of portraits made from gum wrappers that are often cited as being analogues to cubism.

The "assembling" of a "transcendent" new car from existing parts is standard practice in customizing. The Hirohata Merc is one exam-ple. The Larry Ernst Chevy is another, built for a Catholic priest from Toledo, Ohio, who drove his brand-new '51 Chevy hardtop to Barris's shop and said "give me something different." It marked one of the beginnings of the eastern turn toward California for advanced styling ideas. Although Ernst got his way and Barris let him keep the continental kit, an externally mounted and covered spare that was a favorite on East Coast cars, for the rest of the car Sam Barris gave him a perfect West Coast treatment including figuring out how to incorporate the continental kit into the design by extending the rear fenders so the kit wouldn't look just stuck on back. The front of the car is assembled with a '50 Mercury grille shell which surrounds a modified floating Canadian Meteor grille. A modified 1950 Oldsmobile one-piece windshield fits into the reworked roof line. In addition the top is chopped, the hood is nosed, and the headlights are frenched. Painted first in a brilliant metallic purple with a light orchid roof, and then a combination of rose and lime green, the resulting "assisted ready-made" is completely unified. Nothing seems out of place, yet it is clearly not stock nor is it trying to imitate any other car, European or American (see plate 9).

The effect of all these changes is more than a sum of the parts. As in collage, the different pieces retain their original identities—Picasso's newspapers are still "news," read by critics for clues to their positioning—so that Hirohata Merc's taillights remain identifiably Lincoln while, at the same time, they are transformed by a new design which redefines the car and the significance of those taillights in it. The same applies to the Meteor grille on the Larry Ernst Chevy. It is as if one is being asked to think about taillights and grilles in a new way,

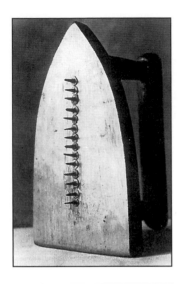

Figure 26.
Le Cadeau (The Gift). Created by Man Ray in 1921. © 2001 Man Ray Trust/ Artists Rights Society (ARS), NY/ADAGP, Paris.

not just as functional elements or as signifiers of status but as having an identity and beauty of their own. Because they don't belong to the original design, they stand out. Because they have been incorporated into a new design they are subsumed. Removed from the context of the original source, they confuse the viewer at the same time providing for a shock of recognition as the effect of the new environment on the lights is understood. By choosing certain parts the customizer changes how we see parts. They become framed. The light bar in a stock 1955 Chrysler grille, for example, is lost in the original overly complicated four-part design. Used by itself as a grille bar in a frenched '49 Mercury grille shell, the bar becomes a simple and elegant sculptural form.

Unlike the engine compartment where the operating principle is basically "form follows function," and where the quest is similar to Brancusi's search for "the essence of things themselves," the collage approach to bodywork based on juxtaposition of appropriated elements allows for an undermining of function and identity (what good do the extra teeth from a Chevy do on an Oldsmobile, or what do nonfunctional scoops from an Impala add to the roof of a Ford) as prime sources of meaning. Instead they create new kinds of meanings in the car, which is, for most people, simply a

utilitarian object to begin with and without much meaning outside of that created by advertising.

Like Man Ray's addition of a row of tacks to the bottom of a flatiron in *Le Cadeau (The Gift)* (see figure 26) which completely obliterates the iron's function of smoothing things out, customizing techniques, severe lowering, for example, often threaten the very ability of a car to negotiate even the smoothest roads easily. Changing a tire becomes a major endeavor. Frenching taillights and headlights turns the normally simple task of changing a bulb into hours of work. Chopping the top greatly limits visibility and some modifications of bumpers render them practically useless. Thus the customizer plays with conventional notions of art as useless and technology as essentially defined by its function. He also plays with conventional notions of what makes a particular car that particular car. Does a Chevy with Oldsmobile headlights, a Buick grille, Packard taillights, Pontiac sidetrim, and a Buick engine remain a Chevy? As with cubist works the balance between opposing ideas is crucial. Although the customizers continually test the limits, a car that goes too far, that is, in fact, not driveable, is less interesting and less valuable than a car that works despite its limitations. The challenge is "how low can you go" and still go. The Hirohata Merc did make it from Los Angeles to Indianapolis.

Le Cadeau is not just a nonfunctional iron, but an indefinable new object that could be many things—an object of torture, a new sort of industrial tool, a weapon, or a backscratcher. In its new form it is disturbing, partly because of the illogical and contradictory joining together of tacks and iron, the materials themselves, and partly because of our inability to solve its mystery, "how is this a gift?" so that we can label it. One of the appeals of creating customs is eliciting that same sort of confused reaction on the part of viewers as happened when the people along the Hirohata Merc's trip east continually asked, "What is it?" Customizers generally didn't care that many people felt, and continue to feel, that customizing somehow destroys the car, turning it into an undriveable leadsled and that it is ultimately a waste of a good vehicle and good money. Instead, like Man Ray, they are interested in arrangements of various objects or the modification of objects to "amuse, annoy, bewilder, mystify, inspire reflection." In contrast to Ray, who didn't, they do want to "arouse admiration for any technical excellence" (in Seitz 1961, 48–49). They are proud of their workmanship and valued for it.

As the rock musician and car enthusiast Mike Ness notes, these cars are not merely or even primarily beautiful, but expressive as well. If they were only pretty, they would be merely decorative. The power that they continue to hold over a large and diverse segment of the population is directly connected to what they mean both individually and culturally.

Customizing transforms the desire for a car from that of merely purchasing, displaying, and possessing a prized object to designing, recreating, modifying, performing, and competing with it. Customizers assert the primacy of the vision of the individual artist over the products of the collective corporate design industry.

It is one thing to update or reconfigure what was seen as an obsolete design, like the Model T's and A's that became the original rods, it is another to set to work improving what was being offered by Detroit as the latest in automotive styling. The stock designs that Barris redesigned were also Mercury's first major postwar styling exercises, purportedly a big advance on prewar styling. The act of altering these designs, the first really new designs in almost a decade, positioned the car builders against great corporate powers and their highly paid design teams. No industry is more American or more tied to Americans' sense of their place in the world than the auto industry. It is virtually the last heavy industry (outside of airplane manufacture) that still survives in this country. No other product is as tied to Americans' self-image, their ideas of status and success. When the customizer erases the name of the manufacturer by removing all insignias, when he decides that the fenders are too short, the roof too high, or the grille all wrong, he is redefining the car in his own image, according to his own vision. Against the vast image creating power of Detroit, this is a Promethean gesture. It is this act of rebellion against the status quo which had so much appeal for working-class car buffs who were in the process of constructing their own identities outside of and against the culture at large.

But, paradoxically, these builders drawn to particular makes of cars were also caught up in corporately determined meanings, defining themselves, for example, as Ford or Chevy men. So, as they immediately began their alterations, often modifying the car beyond easy recognition, they were still clearly influenced by the image of the cars that Detroit had successfully marketed. Some designs, early fifties Plymouths, Dodges, and early fifties Pontiacs, for example, were rejected by builders, as much for their being associated with conservative, family, and corporate values as for their looks, while other cars, especially Fords and

Mercurys, were chosen for car-building projects because they were connected with images of performance and style that fit their own values. (The affection Latino "low riders" shower on Chevys, which can be traced back to the late forties, can be seen as an act of self-definition that situates them against the Anglo preference for Fords and Mercurys.)

In their pursuit of an individual style customizers also tended to choose makes that were popular. Thus, the choices they made were also in some ways safe. They operated within limits that had been set by a corporate structure that inspired the same kind of brand identification one could find almost everywhere else in the consumer culture, from detergents to colas. There were many safe choices to make as a customizer who wanted to follow rather than lead. Olds lights on a '53 Ford, as well as Buick side trim, Dodge Lancer hubcaps, and dual spotlights are just a few standard additions that involved no risk. There were often limits to rebellion.

But even a safe choice within the custom world was likely to be judged negatively by the general culture. Customizing a car was seen as ruining its looks, making it unsafe, and, most significantly, destroying its resale value by those outside Kustom Kulture. And so even by mildly customizing a car with predominantly safe choices a young builder could separate himself from the "straight" world (parents) and guarantee inclusion in the local Kustom Kulture.

It is the challenges customizers present to corporately created meanings and values that really distinguishes them from ordinary consumers. As they altered their desired objects, transforming them and erasing their marks of identification, even renaming them, they cre-

ated a new language of car design. Each decision in some way undid meanings which constituted the underpinnings of consumer culture, like "new is better than old," "fancy (read *expensive*) is better than plain (read *cheap*)," and "Cadillac is better than Chevy." They used parts from older cars to "update" newer ones. They used parts from the more despised brands to enhance the design of their preferred choices. They removed the chrome which added value (cost) to the original car, while chroming parts of the car, like the engine, where, to the ordinary driver, there would seem to be no value at all. They reassembled the products of a billion-dollar industry in a spirit of determined play that declared that Detroit designs were inferior to their own.

One way to assert that mastery of car design was no longer in the manufacturer's hands was to give the car a new name. Like a work of art. After removing the names that Detroit had spent thousands of dollars creating, customizers chose their own names that ranged from the exotically foreign—"Polynesian," "Sahara," "Aztec," "Jade Idol," "Oriental," and "Grecian," to the sentimental—"Miss Elegance," "Blue Angel," and "Moonglow." They could build on existing imagery—"Outlaw," "Beatnik Bandit," and "El Diablo," or they could be fairly mundane—"Dream Truck," "Hirohata Merc," and "the Sam Barris Buick." But even in the simplest designation there is an important value. The Hirohata Merc will always be "the Hirohata Merc," no matter who owns it. The same is true of the Sam Barris Buick or any other important car.

What the customizer substitutes for the values of ambition and conventional status is self-expression, something he can determine for himself. The self-expression of the customizer is clearly not the same as the self-expression of a major innovator like a Picasso or Duchamp, but, then, the self-expression of most artists is unlike theirs as well. Customizers worked within a fairly narrow vocabulary of options, or styles. A car could be lowered in the rear, or the front, or even all around. Each choice gave a decidedly different look to the car. And a surprising combination always created excitement.

Even by taking a relatively safe route, a customizer could individualize his car with an unusual color or wild pinstriping or by simply lowering the car radically. A mildly lowered, de-chromed, '50 Ford sedan painted a deep maroon was admired, but it would brand its driver as somewhat conservative, if tasteful. It would admit him to the club. He would earn a name. But just a little lower and the car would be something special. Slammed (lowered almost to the ground), the car would be truly distinctive, and the driver might be known in towns twenty or more miles away.

In the 1950s the real accolades, however, were reserved for the builders of full radical customs, where the whole was redesigned. Admired for taking big risks, for not every radical custom was a work of art—many were outright design disasters—the builders of cars like the Hirohata Merc set the standard for a generation of builders. They made the cars that were known, and discussed, throughout the country. They made the cars that kids would drive hundreds of miles just to see.

At a time when Detroit didn't have to care very much about the craft of building because cars were traded in so frequently and there was no real competition, the customizer believed in the perfection of the craft of car building as well as of its art. While Detroit could get away with poor workmanship, a customizer couldn't. No one expected a perfect car from Detroit. If it ran, most people didn't care if the chrome was even or if there was a wider gap between hood and fender on the left side than on the right. Customizers not only altered the looks of Detroit cars, the best also perfected them. It bothered them when things didn't match. It was another way of asserting their own values against the common wisdom. As any practical person knew, cars continually lost value from the moment they were driven out of the showroom, it didn't pay to fix them; and customized cars lost value much more quickly than stock cars, so it made no sense to make them look better. The marketplace didn't recognize perfection or imagination.

By the mid-fifties, as rock 'n' roll began to dominate the music charts, hot rods and customs moved further into the center of youth culture. Masterpieces abounded. Styles proliferated. Kustom Kulture was no longer a regional phenomenon as it entered what Larry Watson calls the "Golden Age of Customs" when inventive car artists created a cultural explosion that continues to be a source of inspiration four decades later.

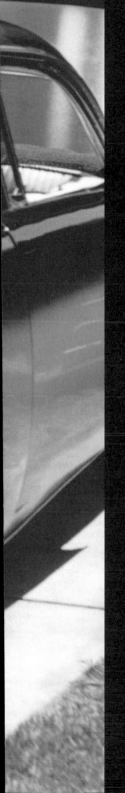

THE GOLDEN AGE
OF CUSTOMS

At the end of 1953, the year the Hirohata Merc caused such a sensation in the car world, the list of the top-ten best-selling records for the year contained not a single song that can be easily connected to any emerging youth culture. The number-one song, the theme from the Hollywood costume drama based on the life of Toulouse-Lautrec, was "Song from *Moulin Rouge*" by Percy Faith and his orchestra. A catchy pop instrumental, "April in Portugal" by Lee Baxter, was number three. The only singing group, hardly doo-wop, who made it to the list was the Ames Brothers with "You, You, You." The top male singers were Eddie Fisher and Frankie Laine. Theresa Brewer, Patti Page, and Joni James each had a top-ten hit.

By the end of the decade a revolution had taken place. Every single one of the top hits of 1959 was either a genuine rock 'n' roll song or performed by a newly created teen idol. As top-ten lists go it is typically conservative and, except for "There Goes My Baby" by the Drifters and, possibly, "Personality" by Lloyd Price, it doesn't contain historically significant rock 'n' roll songs. The list doesn't include "What'd I Say" by Ray Charles or "Back in the U.S.A." by Chuck Berry or "Since I Don't Have You" by the Skyliners, which were all hits in 1959. Also missing are the Isley Brothers' classic "Shout," Phil Philips's "Sea of Love," and Bobby Darin's "Dream Lover." The list, however, is representative of the state of rock 'n' roll at the end of the decade in the year

Buddy Holly and Richie Valens died, after Elvis's entrance into the army and the scandal of Jerry Lee Lewis's marriage to his teenage cousin, and after the image makers began creating teen idols on pop assembly lines. So the list contains two hits by Paul Anka ("Put Your Head on My Shoulder" and "Lonely Boy") and one by Frankie Avalon ("Venus"). Bobby Darin's crossover smash "Mack the Knife" was the number-one hit of the year. Other group songs, besides "There Goes My Baby," are by the Browns ("Three Bells") and the Fleetwoods ("Come Softly to Me"), both featuring sweet close harmonies, closer to the Chordettes than to the Cadillacs. Completing the list are Santo and Johnny's haunting steel guitar instrumental "Sleep Walk" and Johnny Horton's semi-novelty song "The Battle of New Orleans." Overall, it is a pretty bland list.

What is significant about the list, however, is not its quality or lack of it, but the startling evidence it provides of the almost total dominance of the music market by teens. By 1959 teenagers no longer existed on the fringes of the culture, forming what today is called a niche market. By 1959 teens were the market. Even in this middle of the road list, adults have been effectively excised. It is clear that record buyers older than twenty-two no longer have much, if any, influence in determining the best sellers. There is no Frank Sinatra, Tony Bennett, Sarah Vaughn, Count Basie, or Dave Brubeck here. Although they would all have top-ten hits in the rock 'n' roll era, their hits would increasingly become mere anomalies, with little impact on the irresistible drift of American culture toward youth. A hit by big bands like Jimmy Dorsey's "So Rare" in 1956 was just that. Equally notable is the absence from the list of a whole generation of younger pop artists, such

as Theresa Brewer, Doris Day, Jerry Vale, Rosemary Clooney, Vic Damone, Frankie Laine, Al Martino, and Don Cornell. Consistently heading the charts in the first half of the decade, with hit after hit, they were seemingly destined for stardom and long careers. By 1959 they were the ones who existed on the fringe.

By the end of the decade, teens had developed a full-blown culture. They looked different, they talked different, and they acted different from even what today are called "twenty-somethings." Unlike their mothers and fathers who adored the music idols of the thirties and forties, the Benny Goodmans and the Glenn Millers, standing paternally by the bandstand—clearly looking like adults—fifties teens created the music themselves and sang about their own culture. Although they borrowed from older blues and country performers, they sang teenage songs—about school, dances, first love, sex, and just hanging out. No longer proto-adults or innocent youth, they created a unique position for themselves in opposition to both the values of maturity and the limitations of childhood. The generation that created this culture would come to influence not only the record charts but every aspect of American life for the rest of the century as well. Their experience was rapidly becoming the American experience.

Rodding and customizing, an important part of this emerging culture, also moved from the fringe to a place a little closer to center stage. Rods were no longer shown in just teen exploitation films, they had become domesticated, a part of the American television family. In an attempt to lure teen viewers to the "Life of Riley," Chester Riley's son Junior was given a neat chopped and channeled Barris-built '34 Ford coupe to exasperate his father with. Bud

Anderson did a little rodding in his driveway on "Father Knows Best." Not only did Rick Nelson sing rock 'n' roll at the end of episodes of "Ozzie and Harriet," but he had a beautiful green Deuce roadster for at least one episode. In 1958 television even had a hot rod star; Norm Grabowski's beautiful T-Bucket (see plate 10) was driven by Ed "Kookie" Burns on "77 Sunset Strip." The car drew as many young viewers as the plots. As a result of the exposure, it became the most famous rod in the country, inspiring dozens of imitators while creating a whole new class of rod.

In the real world, drag racing was well on its way to becoming a major professional sport and not just the pursuit of devoted amateurs, although the strip was still a place where almost anyone could drive up to see what his car could do in a quarter mile. Strips had been opening throughout the decade from Maine to California. In 1957 *Life* magazine reported that there were 130 strips in operation in forty states. *Life* estimated that they drew more than two and a half million spectators and over 100,000 racers. The article counted 15,000 car clubs which were adding about 1,500 new members a month. Some of the more famous drivers traveled as many as 60,000 miles a year getting to races. Strip owners had begun paying appearance money in order to ensure that the best drivers and the fastest cars would race at their strip. Prize money became more than a token amount to accompany a trophy. Even a top prize of one thousand dollars for winning top eliminator was a significant amount of money in 1959 that allowed builders to continue to improve their cars and their elapsed times.

The rapidly growing auto parts industry began to see advantages in backing the most successful drag racers. In exchange for token amounts of money by today's standards, decals from cam makers, tire manufacturers, and oil companies began to appear on dragsters.

Drivers were becoming stars. And California no longer had a monopoly on cars or drivers. Don Garlits and his series of "Swamp Rat" dragsters from Florida successfully challenged west coast cars. His speed of 183.66 mph at the end of the quarter mile in 1959 was the fastest ever run to that point. Nicknamed "Big Daddy" in the early sixties, he would soon become the most famous and successful of all drag racers, the Babe Ruth of drag racing, who introduced many innovations to the sport. The Ohioan Arfons brothers and their wild airplane-engine–powered dragsters also drew a lot of attention. Other important drivers arrived on the scene from Michigan, North Carolina, and Texas.

The National Hot Rod Association no longer completely dominated the sport. NASCAR briefly flirted with drags. In 1956 the American Hot Rod Association (AHRA) was formed to compete with the NHRA as a sanctioning body. The AHRA, in contrast to the NHRA, allowed the use of the more powerful, and more dangerous, nitromethane fuel which allowed the AHRA to leap ahead of the older body in top-end speeds and elapsed times. *Hot Rod,* closely tied to the NHRA and its emphasis on safety and regulation, largely ignored AHRA events, and the competition became intense and bitter. Because of the excitement created in AHRA events with runs approaching two hundred miles an hour in the quarter mile, the NHRA retreated and approved fuel cars in the early sixties.

Drag racing nevertheless still had difficulties with its image. Even as late as 1957 there was significant opposition to the very idea of drag racing even away from the streets as a sport on sanctioned strips. Despite the fact that organized drag racing is a relatively safe form of auto racing, the National Safety Council (NSC) issued a bizarre recommendation aimed specifically at drag racing—stock cars, sports cars, and Indy racing, all with many more fatalities than drag racing, were not included: "The National Safety Council opposes speed contests. Since speed violations are so often involved in traffic accidents, the National Safety Council cannot condone speeding even in the name of competition" (Maremont 1957, 15). The Council urged rodders to pursue economy runs and offer driver clinics instead of drag racing. Needless to say, the NSC didn't win many hearts or minds among hot rodders.

The overall growth of the economy at the end of the decade played a crucial role in the development of a car-based youth culture. In 1957 *U.S. News & World Report* surveyed the economic accomplishments of the preceding ten years. The results inspired the editors to trumpet "10 Amazing Years":

The last year of an amazing decade is about to end. . . .

In one brief 10-year period, America's face was remade. Vast suburban areas sprang up to receive millions of Americans pressing out from cities. Ribbons of superhighways were laid across the country. A huge expansion of air facilities tie the nation into a compact unity.

Whole regions changed their complexion. Deserts were turned into boom areas. Power was harnessed on a stupendous scale to ease the burden of work.

Nearly 30 million added people were provided for, and on a steadily rising standard of living. A car was put in every garage, two in many. TV sets came into almost every home. There was a chicken, packaged and frozen, for every pot, with more to spare. Never had so many people, anywhere, been so well off. (in Satin 1960, 16)

Fueled by the growth of an economy that put more money in their hands (about $10 billion in 1959), teens were able to spend more time and more money with other teens and create their own culture as an alternative to one based on safety and security. As a result teen life became more and more separate from the adult world. There were movies aimed at them, as well as magazines, books, drive-in restaurants, clothing stores, and radio stations that catered almost exclusively to teen taste.

One of the most visible signs of teen opposition to the dominant values of success and security was found in the cars they chose to drive. More and more they were choosing rods and customs. By the end of the decade driving a car was a necessity if a teenager was going to have a social life. And teens were no longer limited to buying old jalopies: "It is taken for granted that every teen-ager will learn to drive and that, if he does not have a car of his own, individually or as a member of a group, he will certainly have access to one" (Bernard 1961, 2–5).

During the second half of the fifties interest in customizing grew at an explosive rate. Significant new cars were being built all across the country by new builders who ranged from driveway customizers to the emergence of a new group of creative professional designer/builders. Northern California builders like Joe Bailon, Joe Wilhelm, and Gene Winfield began to compete with George Barris for the title of "King of Kustoms." Among the twenty-eight candidates for "Custom of the Year" in 1958, *Motor Life* selected four Bailon and four Winfield customs and six by Barris. Painters like Von Dutch, Dean Jeffries, and Larry Watson fundamentally changed customizing by making paint treatments equal in importance to bodywork in re-working stock designs. These builders and painters defined the Golden Age of Customs—with each producing a number of distinctive masterpieces.

Although customizing was spreading quickly across the country, California remained its artistic center. It is interesting to note that of the twenty-eight candidates for *Motor Life*'s 1958 award only five were not California cars. But there was a growing number of builders outside of California who were not slavish imitators of the California style. The Alexander brothers in Detroit and Darryl Starbird in Kansas began to build cars of national significance. Bill Cushenberry left Kansas in 1958 where he had been building customs and dragsters to open a shop in Monterey where he soon became the preeminent builder in central California. Bodymen Bill Hines and "Korky" Korkes and painter/photographer Andy Southard all built interesting cars before they found the lure of Kustom Kulture irre-sistible and headed west.

In addition to major shows like the Oakland Roadster Show on the West Coast, there were now major shows in Hartford and Detroit, as well as in Nebraska and Kansas where new cars could inspire backyard builders. By 1959 there were more than ten magazines devoted in whole or part to customizing. In addition to the older *Hot Rod, Rod & Custom,* and *Car Craft,* there were *Custom Cars, Custom Craft, Rods Illustrated, Custom Rodder, Rod Builder and Customizer, Rodding and Restyling,* and *Speed and Custom.* In addition *Motor Life* and

Cars devoted a lot of attention to rods and customs. There was sufficient activity in the East that three of the magazines, *Custom Rodder, Rod Builder and Customizer,* and *Rodding and Restyling,* could concentrate on cars built in Michigan, New Jersey, New York, and New England. All these magazines covered new cars, new trends, big shows, and one or two "show how" features each month. A cross between *Artforum* and *House Beautiful,* a typical article in these magazines might cover "styling the new Thunderbird" or "what's new in side trim?" or "how to use expanded metal." Each issue also included photo essays on three or four outstanding cars.

To attract an even younger audience trading card companies began offering custom car and hot rod cards, endorsed by George Barris. Plastic car models designed for the youthful customizer became a huge business. By the sixties the model business had grown so big that car builders were being driven by the need to come up with wackier and wackier cars to satisfy the companies who were trying to please their customers—twelve-year-old boys. In the mid-sixties *Rod & Custom* would devote almost as much attention to model building as it did to car customizing.

The impact of Detroit's exploitation of the Kustom Kulture also helped shaped the growth of customizing. By the mid-fifties Detroit had become more attuned to the growing market for flashier and higher-performance cars, influenced, at least in part, by customiz-ers. The year 1955 marked the first appearance of what would become the consummate fifties cars: much chrome, wild colors, gigantic proportions and, of course, the fin. The 1958 Lincoln Continental Mark III was 229 inches long (more than 19 feet!). True fins, not the little bumps on the backs of early fifties Caddys, dominated Detroit automotive styling and seemed to grow every year. By 1957 almost every manufacturer had a model with some sort of fin. Every configuration was employed. There were vertical, horizontal, angled, and bigger fins. And chrome was everywhere—side trim multiplied, hood ornaments became engorged, and taillights were encrusted with the silver metal.

The year 1955 also marked the appearance of Chevy's first V-8 after decades of offering the same basic six. Soon there were a number of performance packages available direct from the factory which offered combinations of hot rod favorites—fuel injection or multiple carburetors, dual exhausts, and stiffer suspension. In 1957 you could buy a 283ci Chevy that produced 283 horsepower—matching the hot rodder's old ideal of one horsepower per cubic inch. Plymouth offered its Fury in 1956 with a 240 horsepower "Hy-Fire" V-8 as a special hardtop model with gold trim. Chrysler began offering its high performance 300 series in 1955 with a 300 horse Hemi engine. Although the luxury 300 series was not directly aimed at a hot rod audience, Chrysler's Hemi engines would soon become the standard engine in top dragsters. In 1955 the Corvette, introduced in late 1953, also finally got a V-8 and the first Ford Thunderbird appeared, giving Americans an option of two Detroit two-seaters.

It was not technical innovation, however, but styling that dominated Detroit's productions in the fifties. Although there is disagreement over this point (Ganahl 2000, 68), many ideas from Kustom Kulture, whether through direct influence or coincidence, were incorporated into the new models: both two- and four-door hardtops with rakish roof lines became a standard body style for all makers; the '55 Chevy came with hooded headlights; and scoops, mostly nonfunctional, were added to hoods, roof lines, and side panels of a number of models. Grille shells began to be integrated with the bumpers on a number of models; the exhaust of the '55 T-Bird exited through ports above the bumper like many customs; dual headlights, first used on the "Wild Kat" pickup by Barris in 1956, became commonplace on production cars by 1958. Dealers offered continental kits as an option. The traditional Detroit range of colors—black, white, red, beige, blue, and green—was enlivened with a whole range of new tints that evoked warmer climates like southern California: pinks, aquas, and salmons, often applied in two tones with the chrome strips used as color dividers the way Barris had done on the Hirohata Merc. Hudson and Packard even tried three tones in an ill-fated move to stay ahead of the competition. At the end of the decade metallic paints were widely available.

Changes in styles accelerated. Model changes had been occurring in three- or four-year cycles, the '49 to '51 Ford and the '49 to '52 Chevy, for example, where one body style received minor trim changes for each new model year until a major change. By the mid-1950s Detroit offered major, sometimes radical, changes from year to year. The '55 to '56 Chevys were fairly close in style, the '57 was a fairly big departure, the '58 constituted another major new direction. There was almost nothing the '59 Chevy had in common with the '58.

Despite the stylistic innovation on Detroit's latest creations, customizers were not deterred from their desire to modify stock models. They still found lots to do. As far as they were concerned Detroit still hadn't gotten it right. Detroit lacked restraint with chrome. There was still much too much trim and too many ornaments that often obscured lines on the new models. And they didn't sit right. Cars always needed lowering. The stock paint in stock colors just didn't measure up to custom colors and didn't even come close to the new paint treatments like paneling and scallops.

With a greater sense of daring customizers turned their attention to a wider variety of vehicles. The line between hot rods and customs became blurred. Barris customized a Model A pickup truck, "Ala Kart," with a completely customized front end including quad headlights which won the "America's Most Beautiful Roadster Award" in both 1958 and 1959 (see plate 11), and he created a custom front end on "The Emperor," a Deuce roadster that won the award in 1960. A little later Bud Pearce built a pickup custom/rod, with an upholstered top and unusual Jaguar engine, out of a 1930 Ford (see figure 27).

Early fat-fendered Fords also received the full custom treatment. Bill Cushenberry's "Matador," a 1940 Ford coupe, is a particularly fine example. Its body was totally reworked: chopped two inches, sectioned four and a half inches, with deep sculpted fender insets and hand-formed front grille (see figure 28).

Contemporary pickup trucks, largely ignored by early customizers, became more and more popular as candidates for the full customizing treatment. Barris's "Kopper Kart," a 1956 Chevy with a radically reworked body, had matching front and rear grilles that were both copper plated.

In 1954 articles began to appear in *Rod & Custom* about a truck project being undertaken by Spence Murray. The resulting 1950

Figure 27.
Pearce Model A pickup. Built by Bud Pearce in the sixties, it follows on the innovations of Ala Kart. Note the upholstered top and the unusual Jaguar engine in addition to the hand-formed front end that is typical of radical customs in the early sixties. This car was an award winner in Detroit.

Figure 28.
Matador. Built by Bill Cushenberry in 1960, it is one of the most radical '40 Ford coupes ever built. The top is chopped four inches, and the body is sectioned five inches. The front end is completely hand formed with a grille made of expanded metal and Lucite bars. The sides feature elaborate flowing sculpted cutouts in the fenders and huge scoops along the sides. The interior is equally sculpted and finished in red and white naugahyde. Courtesy of Petersen Publishing.

Figure 29.
The *R&C* Dream Truck. A style guide to the late fifties custom, it features all the key elements: sculpted fins, hand-formed front and rear grille shells, hand-fabricated grilles, molded front and rear ends, radical bodywork such as top chopping, sectioning body and hood, and finished with candy scallops over pearl paint. The remarkable thing about the car is how well it holds together despite the number of builders who were involved in the project. A case where too many cooks didn't spoil the broth. Photo by George Barris.

Chevrolet truck was closely monitored by the magazine, which covered the progress of the changes in thirty-six articles over the next four years. The truck came to be known as the "*R&C* Dream Truck." Under the direction of Murray, most of the top customizers had at least a part in the final creation. The truck was chopped by Sam Gates, initially sectioned by Gates, and completed by Valley Custom, which also did the dashboard. The front and rear treatments, including quad lights, still rare at the time, and molded hand-formed front and rear grilles with hand-formed taillights were done at the Barris shop. Gene Winfield handled sectioning the hood, reshaping the wheel wells, and removal of the running boards. Bob Metz

of Indiana created the fins and the rear panels and transformed the car from a somewhat ordinary custom into something strikingly new. Bill Colgan installed the white and purple interior. Dean Moon built the Chevy V-8, one of the earliest swaps of the new Chevy engine into an older custom. Barris applied the light metallic purple paint, and Dean Jeffries applied the dark purple scallops and pinstriping. The "Dream Truck" became one of the most popular and influential customs of the fifties, drawing as many as a million spectators until it was severely damaged in a towing mishap on route to a show in the midwest. It represents the most advanced ideas of what would become the dominant style of the golden age of customs. It has recently been restored (see figure 29).

With the increased number of models and trim levels provided by Detroit, customizers were blessed with an abundance of parts to use on the older models they still favored: the '49 to '51 Mercs, '49 to '52 Chevys, and Shoebox '49 to '51 Fords. Packard Clipper taillights, Plymouth grilles, and Pontiac side trim, as well as a host of other parts, could be used to give a new look to older cars.

Some customizers seemed to find a challenge in the new Detroit designs as if the big car manufacturers had upped the styling ante. The ubiquitous fin that seemed like an afterthought on a stock '57 Dodge became a pair of elegantly curved panels that look as graceful as the arms of a Chinese fan dancer on Bill Hine's "L'il Bat," a '51 Ford coupe, a car that never was meant for fins and which never should have looked good with fins, but did (see figure 30 and plate 12). Joe Bailon, Bob Metz, Gene Winfield, and Anthony Abato all did some interesting work with fins.

In the mid-fifties stylistic dynamism, the changes in style that signify a vital art form,

Figure 30.
L'il Bat (two views). A 1951 Ford built by Bill Hines in 1959. It later received scallops. It is the swoop of the fins that make this car so unusual and special. The rest of the car is fairly conventional.

reached its zenith, although Pat Ganahl disagrees again. For him customizing was essentially over by 1955. Because of the attractiveness of Detroit's new models, traditional customizing had no real function: "Other than the chrome-laden '58 Buick and Olds, which were Harley Earl last-gasp blunders, most of these longer, lower, wider, wrap-around window, super-finned new cars outdid traditional customs in every way. They made them look dowdy and dated. They were finished" (Ganahl 2000, 68).

He is correct about the slow demise of traditional customs, the early Westergard- and

Barris-styled Fords and Mercs, but not, I think, about customizing in general. As more and more new cars were customized and more new models were introduced, the dominance of the Westergard/Barris style was broken, even though it remained influential. There was a whole range of cars from mild to radical, that still relied on the traditional Westergard/Barris techniques. Duane Steck's 1954 Chevy,

Figure 31.
Moonglow. Built by Duane Steck in his driveway, it is a testimony to ingenuity and understatement. With a top chop, frenched Chrysler taillights in extended fenders, radical lowering, and additional grille teeth, it is a reminder, against some of the excesses of the "Golden Age," of the continuing power of the early fifties style.

Figure 32.
Aztec. This 1955 Chevy owned by Bill Carr was the result of a collaborative effort at the Barris shop that lasted more than two years. Sam Barris chopped the top. Carr, Bill De Carr, and George Barris worked together on the design. All contributed in the construction. George Barris painted it a "Golden Honey," which he blended himself. The amount of work is impressive from hand-formed front and rear grilles to the elaborate fins. It was selected by readers as the *Motor Life* "Custom of the Year" in 1958 beating out a lot of famous customs, including the Dream Truck. Photo by George Barris.

"Moonglow," is a notable example (see figure 31). By mid-decade fresh ideas opened up customizing to a much wider range of options. There were new individual styles from emerging builders and more clearly defined regional styles that served as models for the customizer who was not quite as original as a Bailon, Winfield, or Wilhelm. Barris himself moved away from his Westergard-based style and stayed at the forefront of the art with cars like "The Aztec" (see figure 32).

No longer did the customizer have to rely primarily on collaging existing parts or cutting away from the stock body as the means of transforming a stock car. A new aesthetic, a kind of expressionism, began to emerge which left no part of the car as it was and which allowed much more freedom to the customizer to create his own fantasy of a particular car. These new directions were closer to the art of true sculpture than assemblage. By the end of the decade many customizers moved away from using stock cars as the starting point and began creating one-of-a-kind cars from scratch.

In the mid-fifties all of the strategies of the traditional custom as defined by Westergard and the Barris brothers were reconfigured and redefined. There were more options for the crucial stance of the custom than before. Cars were still lowered. Cars always look better lower (one has only to look at cars from the sixties when "jacking" them up became the fashion to see that). But no longer was the standard to lower the car more in the rear than the front as was done in the early fifties with the various Barris Mercs and the Larry Ernst Chevy. In the East lowering the car more in the rear remained the standard for much longer than in California where customizers experimented with lowering the car evenly all around or adding a rake to the car by lowering it more in the front than the rear. By the end of the decade California rakes often became so severe that cars often looked like they were perpetually in an emergency braking situation or always going down the side of a steep mountain.

Lowering the car evenly or raking it allowed for more emphasis on the wheels. The wheels didn't receive much attention in the early fifties when rear wheels were usually completely covered with massive skirts. The front wheels typically received simply a new pair of hubcaps that were favored by customizers: Caddy caps, Olds Fiesta, or Dodge spinners. But the new stance, particularly with a rake, focused equal attention to all four wheels. A car lowered all the way around could look good with or without skirts, but as the decade progressed skirts became rarer on the West Coast. On the East Coast the appearance of huge bubble skirts, originally formed from scrap car hoods, worked well with the rear tilted stance favored there and skirts continued to be widely used long after they fell out of favor on the West Coast. Skirts, especially bubble skirts, didn't work well with a rake. A comparison between Gene Winfield's and Dave James's '56 Chevies reveals the small, but significant, stylistic differences between the two coasts (see plates 13 and 14).

While changing hubcaps remained the most common modification to the wheels, California customizers began to experiment with new wheel treatments. Rather than merely replacing one hubcap with another, they began to modify their favorites by adding spinners and bullets and/or by color chroming them. An open wheel look became

one of the most popular ways to show off wheels as wheels. Wheels without hubcaps were painted contrasting colors or they were chromed, like the parts of an engine, to emphasize their "wheelness" rather than hidden behind caps. Often the wheels were reversed, turning them inside out which required some modifications. This gave them a deep sunken appearance that worked well with chrome. Sometimes parts of the wheel were sprayed with transparent color, tinted gold or blue or red. Bullet centerpieces, called "spiders," were often added to the wheels as well as spinner bars. At times the wheels approached becoming pure sculptures in their own right (see plate 15).

Even the choice of whitewall tires was important. The "wide whites," favored by early fifties customizers gave way to narrower and narrower whitewalls until, by the end of the decade, whitewalls were hardly more than stripes.

Because the wheels received more attention, the wheel openings themselves became important as frames for the wheels. Sometimes they were reshaped or cut out in a semicircle, known as "radiusing," to outline and highlight the wheels. Gene Winfield added concave panels, painted a contrasting color behind the front and rear wheels on LeRoy Goulart's '50 Ford sedan, for example, to draw the eye to the wheels and wheel openings (see figure 33). Cushenberry had done something similar with his '40 Ford.

The collage techniques of replacing the grille, modifying or replacing the bumper, changing side trim, and so forth that typified earlier customizing, were replaced with much more elaborate front-end treatments as customizers began to reshape their cars totally.

Figure 33.
Goulart Ford. Built by Winfield in 1958. An earlier
version lacked the sculpted concave panels behind
the wheels. Courtesy of Gene Winfield.

Front-end treatments became much more
sculptural, often completely hand-formed, with
swooping curves and peaks surrounding grilles
made from everything from drawer pulls to
utility bars. The visual clutter of bumpers was
often eliminated completely.

Customizers no longer relied completely on
existing parts to use in reconstructing the front
end. Hardware stores were pillaged to find
anything from drawer pulls, chrome rods, and
bullets to expanded metal sheeting that could
be used in constructing a new grille. These
parts were often color chromed as well. Dual
headlights, even, although rarely, triple headlights, vertical, horizontal, or canted, sometimes separated high and low, were used to reconfigure the front ends of even older cars like
early forties Fords. The result was an entirely
new front end where grille, grille shell, and
headlights all flowed together in a completely
integrated design.

Hoods were peaked, scooped, sectioned,
and reshaped. Headlights were tunneled and
hooded and peaked and beaked. Scoops were
added everywhere. Fenders were reshaped in
art nouveau curves or cut away in strong geometric forms that shared modern architecture's
love of the right angle. The front ends were
rolled and panned, that is, smoothed and
molded, so that the sharp edges revealed when
bumpers were removed were softened and tapered (see figure 34).

The treatment of the rear ends mirrored
what was happening in the front, reflecting a
much greater sophistication in design, one that
extended beyond the early idea of finding the
essential lines of the original and enhancing
them with the right parts and the right attention to finish. These new customs were more
about invention than redesign. Much more attention was paid to matching front-end treatments in the rear. Often hand-formed, completely nonfunctional, grilles were added to the
rear to match the front. They were made of the
same found materials: bars, bullets, knobs, and
mesh. More effort was spent on fitting the
rear-end design together so that taillights were
integrated with the rear grille and whatever
bumper system might be used. Rears were also
often rolled and panned.

Gene Winfield, who opened his first shop in
1945 and who is still an active customizer, began the process by seeing the car as a whole: "I
wanted the rear end to work well with the
front. You had to see it as a whole." Not everybody approached it that way, particularly in the
East. "The problem with many East Coast customs of that era," according to Winfield, "was
that they seemed to approach the car in parts.
'This is what I want to do with the taillights.

This is what I want for side trim.' But they didn't think about how it would all come together" (Winfield 1998, interview).

Not every customizer, even in California, had Gene Winfield's clarity of vision. The new freedom that customizers achieved by relying less and less on swapping parts and more on their own skills in fabrication placed much more emphasis on their own imaginations and more weight on their technical prowess to solve the problems that their intricate new designs presented. Not everyone was up to it. Sometimes the modernist credo "less is more" was replaced with "more is more" (see plate 16). The weird pink Frank Maratta Mercury, built in Hartford, Connecticut, was so ugly that it was often cited, unfairly, by California customizers as an example of the overall inferiority of East Coast design (see figure 35).

Even George Barris made missteps. Although not everyone shares this view, his updating of the '48 Studebaker four-door "Grecian" into "the Modern Grecian" resulted in a car that looks merely heavy rather than menacingly massive like the Hirohata Merc. The front end is too busy. The grafting of the Olds

Figure 34.
Gimenez '56 T-Bird. Built by Joe Ortiz in 1961. It is not the most radical T-Bird, but it illustrates many of the typical strategies of the time: canted quad headlights, molded front end, tunneled rear fins, minimalist bumpers, chopped top, and reversed wheels. Courtesy of Petersen Publishing.

Figure 35.
Maratta Merc. Built from a 1948 Mercury by Frank Maratta of Hartford, Connecticut. The one thing it shows is that the "radical complicated" style didn't die out after all. Courtesy of *Motor Trend* magazine.

Figure 36.
The Beatnik Bandit. The most famous of Ed "Big Daddy" Roth's many wild show cars. Courtesy of Greg Sharp Collection.

Figure 37.
Classic interior. The mildly rolled and pleated naugahyde worked in 1957 and still works today.

grille to the front bumper might have worked with a simpler grille treatment, but the way that Barris put it together the front end has lost its focal point and its force. The translucent plastic headlight covers might work on a more futuristic design, but they don't help the older boxy shape of the Studebaker. In addition they cap the front fender lines abruptly and just don't work well with the rearward tilt of the car. The biggest failure is the fins, which look like someone dropped a pair of wings on the rear that would better suit one of Maxfield Parrish's nymphs than this car (see plate 17).

When *Car Craft* picked its top customs of 1961, only one, a Jim Galvin–built '49 Ford from Illinois was done in the early fifties collage style—Corvette grille, Pontiac split bumpers, DeSoto side trim, Edsel taillights, and Dodge Lancer hubcaps, along with all-around lowering, a chopped top, fender skirts, striped rolled and pleated interior, and painted in a monochromatic Orchid Mist lacquer. The only concession to contemporary styling was the use of canted quad headlights adapted from a mail-order conversion kit.

Even though they follow the same general route to creating a custom, each of the others is unique. None of the nine has a true bumper. None uses skirts to cover the rear wheel openings. Each has a molded front and rear end; four have matching rear grilles. Each has a hand-formed grille using either tube steel bars or expanded metal, sometimes with clear plastic knobs or other hardware. Three sport chromed or painted open wheels. Four of the others feature chromed reversed wheels with simple baldy caps. The most famous of this top ten is undoubtedly Ed Roth's "Beatnik Bandit," a completely handmade fiberglass-bodied roadster with a plastic bubble top and a central control stick for turning, braking, and acceleration (see figure 36). As evidence of the increasing quality of customizing across the country, half of the cars selected by *Car Craft* were built outside of California.

Perhaps the area of greatest excess in the mid to late fifties was in interiors. In early fifties customs the original cloth upholstery was often replaced with rolled and pleated naugahyde. Favorite colors were white and black. Pink was sometimes used with purples and violets. You could also find stripes and patterns like hearts sewn in as well. Package trays, door panels, and visors were often upholstered to match the seats. Dashboards were repainted and pinstriped. New gauges were sometimes added as were newer steering wheels. Teardrop knobs like the ones designed by Bob Hirohata for his Merc were a common substitution for the stock ones (see figure 37).

But in the late fifties, custom interiors, often influenced by the big shows that were competing for the most radical cars by offering appearance money, became more and more ornate and outrageous. The design sense that ruled when customizers modified the exterior of their cars, the modernist ideas of simplifying the basic form and emphasizing the essence of the object, seemed to disappear as soon as they opened the car door.

In the most extreme cases, instead of the low nap solid color or piped car carpet with, perhaps, a naugahyde insert that graced customs like the Hirohata Merc, plush carpeting, even shag, some approaching the length of angel hair, began to appear at shows, often in displays that featured everything from palm trees, beach scenes with real sand, and early versions of Astroturf to bikinied mannequins all set off with mirrors and lights.

Fifties barrel-shaped TV chairs were re-upholstered and attached to Chrysler swivel mechanisms to function as bucket seats. Cheap versions of modern plastic chairs like those first designed by Charles Eames were upholstered and placed on raised swivels. Hand-formed chairs with severe "ess" curves, like the new lounge chairs that were popping up in American dens, that made driving almost impossible, became a brief fad. Customizers discovered that supermarket shopping carts could be converted into bucket seats by cutting away the basket and upholstering the frame. The new interiors took on the look of shotgun marriages between Hollywood bedrooms and rocket ship cockpits.

While the basic materials stayed largely the same as in earlier customs—naugahyde and frieze—the use of these fabrics got wilder and wilder. Rather than choosing frieze or naugahyde the customizer often used both. Enormous buttons in contrasting colors were also widely used to add a deeply tufted quality to the upholstery. The colors reflected the current domestic interior palette, the colors that mean the fifties today—electric reds, rich golds, bright pinks, brilliant greens, and vivid fuchsia. Dashboards were upholstered, as well as doors, roof, pedals, and package trays. Matching upholstery panels were sometimes attached to the inside of wheel wells, around lakes pipes, and under the hood.

The upholstered dashboards were often hand formed in free-formed shapes. Steering wheels were chopped in half, often imitating an airplane's controls. Center consoles were constructed that separated the bucket seats. Televisions, telephones, and record players became standard accessories, especially in show cars (see plate 18).

But, overall, the area of innovation in the Golden Age which had the greatest impact on the direction of customizing was in the radical changes taking place in the uses of paint. The dark colors—blacks, maroons, and blues—favored by early customizers were employed to show off the quality of bodywork as well as being attractive in themselves. Nothing reveals flaws—every ripple and every ding—in the surface of a car more than many coats of hand-rubbed black lacquer. But there was nothing particularly expressive about these flawless monochromatic paint jobs.

By 1954 things had begun to change. Kenneth Howard, known to everyone as "Von Dutch" or just plain "Dutch," began to revive the art of pinstriping on customs being finished in the Barris brothers shop after he had gained some recognition striping custom bikes. Pinstriping, thin accent lines, had been used on vehicles for decades. Boats, fire engines, even bicycles, as well as cars, used the stripes to emphasize the basic original contours of the vehicle. Functioning as a kind of underlining or italics, striping was about emphasis rather than defiance or creativity. Pinstripes are used widely today on production cars in much the same way.

What Von Dutch did was reinvent pinstriping as an expressive rather than a merely decorative medium. Using a thin tapered sword brush, he began to draw on cars with an exuberance and a freedom unprecedented in car design. Sometimes he was so exuberant that Barris would have to keep an eye on him to prevent him from striping everything in sight as he had done with the Barris shop truck, a '49 Ford Woody, that was completely striped by Von Dutch in a marathon striping session that lasted all night. When it appeared on the cover of the March 1955 issue of *Rod & Custom,* it gave him his first national exposure which, in turn, created imitators across the country (see plate 19).

Von Dutch was the first genuine surrealist to appear in the world of car customizing. His Salvador Dali–like flamboyance and eccentricities added to his reputation as a striper. He lived and worked out of a converted bus. Like a Rimbaud at the height of his fame he walked away from striping and seemed to disappear, leading to rumors that he had died. His name became a verb as in "I want my car to be 'Dutched.'" From his personal logo, the "Flying Eyeball," to abstract figures and animals and the purely visual rhythms that became strange landscapes painted on the fronts of Fords and Chevys, he understood that his designs, like surrealist "automatic drawing," were not only interesting in themselves, but conveyed social and artistic messages about human freedom and expression: "Modern automobiles need some human element on them. Without it they look like they've been ground out by a mechanical monster—which they have! I treat striping brushes like a musical instrument and whatever I stripe becomes a melody" (in Stecyk 1993, 22).

Like the most expressive graffiti, striping is both transgressive and aesthetic. Where graffiti claims public territory for the artist—walls, subway trains, and billboards—the pinstriper imposes his vision on a product of modern industry that is owned by an individual. Because the most common locations for striping are on the nose and the deck where the chrome emblems had been removed, the striper replaces the standard identical sign of meaning favored by mass industry, the logo, with the unique marks of a particular human hand. But unlike graffiti, which is an act of invasion, striping is an act of possession as well as an act of patronage where seventeen-year-old kids hire artists to draw abstractly on their cars. This was an act few parents understood, like tattooing today, which is an even more transgressive decoration.

Although the ideal in striping was to create lines which were balanced and symmetrical, it was a mistake to make them too perfect. The decals that mail-order houses offered to customizers were perfect, but they had no real value or status. The imperfections of the line, the minute irregularities, and even the slight mistakes made it clear to anyone who knew striping that this was real pinstriping, created by a single hand. These slightly imperfect lines on the perfect surface of the car create interesting contrasts and contradictions, suggesting the intersections of the personal and impersonal and the manufactured and the created that modernist artists like Schwitters, Man Ray, and Picasso had been exploring for years. As the culturally astute Von Dutch said, "My striping was the first modern technique to be really popular" (in Stecyk 1993, 20).

Striping soon became a rage, and Dean Jeffries, Tommy the Greek, and Larry Watson, each with his own individual style, joined Von Dutch as the preeminent stripers in California. Before long there were stripers from coast to coast and pinstriping had become a standard way of finishing and embellishing a car.

Von Dutch also reinvented another standard technique of car decoration, the use of flames. Like striping, flames had been used on vehicles for quite some time. Race cars had often used flames, usually red or red tinged with yellow and orange, on the hood and along the side near exhaust pipes. World War II fighter pilots were also fond of flames. Here the

Figure 38.
Crab-Claw flamed Ford. Also known as "Curly Flames." Jeffries painted these innovative flames on a modestly customized 1949 Ford owned by Bill "Smiley" Polk. One of the first all-over flame jobs. Even the roof was flamed. Photo by George Barris.

flames were fairly literal, although not always executed with skill, signifying that this engine was "hot." When Von Dutch was asked to fix a fading paint job on Earl Bruce's Mercedes 300 SL, his solution was to flame the whole car. No attempt was made to connect the flames to the engine as had been done before. The flames seemed to come from below as if the car were sitting in a pit of fire. The colors themselves reversed the conventions of flame painting—the flames were stark white on a dark maroon body (see plate 20). It caused quite a stir. "People couldn't accept a flamed 300 SL Gull Wing back then. They thought it was desecrating a shrine" (Stecyk 1993, 23). His flame job on the Barris shop wagon was equally controversial and influential.

Influenced by Von Dutch as well as taking his place at Barris's shop, the young Dean Jeffries soon followed with the "Curly Flame

Figure 39.
Flames within Flames (detail). With the Carol Lewis '56 Chevy, Jeffries extended his exploration of flaming by adding flames inside the flames on this crab claw flame job. Photo by George Barris.

Ford," which was also flamed "all over," including flames on the hood, trunk, and roof as well as all along the sides. Jeffries added red tips to the pattern of curved white flames which also became known as "crab claw" flames (see figure 38). Soon Jeffries was doing flame jobs with much more elaborate patterns that played with the figure-ground relationship so that it was difficult to determine, for example, if his '47 Mercury had white flames on a gold body or vice versa. "It started here," he remembers, "on just my louvers—you would think if a car caught fire the flames would come out there. Then you keep going. You keep creating more and more out of simple little flames—flames inside of flames" (Jeffries 1998, interview).

Very quickly flames went from being a very illustrative form of decoration to an exploration of design for its own sake. Although there were still beautifully done flame jobs like Bob McCoy's '40 sedan that used the traditional colors—yellow to orange to red flames in the conventional location (the front of the car)—flames could now be any color, and their connection to any form of fire could be very remote.

But these painters often began by becoming students of fire. Like Cezanne looking at Mont St. Victoire, Jeffries and others studied actual flames. "You know you really can't paint a fire. But you get ideas. I really watched fire for years—how there's flame in a flame in a flame—eyeball one spot of it and you see so much. You just tried to make a design and still not be stupid looking" (Jeffries 1998, interview). On Carol Lewis's '56 Chevy he added fire within fire, changing the scale as well as the patterns of flames (see figure 39). His own '49 Mercury was equally complex with flames within flames combined with striping and surrealistic graphics—detached hands pulling the striping off the front fenders.

Crab claw flames quickly evolved into streamer flames. Then Larry Watson introduced "seaweed flames" on Al Lazarus's '55 Chevy and perfected them in 1958 on Jack James's amazing 1957 Buick. These were long sinuous and delicate streams of multicolored hand-rubbed enamel rubbed out with chrome polish. They raced along the hood, over the hood and across the sides like multicolored pennants in the wind (see plate 21). This shift in the way flames were used marked a move, mirrored by abstract expressionist painters in

New York, from working in a conventional space (flames near the engine) to "all over" painting where the whole canvas (car) received the same attention. It also led the way to more abstract uses of paint as pure color and shape with the creation of scalloping, paneling, and blends.

In 1956, when he was only seventeen, Watson began work on a 1950 Chevy coupe that he used to visit in the shop after class as it was being built. Designed by Watson and built by Jay Johnston and Ed Schelhass, it endures as one of the most perfect semi-customs ever built. It was the ultimate high school ride. The bodywork was modest. It was not chopped or sectioned. There is no attempt to alter the basic lines of the stock Chevy. Initially the car was lowered six inches all around; Buick side trim was added; and inverted frenched '54 Mercury taillights, which he loved on Lyle Lake's Buick, the "Blue Danube," "just had to be used." A '53 Chevy grille opening was added and a '53 Chevy grille bar with thirteen teeth. The original car was painted Rose Mist over white ivory lacquer. After the car was run into by a drunk driver, Watson had Jay Johnston mold the grille shell, and Watson shaved the teeth so that he was able to squeeze an extra four teeth into the grille. "People wondered how I got seventeen teeth into that grille. Thirteen was the maximum, they thought." The effect was striking—an insanely toothy grin.

The new version was painted two shades of metallic grape thus the name "Grapevine." Watson was determined to have the lowest car in California, but one day a low four-door Fleetline pulled alongside the Chevy, and Watson asked his friend to check it out. "'It's lower, Larry,' he said." So Watson took the car into the shop that night and got three more inches in the front and two in the rear to drop it a total of nine inches in front and eight in the rear. He never found a lower car.

The Chevy not only earned Watson a lot of attention on the street and around the Clock Drive-in in Bellflower, it led to his career as a painter. He had painted a dragon and some roses on his dashboard and a friend wondered, if he had that much artistic talent why wasn't he striping? He went down to see Dean Jeffries at Barris's shop and asked about paint and brushes, and Jeffries said, "What the hell are you trying to do, run me out of business?" "And I said, 'No, I just want to stripe my little Chevy.' And I did and people come up to me and said, 'How'd you afford Dutch?' They didn't believe me when I said I did it" (Watson 1998, interview). Eventually they did believe him and he began to stripe cars in his driveway, in parking lots, and at school, at five dollars a job, before he opened the first of his many different shops. He had become fascinated with paint and being a painter. From striping he moved on to flames and scallops—abstract organic and geometric shapes, usually tapered, that highlight various areas of the car such as headlights or that are applied like flames. He eventually finished his '50 Chevy with swooping art nouveau silver scallops outlined in black (see plates 22 and 23). Watson remembers how scallops came about:

In 1956 we were doing striping and this guy come in with a '54 Chevy, Bob Shremp, from Norwalk, had Branson's Bodyshop nose and deck it, and it was painted. But it had runs on the hood and back of the splash pans. I said, "Well, flames aren't going to cover it up so we'll scallop it." And he said, "What are scallops?" "You come back tomorrow and I'll surprise you." He hit the Bellflower Clock and the next

day there were two cars at my shop waiting for scallops. They just skyrocketed. (Watson 1998, interview)

Watson's reputation was beginning to grow to the point where he could experiment without worrying about what his customers demanded. They just wanted a Watson paint job. "They gave me carte blanche. They had to have one of my candy or pearl paint jobs. They'd just pull up and give me the keys. They'd say, 'I don't care what you paint it. I know you got something going on in your head.' And that was it. That way I could create what I wanted" (Watson 1998, interview).

Watson was obsessed with color and his color sense is remarkable, with strong connections to the painters Mark Rothko and Frank Stella, who also made careers as colorists. Forty years after a paint job he can recall the formula for the colors instantly: "I'd lay in bed at night and I'd think about what I wanted to do. A candy lime faded into a yellow pearl. And something for contrast—a candy grape, an orange. I'd keep thinking about stuff like that. That's what kept me going. It was exciting for me to create a new color. I was never bored" (Watson 1998, interview).

Watson took immediately to the new candy apple red, the first of the candy colors, which would change custom painting and customizing dramatically in the late fifties. Although there are a number of competitors for the title of inventor, Joe Bailon is generally acknowledged as the one who made the key breakthrough. He hoped to imitate, not a candy apple, but the brilliance of a taillight reflecting and projecting light. As Bailon himself describes it:

I just wanted something that looked like a taillight. Bright. In my younger days I was following a

'39 Ford, and I said to myself, "Gee, wouldn't it be great if the whole car looked like that taillight?" That was when I was doing my '41 Chevy, so I painted it ruby maroon with metallic over yellow, and I got it really bright.

But I wasn't satisfied. I kept toying with it, playing with different materials, various silver and gold powders, but nothing worked. Finally one day I got the right gold powder. I dropped some Sherwin-Williams Brilliant Maroon dye on it. Boy, that was it! It looked like it lit up, and Holy Moly! Immediately I painted a piece of a fender—I primed it, then I put the gold on, and then the red over it, and that was it! 1956! . . .

I blew it. I'd be a millionaire right now if I'd patented it. (Bailon 1991, 65)

The new candy paints produced a finish with a brilliance that literally stopped traffic on the streets of California. Watson also embraced the new expensive pearls, which contained ground fish scales for a translucent pearl-like finish, with enthusiasm and invention, often combining candies and pearls.

And he created new colors: candy root beer, black pearl, candy raspberry over platinum pearl, green gold murano pearl, and the candy blue, "my best," used on Duane Steck's "Moonglow": "I used a silver metallic base and the brightest pearl and I shot the candy as light as possible."

He also created new ways of painting. Wanting to create "the next new thing," in 1958 he invented paneling. When the original candy burgundy paint faded on his brand-new 1958 Thunderbird (one of the big disadvantages of the original candy paints was their tendency to fade), he taped the car and sprayed wide stripes along the contours of the car with white pearl and candy wild grape.

Then he outlined the grape in white. The result created a sensation (see plate 24).

Watson describes sitting at a light in Bellflower and noticing that the driver of the car couldn't take his eyes off the T-Bird. Watson sat through the green light and so did the driver. He never moved. No one honked. Cops would pull him over just to admire the paint. Some of Watson's panel jobs, like the one he did for Floyd DeBore, used as many as eight or nine colors, all balanced and coordinated so that the result never looked like a circus car or an advertising stunt. He extended paneling: combining panels with flames and panels with fogging. There were still more innovations in the early sixties: metalflake, rainbow painting, lace painting, and web painting (which was like striping with a gun). "I stayed as a painter. I didn't get next to a torch, just my brush and my spray gun. There were a lot of body shops that did good work," he says.

The innovations of Von Dutch, Jeffries and Watson changed the nature of the act of customizing. No longer was the paint job simply a way of showing off good bodywork. In addition to being material to be assembled and sculpted, the car had become a shaped blank canvas where color, shape, line were played with and against the surface of the car itself. Paneling, for example, because of the ways that different colors act on the eye, added contours to flat surfaces. Flames played with dimensionality, adding depth as one flame disappeared behind another. Pinstriping used the surface of the car as a place for making marks. Watson's relatively simple panel job on his '58 Thunderbird stopped traffic and won awards even though the body of the car was basically stock.

But Watson's inventions, and those of Von

Dutch, Jeffries, and Bailon, as they changed the practice of customizing, ironically, also helped speed its demise. Nothing more than paint was needed to cause a sensation. Paint is cheaper than metalwork. The "Curly Flamed Ford" was barely nosed and decked. Modern cars were more difficult and more expensive to chop than early fifties cars with their relatively square roof lines, but they could easily be radically painted. The paradox of the golden age of customs is that, at the same time the most imaginative builders were radically altering stock cars with an unprecedented freedom and unfettered imagination, the average out-on-the-street-cruisin' custom freak opted for something more like a Watson custom: minor bodywork, bolt-on accessories, lowered but with special paint.

At the same time, the most creative builders kept moving beyond redesigning stock cars to creating new cars with an expressionistic exuberance that was as much about producing a kind of shock as about creating beauty. Designs became more outrageous and more removed from ordinary cars.

Kustom Kulture has always had an intrinsic affinity with surrealism. It is the one modern art movement that customizers overtly and directly connect with. With the appearance of Von Dutch and Ed "Big Daddy" Roth, that connection becomes an identification. Von Dutch's flying eyeball logo and the wild caricatures of bulging-eyed monsters that Ed "Big Daddy" Roth air brushed on sweat shirts are an easy to read marriage of cartoon and realism. Both Roth and the painter Robert Williams explore, as did the surrealists, the terrain of the forbidden—the unconscious—where the grotesque, the erotic, the violent, and the bizarre constitute the real. Williams adds a strong allegorical

component to his work, offering cautionary tales that critique central myths of the rodding culture like "live fast, die young." In contrast to the surreal dreamscapes of Dali, Delvaux, and Magritte, which are often filled with an unearthly quiet, a moment of strangely frozen calm, the work of Roth and Williams is a wild, exuberant, loud, and manic celebration of the distorted, deformed, and repulsive. Much of this energy comes from the cars that form the dynamic center of so many of their images. Through surrealism Roth and Williams capture the "dynamism of an automobile" in ways that the futurists never imagined (see plates 25 and 26).

Von Dutch's striping was improvised like surrealist "automatic" drawing, and Roth's early handmade cars, which seem like intruders from another car universe, are deliberately surrealist sculptures that, for the most part, take their inspiration from a fantasy world that also has its origins in science fiction (see plate 27).

Salvador Dali is clearly the master influence here, especially in the fantasy drawings of Roth and in Williams's paintings. But there is another aspect to surrealism beyond the fantastic which Kustom Kulture also connects with, although not quite so consciously. The first surrealists weren't interested only in painting an alternative universe—unreal, grotesque, and even obscene—a shocking, and sometimes comic, dream world where watches melt on trees and a woman's body grows out of the landscape. Equally important to them was altering our perceptions of the ordinary world by subtly challenging our assumptions and expectations about the real. One goal of the original surrealists was to discover the surreality of ordinary life and ordinary objects. By playing with our sensibilities and our habitual ways of looking at the world, the surrealist alters our sense of the boundaries between reality and fantasy, between waking and dreaming. Because of surrealism the world, even reality itself, changes. What can be imagined exists. What emerges is a surrealism of everyday life which conflates the fantastic and the ordinary. As André Breton, one of the founders of surrealism, states: "The admirable thing about the fantastic is that it is no longer fantastic: there is only the real" (Breton 1934, 414).

René Magritte's *Empire of Light*, for example, depicts a very ordinary residence, rendered according to the conventions of realism. It is night. A street lamp is lit. Its light reflects off the surface of a pond in front of the house. What is surprising is that up in the sky it is the middle of the day. Above the house is a bright blue-gray sky dotted with puffy clouds. Once you see this painting, you will find it repeated on ordinary streets at dusk in the "real" world again and again.

Magritte alters our sense of the real by dislocating reality not escaping from it. In other paintings he fills a room with a giant green apple or an equally immense rose. Business men, absolutely identical to each other, rain down on an ordinary street of identical townhouses. A man looks into the mirror and sees the back of his head. Magritte paints a nude woman whose body is covered with what might be wood grain or animal stripes. He would have appreciated flames that look like seaweed or crab claws covering a Ford sedan.

Almost every custom is surreal in a Magritte way. Customs painted in rainbows of colors or paneled in candy or pearl or flamed or sculpted with nonfunctional scoops or shaped into forms that drip over hoods above grilles dotted with chrome drawer pulls are like Magritte's nudes and landscapes in that they play with our perceptions of the real, our sense of familiarity with the most common of objects and with our basic notions of what a something is (this isn't what cars look like; this is clearly a car; this isn't what a Chevy looks like; this is apparently a Chevy). Also like Meret Oppenheim's surrealist object—a fur-covered cup, saucer, and spoon—the custom combines an ordinary object with equally ordinary but unexpected materials producing something, however illogical, that actually exists. This happens when customizers upholster wheel wells and lakes pipes or when they chrome undercarriages. Like Magritte and Oppenheim, customizers begin with one of the most mundane of objects—one of the 185,000 '55 Chevy two-door hardtops GM produced, for example, and transform it into a candy apple with pearl scallops. It becomes something fantastic, something real . . . something surreal.

The one whose cars blur the distinctions between dream and reality most tellingly is not Ed "Big Daddy" Roth, whose work *is* more about the fantastic than the surreal, but Joe Bailon.

Bailon is an expert bodyman as well as a fine painter. He had made his reputation in 1952 with "Miss Elegance," a radical '41 Chevy. Bailon built hundreds of cars in his shop. "The Mystery Car," a scooped, molded, and reshaped candy '51 Ford with frenched sidepipes, and Joe Boliba's strange grilleless '56 Chevy convertible, which uses a DeSoto grille for a bumper, are just two of the unusual, immediately recognizable cars that bear the Bailon signature. Although he followed

Figure 40.
Scoopy (front view). One of Bailon's more outrageous works. The concave oval tube grille is clearly anthropomorphic, offering a voluptuous mouth. Courtesy of Petersen Publishing.

Figure 41.
Scoopy (rear view). The rear matches the front shape, but places exhaust pipes in place of the mouth of the front, making, at least obliquely, a mildly obscene visual pun. Courtesy of Petersen Publishing.

many standard customizing practices in his cars, he was always something of a maverick and an innovator. At the same time that Roland Barthes was writing *Mythologies* (1957), which applied semiotics, the study of signs and their

meanings, to everything from the face of Garbo to the new Citroën, Joe Bailon was playing with all the terms that made up the custom vocabulary.

Perhaps the most original of all his creations is "Scoopy," a custom where it is impossible to find a single part of the car where Bailon shows restraint. Although the basic shape of the original '58 Chevy Impala remains largely intact, each line is stretched, curved, altered slightly, or radically modified so that finally "Scoopy" becomes a kind of "Impala through the Looking Glass," distorted and exaggerated, bent and stretched, and smoothed and broken. It functions like the surrealist mannequins of André Masson and Salvador Dali which also violate classical notions of beauty and harmony to get at the fetishistic meanings of the body by adorning the mannequin's form with shells and chains and hair and bits of lace, even cages—any sexually laden material will do. Bailon also uses a given body (of a car) to extend, expand, and ultimately undermine the purely automotive fetishes of customizers—scoops, pipes, fins, teeth, and frenching. Like so many surrealist artworks which are seldom truly abstract and often refer to the human body, there is a strongly anthropomorphic element to Bailon's joyous riot of a car. Head on one is struck by the wide-eyed headlights and the voluptuous mouth formed by the oval tube grille with a mesh center—Impala as Jayne Mansfield. The new white roof looks like an elegant hat made of surfboards. The body itself is covered with openings, cuts, and curves, which remind us of orifices and wounds. The final effect is much more disturbing than its cute cartoon name would suggest (see figures 40 and 41 and plate 28).

The original Impala was distinguished by faux scoops on the roof and along the rear side panels. Bailon's decision to cover the car with scoops—forty in all—double scoops above the stock headlights, double hood scoops, and a giant scoop to house the rear license plate, transform a potentially functional design element which Detroit had already made merely decorative into an absurd commotion of scoops. And teeth, a favorite of customizers, are also everywhere—on the fenders, on the hood, on the roof. Exhaust pipes, frenched above the front wheel wells, emerge along the bottom of the front door. Where a few tubes had been used to form grilles before, Bailon curves six tubes, front and back, to form a symphony of bumpers and grilles. Finished off in Bailon's signature candy apple with white scallops (reversed on the roof), it is one of the busiest cars ever built.

Bailon created "Scoopy" when Frank Caraway, who wanted to win at Oakland, asked him to rework "Scoopy Doo," the first version of the Chevy. It didn't win. Even today it can evoke strong negative reactions. To some it is as ugly as the pink Maratta Merc. It is not beautiful nor is it particularly menacing. Rather, it is disruptive. It is a surrealist joke, and surrealists loved jokes, especially ones that played the absurd against the forbidden. This joke works because Bailon knows his materials and how to play with them.

At the opposite end of the artistic spectrum from Bailon's exuberant play is the work of Gene Winfield. Winfield is the Brancusi of the custom car world. Brancusi, noted for his profoundly simple sculptures like the *Bird in Space* series (see figure 42), believed that "simplicity is not an objective in art, but one achieves simplicity despite one's self by entering the real sense of things." From the very beginning of his career as a bodyman in 1944 to the '61 Cadillac Winfield exhibited at the 1999 Oakland Grand National Roadster

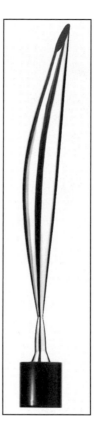

Figure 42.
Bird in Space. Sculpted by Constantin Brancusi c. 1924. © Philadelphia Museum of Art: The Louise and Walter Arensberg Collection.

Show, his work has always demonstrated this "essential" simplicity. Although he created dozens of exceptional cars from Lanny Erickson's '56 Chevy to LeRoy Goulart's '50 Ford, his masterpiece is undoubtedly the "Jade Idol," which was built for Leroy Kemmerer in 1960.

Beginning with a fairly unpopular, as far as customizers were concerned, 1956 Mercury two-door hardtop, a particularly boxy design, from Ford's middle division with a middle-class appeal (see plate 29). Winfield creates a completely new car which shows Detroit how to handle fins. Even though it makes extensive use of standard late fifties practices—molded front and rear ends, hand-formed front and rear grilles, and open wheels—the "Jade Idol" transcends its time period. Often compared to Italian designs and picked by *Rod & Custom* as one of the twenty best rods and customs ever, it continues to look contemporary even in the nineties (see plate 30).

The "Jade Idol" is the apotheosis of an American production car envisioned as pure form. Created during a period of unrestrained expression, it is defined as much by what Winfield doesn't do as what he does. Nowhere is there the chrome, the scoops, or external exhaust pipes, anything that might detract or interrupt the lines of the car. There is no striping. No spotlights. No fender skirts. Winfield leaves the roof line stock, but sections the body four inches, creating a completely different set of proportions in the body. He grafts '57 Chrysler fenders, which sported about the largest fins of the era, but on the "Jade Idol" the fins seem to flow in one continuous line from the tip of the front fender to the extended rear peak, hardly rising. They are organic to the design not an add-on. It is only at an angle that their full force is revealed. The front and the rear balance each other perfectly. The front and rear grilles are restrained and simple as are the headlight and taillight treatments.

What sets it all off is the paint. The car is painted in one of Winfield's signature blend paint jobs, which he continues to do today. Blends involve as many as nine different colors (Winfield doesn't remember how many exactly he used on the "Idol"), flowing into each other in a mist of tints like the blocks of color in a Mark Rothko painting. Here the range is from white through various greens to black.

But as striking as the paint is, the final form of the car, how lithe and light it appears, especially when one considers its humble hulk of a beginning, is its crowning achievement. It is hard to find a single misstep. There is nothing formulaic about Winfield's approach to customizing. For him it is about putting himself right there, totally facing up to the need to invent. "I would look at a car and study it for hours and generate ideas by just looking at it— I could see this with the grille, that with the rear. I can visualize it. See the pictures in my mind. Then I would see the total concept and sometimes there would be variations afterward, but I knew what I was going to do." The

process was not just about serving a client. Winfield wanted to bring his vision to reality. Sometimes, if a customer's wallet didn't match Winfield's conception, he would say, "Let me design the work." "I would tell them to go away and leave me alone. I would tell them 'I will paint it until I like it even if it takes an extra week. Leave me alone.' And they did" (Winfield 1998, interview).

The golden age of customs ended in the mid-sixties when the practice fell victim to a number of forces both within and without the Kustom Kulture.

In the mid-sixties Detroit stepped up its marketing to the youth culture creating a whole generation of cars known as factory hot rods or muscle cars. In 1964 Ford introduced the Mustang, one of the most successful sporty cars ever built. Also in 1964 Pontiac introduced the legendary GTO, the first true muscle car, which packed a 360 hp, 389ci V-8 in a mid-sized Tempest body. Soon there were GTXs and Roadrunners from Plymouth, Torino GTs from Ford, SS Chevelles and Novas from Chevy, Super Bees and Chargers from Dodge, 4-4-2's from Oldsmobile, and even hot Ramblers. In 1963 the Corvette became the Stingray.

These cars were high-performance factory-built street rods that could be driven home from the showroom with 450 horses under the hood. In the sixties Detroit also borrowed much of its styling from the California car culture. Integrated headlight, grille, and bumper designs became common. The pans on the Mustang, Camaro, and Stingray were rolled, or at least they appeared to be. By 1968 there were molded, bumperless looking GTOs and Camaros competing with the sculpted fastbacks from Dodge and AMC. Chrome was no longer the only way Detroit had of adding design to a car's lines. Sculptural hood ornaments were eliminated as many of the factory hot rods like the 1967 Camaro and Buick Riviera were dechromed. The Roadrunner eschewed all decoration except a small graphic of the cartoon character just the way Plymouth imagined street rodders would have done it. Custom-like scoops appeared on the hoods of the Roadrunner and Buick GS's. Even the open wheel look was imitated by Detroit with factory mag wheels. By the mid-sixties even customizing magazines began to wonder if these new models left anything for the customizer to do.

Enthusiasts embraced the new cars. (They still have a strong following.) Customs in the style of the Hirohata Merc began to seem seriously old-fashioned. Hirohata's Merc had wound up on a used car lot. Other customs met worse fates. The new look was a performance look taken from the dragstrip. Imitating the stance of gassers (forties coupes that were set up high in the theory that rapid weight transfer upon acceleration would aid in traction), Mustangs, Roadrunners, and hot Chevelles were jacked up sometimes as absurdly high as fifties customs had been low. All that was required to look cool was to have the right stance and a set of hot wheels with big wide tires on the rear—a street racer look—as hot rodders evolved into street rodders. Those who favored some customizing settled for the wide range of painting options available—true candy, pearls, and the hot new metalflake colors. There wasn't much work for bodymen.

The bodymen themselves had been moving away from the daily drivers that had been the bulk of their work since the late fifties. A number began to work in movies and television. The customs they did create were often unique, just for show, hand-formed experimental cars. Their creation was fueled by the need that model companies had for more and more unusual cars and that car shows had for more outrageous cars as gate attractions. Ordinary street customs were no longer big draws. The results were often more closely connected to science fiction movies than modern art. The futuristic began to replace the futurist. Almost every important builder took his turn with these high concept cars.

Ed Roth had led the way with his "Outlaw" and seemed to introduce a new car for each show. But while the "Outlaw" shared strong connections to traditional rods, looking like an updated version of Grabowski's T-Bucket, his later efforts, like "Beatnik Bandit" and the "Road Agent," became more and more science fiction until they began to resemble flying saucers more than cars. "Rotar," for example, is a tiny single seater spaceship that floated on a cushion of air (refer back to plate 27).

Barris created his share of concept cars, also producing the "air car," "XPAC 400." With its sweeping bat wings it looked more like a manta ray than Jeffries's "Manta Ray," an open-wheeled roadster with a hand-formed body with elegant curves that just hinted at being fenders. Gene Winfield made the "Reactor." Bill Cushenberry created his bubble-topped "Silhouette" that Tom Wolfe praised in 1963. Darryl Starbird of Kansas was a particularly prolific builder of these concept cars such as the "Predicta," based on a '56 T-Bird body, which featured the first bubble top. It had stronger traditional custom elements than his more adventurous creations like the "Scorpion" and the "Ultratruck," which owed nothing to existing production cars (see plate 31).

Although there were no restrictions on what these cars could look like (they were, af-

Figure 43.
The Red Baron. One of the most successful of the many concept cars that came to replace street customs as car show draws in the sixties and seventies; inspired one of the most popular model kits. Owned by Bob Larivee Sr. for more than thirty years. Courtesy of Bob Larivee Sr.

ter all, concept cars rather than customized production cars), they demonstrated a number of common elements. These concept cars tended to be open one- or two-seaters. Flip-up bubble tops were common. Engines tended to be exposed. Fenders tended to be vestigial if they were used at all. The most popular shape seemed to be some variation of the wedge, which had replaced the teardrop as the latest in aerodynamics. Various asymmetries were incorporated into many of the designs.

These hand-formed cars began to compete for the prestigious America's Most Beautiful Roadster Award (AMBR) in the sixties, frequently beating out more traditional rods. Tex Smith's sleek "XR-16" won in 1963. The twin Pontiac-powered "Invader," built by Bob Reisner, won in both 1967 and 1968.

While these cars are certainly imaginative and quite beautiful in their own right, and while, in some cases, they are truly engineering marvels (Dave Puhl's "Illusion" stands out in this regard, a completely asymmetrical design from drivetrain to body that really worked), they have more to do with a Hollywood vision of the future than with the ordinary car world. Because they had so little to do with the average car bought at the local showroom, these customs lost the tension between the familiar and the strange, the ordinary and the unique, the dream and the reality that make customs created from Mercs and Chevys and Pontiacs so powerful. By becoming completely one of a kind they just became odd, fantastic instead of surreal. Ganahl is right about this: the shift in attention from street customs to hand-built show cars radically altered the practice of customizing and not always for the better (Ganahl 2000, 73).

Surrealism, at least one Kustom Kulture version of it, did prosper in the early sixties—cars made in the shape of pool tables, outhouses, German helmets, coffins, guitars, skulls, and just about anything that anyone could conceive of. In the end they are more joke than dream (see figure 43).

The whole cultural landscape, not just cars, changed in the sixties as well. The slogans of the fifties teenagers who had become rockers in the sixties changed from "Rock and Roll Is Here to Stay" and "Fun, Fun, Fun" to "The Times They Are a-Changin'" and "Strawberry Fields Forever." The Beach Boys stopped singing about cars and began singing about vegetables. In the face of the upheavals of the decade, all automobiles, custom or stock, no longer seemed so important or so cool. The American car began to symbolize something bloated and arrogant, even criminal, to much of the counterculture and to the growing environmental movement. An increasingly popular view was that Detroit produced gas-guzzling dinosaurs that deserved to become as extinct as the T-Rex. Much of the animus against De-

troit seemed to be a displaced attack on the might of the American Military-Industrial Complex during the Vietnam war.

The VW Bug, with peace sign or without, became the definitive sixties car symbol. The VW bus became both a symbol of the counterculture and its basic transportation. They both said that style didn't matter, horsepower didn't matter, size didn't matter; what mattered were gas mileage, reliability, and longevity, but what really mattered was that they weren't made in Detroit.

To gauge the difference between the sensibilities of the late fifties and the late sixties it is interesting to compare George Lucas's *American Graffiti* (1973) with its sequel *More American Graffiti* released in 1979. In the first, set in 1962, the cars are practically main characters. Each character is defined to a large extent by his car—the intellectual drives a Citroën, the head of the Pharaohs a chopped '51 Merc, the nerd a motorscooter. The whole movie centers on a single night of cruising, at the end of the summer of 1962—the year before the Kennedy assassination, before the arrival of the Beatles, before *The Feminine Mystique*, before the world would change forever. The movie is about rites of passage and the end of an era. There is no mention of politics or social issues more serious than the impact of the Beach Boys on rock 'n' roll. This is a self-contained culture with its own heroes and villains. Adults are invisible, ridiculous, or irrelevant. Geography is defined by high schools and junior colleges.

In the sequel the Vietnam war and civil rights protests dwarf not only the cars but the characters. Disjointed and disconnected both in time and space—the film intercuts episodes that occur on four New Year's Eves 1964 to 1967—the film attempts to mirror the confusions of a generation's facing up to a much larger and more serious world. The original focuses on a ritual event in mythical time. The sequel falls out of myth into a more disturbing reality. The original was one of the most successful films of all time; the sequel was a box office failure.

Surprisingly, the original *American Graffiti*, despite its strong feeling of things coming to an end, was a significant factor in the seventies revival of interest in the fifties in general, and rodding and customizing, in particular. Although the seventies are themselves currently basking in the warm spotlight of nostalgia, they began with Vietnam, the war that wouldn't end, just as it was heating up again with the bombing of Cambodia. The decade began with the collapse of radical politics in the aftermath of campus bombings, political kidnappings, and bank robberies. The seventies were the decade of the Pentagon Papers, Watergate, and disco.

The seventies also brought gas shortages, high inflation, environmental as well as safety concerns surrounding American-built cars, and the triumphant invasion of the U.S. market by the Japanese car makers. Not only did it look like rodding and customizing were on the road to extinction, but the American auto industry as well.

In this depressing atmosphere it is hardly surprising there was a growing need to escape to a more confident and more placid time. America seemed to settle on the fifties as that time. Teen life had largely disappeared from the sixties cultural landscape. *Teenybopper* originated as a term of derision invented by twenty-two-year-olds. Youth culture had aged in the sixties. Rock music was largely played by musicians in their twenties and thirties. The

Woodstock Generation, fifties teenagers grown up, came to dominate the landscape. They had moved into a much wider world with much deeper concerns than teen life. Taking on the war, racism, and capitalism, protecting the environment; transforming campus and electoral politics; and creating their own counterculture, they didn't have time to worry about something as mundane as new wheels for a Chevy convertible. But by the mid-seventies a reaction against the sixties began to take shape. The counterculture began to look pretentious, hypocritical, and caught up in its own contradictions. It was difficult to proclaim "Make Love Not War!" after Charles Manson, after Altamont, after the SDS "Days of Rage," after the Jonestown Massacre, and after hippie capitalism.

George Lucas offered an antidote with *American Graffiti*, just as the war in Vietnam was finally coming to an end. The film saw the beginning of the sixties with a mood of loss and regret rather than anticipation. The film was as elegiac as it was celebratory.

American Graffiti began a flood of fifties themed movies: teen gang movies like *The Lords of Flatbush* (1974) and *The Wanderers* (1979); evocations of the days of early rock 'n' roll like *American Hot Wax* (1978) and *Let the Good Times Roll* (1973); movies that dealt with the lives or meaning of fifties icons like *James Dean* (1976), *September 30, 1955* (1978), and *The Buddy Holly Story* (1978). High school reappeared as the setting for a number of other films, with echoes of the fifties—*Cooley High* (1975), *Rock 'n' Roll High School* (1979), and *Malibu High* (1979). *Grease* made its appearance on Broadway. Fifties revival groups like Sha-Na-Na and Flash Cadillac were moderately successful. There was a small *a cappella* revival as well. Seventies groups like the Ramones revisioned fifties rock 'n' roll in leather-jacketed punk to counter the example of "serious" art rock groups like Yes, ELO, and the Moody Blues in chiffon, who seemed to think the more rock sounded like Bernard Herrmann the better. In so doing they helped give birth to new wave and punk.

The focus on contemporary teens and teen life increased by quantum leaps in the eighties to the point where Jonathan Bernstein calls it "The Golden Age of Teenage Films" in his book *Pretty in Pink* (1997). The decade also saw a number of fifties revival films, many by important directors, including Francis Ford Coppola, Rob Reiner, John Sayles, John Waters, and Barry Levinson, films like *The Outsiders; Diner; Stand by Me; Rumble Fish; Baby, It's You; Hairspray;* and *Dirty Dancing.* (Although these films often take place in the early sixties, they are essentially fifties movies like *American Graffiti*.) In the eighties, there was a return to the serious contemporary teen film in movies such as *River's Edge* and *The Wild Side*, which attempted to replicate the themes of *Rebel without a Cause* in an eighties context. In addition there were the fifties fantasy films, *Peggy Sue Got Married, Back to the Future, Heavenly Kid, Mystery Train,* and *Heartbreak Hotel*, in which the fifties or fifties icons take on a mythic importance. Finally the eighties marked the appearance of the films of John Hughes and his imitators, films that more lightly treated fifties themes of warring taste cultures in films like *Sixteen Candles, Pretty in Pink, The Breakfast Club,*

and *Valley Girl,* but in contemporary settings. *The Outsiders* without the violence or the moodiness.

In the nineties interest in the fifties continued unabated as the decade's icons seem to have become a permanent part of the imagery of our culture. Elvis continued to appear as a cross between a guardian angel and an all-knowing divine being (*True Romance, Wild at Heart,* and *Finding Graceland*). Even after forty years Brando's Johnny in *The Wild One* and James Dean's Jamie in *Rebel without a Cause* still have power and influence successive generations who do not see them as figures of nostalgia.

James Dean, for example, continues to represent the model for many young actors and continues to sell sneakers, khakis, and cars forty-five years after his death. He also continues to inspire songwriters and filmmakers. According to one source, there have been at least sixty-six recordings of songs about Dean or which mention him, from artists as diverse as Eydie Gormé and Bruce Springsteen to the Goo Goo Dolls and Madonna. Fifties weekends from Reno to the Meadowlands attract hundreds of thousands of participants and continue to grow. The reasons for the permanence of the fifties, its icons and imagery, its culture and history, and for the continuing passionate interest in fifties rods and customs are deeply intertwined.

In the midst of this cultural intoxication with youth, rods and customs have risen from the grave. But the contemporary Kustom Kulture is no longer simply about cars or being a teen. It has become part of a culture of nostalgia.

BACK TO THE FUTURE

A four-page advertisement for the Mossimo clothing company appeared in the men's fashion supplement of the *New York Times Magazine* in the spring of 1999. Except for the Mossimo logo there is no text, just a sequence of four related full-page photographs. The first image is a close-up of a 1951 Mercury club coupe steering wheel with a prominent V-8 in the center. In the background are the gauges, including an after-market tachometer mounted on the steering column. Although the photograph is in color, its feel is very black and white (see plate 32).

The second image captures a young man, looking a little like a cross between Matt Dillon and Ben Affleck, dressed completely in black, presumably Mossimo. His eyes are closed. His arms are stretched out to the side as if he were a bird testing the air. There is a self-satisfied smile on his face. Directly in back of him is a three quarters' view of the black Mercury, from the front door back. The car is mildly customized. Lowered with full skirts, it is the same color as the James Dean Mercury in *Rebel without a Cause* and similarly modified, although a bit newer. In the car a buddy sporting a nineties version of a fifties flattop haircut, looking a little like a blonder Matt Damon, is also in black. As he leans out the window with arms crossed, he skeptically observes the actions of his friend. The car has stopped in the middle of a dry lake bed, just like the ones where the original hot rods raced.

The third image is of the interior of the Merc through which the almost colorless empty landscape surrounding the lake bed is revealed. The interior is a perfect example of an early fifties custom interior. The metal trim is painted a deep maroon. The upholstery is white naugahyde set off by modest pleats in the side panels and a thin chrome strip. In the picture the steering wheel is not visible, just the tops of the front seats.

The last image is a three quarters' frontal view of a very contemporary young woman with the dry lake beds in the background. She has straight auburn hair. She is wearing a slight dress, presumably Mossimo, with a lacy bra top that also features a very pale blue ribbon in the middle. Below the bra the dress is striped in narrow bands of muted colors and thin, contrasting black stripes that match both the car and the landscape. Her head is tilted to her right. There is a slightly challenging look on her face. She is not smiling. Although she is dressed provocatively, this is no voluptuous sex goddess. She wears no lipstick or eyeliner. Freckles are clearly visible above her nose. She could be sixteen.

The fact that Mossimo uses these images to entice a generation whose parents were barely born when Mercs like this one were first being customized shows how deeply ingrained fifties culture and its imagery are even after half a century. These are subtle and sophisticated images that are knowing in ways beyond the clichés of typical fifties images in advertising: the big-finned Cadillacs, the poodle shirts, garish colors, drive-in restaurants, the sleeveless sweaters, and the plain front leather jackets such as the one worn by "The Fonz" (which are not only clichés but often inaccurate or misleading).

And it is more than just the images themselves which evoke the fifties; the logic of the sequence of the ad as it pairs and contrasts images of interior/exterior, male/female, color/black and white, and fifties/nineties thrusts a fifties social structure based on sexual/power differences into the nineties. The pairing of the image of the steering wheel, speedometer, and tachometer with their strong associations with speed, power, and control, as well as the use of a custom with its implications of masculine style and cool, with the two males suggests the construction of an image of potent male sexuality that combines the two decades as it builds on implied connections between James Dean and more contemporary male icons.

The young woman's pairing with the interior is equally telling. She is not connected to images of control and power but to the feminized interior space of the pristine passenger compartment: seats, upholstery, color, and curved windows. It is the rear window that is her focal point as well as the equally significant back seat with all its sexual associations. Her lacy white bra top connects her to the white material of the interior as the black clothes of the males link them to the hard exterior. This is not a unisex view of the world, but one in which there are clear differences between males and females, where sexual roles are as different as color and black and white. At the same time these images take us back to a world of sexual difference constructed along stereotypical lines, Mossimo inverts these differences by having the male pose, eyes closed and arms outstretched, like a dreamy romantic, while the female confronts the camera head on with a look that mimics "tough" guy poses.

Mossimo makes no attempt to explain this conjunction of decades, to answer the questions: why are there contemporary people in some sort of fifties world? why don't these images look like history? The images speak for themselves. In a kind of fantasy, a dream, that exploits a new form of nostalgia that doesn't depend on living through a period, just on being able to read it, the images disengage our conventional experience of time.

This confusion of fifties images and icons with contemporary culture has been going on for almost three decades. It is a form of cultural time travel where one decade informs, subverts, refreshes, and redefines another. Time now exists in fragments—bits of style, collections of objects, sampled chunks of sound—which we assemble and reassemble to fulfill our needs rather than to gain perspective on "what happened." As William V. Dunning writes in *The Roots of Postmodernism:* "Time has become so fragmented in the postmodern age that we see it in pieces. We cannot think of it as cohesively linear as we did for four hundred years. . . . Time has become so fractured, like a hapless Humpty-Dumpty, that we cannot put it back together again" (Dunning 1995, 265).

In the 1985 film *Back to the Future,* Marty McFly (Michael J. Fox) goes back to 1955 (the time travel machine is, appropriately, a car, a DeLorean) to rescue his own past in order to ensure his own future, his very existence, in fact. To do so he has to fend off the advances of his own mother, who finds him irresistible, while he makes his nerdy father cool enough to attract her sexually so that he will, in fact, be born. Along the way he also "invents" Chuck Berry's sound. Thus, he fulfills a kind of double Oedipal fantasy, surpassing both his biological and his cultural fathers.

The film tells us that we are certainly more sophisticated and cooler than they were in the fifties, but our origins are there, in any case, which we can't ignore if we are going to survive. In much the same way Elvis Costello, who owes much more to *his* nerdy cultural father, Buddy Holly, than he does to the King, whose name he took, invented his pop identity by going back to the fifties, transforming geekiness into cool.

A year later, in 1986, Peggy Sue (Kathleen Turner) reconsiders her life choices in *Peggy Sue Got Married* after she collapses at a high school reunion and "wakes up" back in the fifties. She returns, cultural knowledge and experience intact, to her television sitcom-like family in a typical fifties neighborhood where a father proudly shows off his brand-new purchase, an Edsel, which Peggy (and the audience) recognizes as a hilariously comic error as her father cannot. She also finds herself back in high school. Peggy Sue is not returned to her youth—she is clearly a woman of some age—but she fits right in. Everyone thinks she's acting a little peculiar, but no one suspects that she is old enough to be the mother of a Helen Hunt. She lives out the suspicion we all have that we have never outgrown high school or its issues, the stuff of nightmarish anxiety in dreams where we are called upon to identify the capital of South Dakota or show up to class unprepared for the big test. In this fantasy, which has become our collective fantasy, Peggy Sue is aware enough to overcome the nightmare as she deals with her husband's rock 'n' roll dreams and reevaluates her initial decision to marry him. She also discovers her soulmate in the person of a pretentious Beatnik type who, after a night of incredibly self-absorbed rant and passionate sex, inspires her to return with renewed purpose and appreciation to her ordinary life. Senior year becomes the effective turning point in her life—twice. Nothing after that really matters.

Time travel works in both directions. You can be a fifties hood in the eighties and nobody notices very much either. A Marlon Brando type (Michael Paré) drives a fifties custom into the urban near future of *Streets of Fire* (1984) and rescues the lead singer of the Blasters, a female rock group, from evil bikers without anyone asking if he is a time traveler. In *Cobra* (1986) Sylvester Stallone plays a contemporary cop who drives a chopped '50 Merc and talks like a refugee from a fifties hot rod movie. The car tells everyone that he is a maverick, a rebel, an individual with no connection to organization men like the Joe Fridays of the world, even if he does wear a badge. It denotes his character as much as James Bond's Aston Martins and Columbo's Peugeot do theirs. David Lynch mixes cars, music, and clothing from the forties, fifties, and eighties to create the timeless small town of Lumberville in *Blue Velvet* (1986).

Outside the movies you can choose the decade you want to define yourself with or against by mixing and matching fashions from different decades—chinos, black leather jackets, buzz cuts, and miniskirts are all in fashion. You can listen to hard rock, heavy metal, disco, punk—each provides a different self-definition. Musicians combine beats from Abba with hip-hop poetry and even revisit the Monkees. Everything is contemporary in a culture where "The Dick Van Dyke Show," "The Mary Tyler Moore Show," "Northern Exposure," and "M.A.S.H." continue to share the same airwaves. Tricky, the British techno pop artist, captures the paradox of postmodern originality in this "back to the future" culture in his song "You're Brand New (You're Retro)." Or as an-

other time traveler, Anne Rice's vampire hero Lestat, recognizes, when he is awakened by the buzz of media—the invisible radio and television signals that fill the atmosphere—"the old was not routinely replaced by the new anymore":

In art and entertainment worlds all prior centuries were being "recycled." . . . In grand fluorescent-lighted emporiums, you could buy tapes of medieval madrigals and play them on your car stereo as you drove ninety miles an hour down the freeway. In the bookstores Renaissance poetry sold side by side with the novels of Dickens or Ernest Hemingway. . . . Countless television programs poured their ceaseless flow of images into every air-cooled hotel room. But it was no series of hallucinations. This century had inherited the earth in every sense. (Rice 1985: 8–9)

The bleedings back and forth of the 1950s into the contemporary world that we find in the Mossimo ad, *Back to the Future, Peggy Sue Got Married,* and throughout the culture, is a general phenomenon that is also mirrored in contemporary Kustom Kulture. It marks the transition from a modernist culture, where the new is valued above all, to a postmodernist one, where "everything old is new again."

Postmodernism is a highly contested term defined in a number of contradictory ways. It is identified as a time period, an approach to style, and a condition. It has been defined in terms of "allegory" (Owens), the "voice of the apocalypse" (Hassan), the obscene "ecstasy of communication" and "simulation" (Baudrillard), and the end of "progress" (Lyotard), to name just a few of the contenders for its distinguishing characteristics. Kustom Kulture's version of postmodernism has much in common with Norman K. Denzin's definition, derived from his imaginary "dialogue with Jean

Baudrillard and C. Wright Mills." The postmodernism that emerges from this dialogue involves "a nostalgic, conservative longing for the past, coupled with an erasure of the boundaries between the past and present; an intense preoccupation with the real and its representations" (Denzin 1991, vii).

Although contemporary rodders and customizers are more celebrants than brooding renegades, their identification with a past (consider the implications of being lost in the fifties) that represents nonconformity in the form of outlaws, outsiders, and rebels and their resistance to the culture of the present, to a certain extent at least, links them with Denzin's description of the postmodern condition: "intense emotional experiences shaped by anxiety, alienation, ressentiment, and detachment from others" (Denzin 1991, vii). Besides being marked by pervasive nostalgia contemporary Kustom Kulture is also inscribed with a number of other key postmodern markers: appropriation, hyperreality, pastiche, intertextuality, and pluralism.

In order to understand the continuing appeal of hot rods and customs at the turn of the new century, it is important to see them not just as beautiful objects or just as works of art, but as symbols that have helped transform old-fashioned nostalgia into a particular postmodern myth of a Golden Age. Because the Kustom Kulture is lost in the 1950s, the Mercs, Chevys, and Fords from that era now represent a kind of prelapsarian state of original youth not just raw material or a medium for creating art. For anyone invested in this decade the cars now stand for a set of values—enthusiasm, purity, nonconformity, and invention—that serve as a corrective to the shortcomings of the present which seems to be marked more by boredom, sameness, and

indifference ("whatever"). The revival of interest in the decade of the fifties as a storehouse of images and styles, a revival that has continued for almost thirty years, is a significant cultural phenomenon affecting all corners of the culture, not just car buffs.

Nostalgia, however, is not a new phenomenon in teen culture. It entered before its first decade was even over. As early as 1958 *Oldies but Goodies,* a series of collections of "old" records, started to appear. Radio stations regularly offered "Blasts from the Past" even if the past had occurred only six months before. As the fifties slid into the sixties, a new genre of explicitly nostalgic songs exploited this longing for the recent past: "I Remember" (1958), "Do You Remember?" (1959), "Those Oldies but Goodies" (1961), "Remember Then" (1962), "Play Those Oldies, Mr. Dee Jay" (1963), and "Memories of El Monte" (1963) all reminded eighteen- and nineteen-year-olds of their lost youth. These songs reflect an old-fashioned nostalgia, the sort that depends on having had experiences in the past, but in a new accelerated time frame. No longer did one have to wait decades before one felt nostalgic for the past. It was now a matter of months.

But songs don't have to be about the past to trigger powerful memories. The intimate connection that rock 'n' roll songs had with all aspects of teen life, as they were played over and over on the radio, at dances, on record players, meant that there were numerous accidental connections between songs and experience that could be recaptured by just the opening notes of a particular song. A kind of cultural imprinting began to occur. To hear "Speedo" or "Since I Don't Have You" or any song, even if it wasn't a favorite, years after it was first heard is to be immediately thrust back to a particular place and time, a particular moment that affects memory in a synesthetic way: you taste sea air, smell the boardwalk, and relive the memories as the song plays on. (One of the criticisms of early MTV was that it was replacing these powerful personal experiences with mediated ones on video.) This powerful connection between song and memory makes even the most banal songs seem deeply moving and significant. This effect is not a unique property of rock 'n' roll—all songs can affect us this way—but by the mid-fifties rock 'n' roll had become the sound track of a generation's life to the point where it seemed everything was accompanied by music.

Once being a teenager took center stage in America's cultural life, the concentration on the numerous passages of youth inevitably made time seem exceptionally fleeting. This was the generation that coined the phrase "Don't Trust Anyone over Thirty" in the sixties. There isn't much of an opportunity for long-term development when youth becomes equated with life, at least a life worth living. One summer vacation, as so many movies tried to convince us, could constitute an epoch in one's life. Living in a culture where adulthood seemed to be one long, unchanging drone from marriage to old age, teens saw their own lives marked by significant events that could be celebrated in song and movies and in memory. From ninth grade to sophomore year, from junior to senior year, life underwent fundamental and profound changes. There were numerous rites of passage along the way, each fraught with meaning and anxiety: reaching puberty, turning sixteen, getting a driver's license or a first summer job, graduating, and entering the service or going to college. The changes in her body alone could make it seem that there was no connection between the girl who turned thirteen in April and

the one who attended her first dance in October. At each stage there were easily memorialized moments: first kiss, first real party, first date, first breakup, and first reconciliation. Each was an occasion for the memory of time lost that is the basis of much fifties sentimentality.

The development of a culture of nostalgia is also related to factors beyond the teen culture itself. Once the United States was economically threatened by Middle Eastern oil sheiks, German car manufacturers, and Japanese electronics firms, it was almost inevitable that the country would begin to look back to a better time when America seemed economically invincible. In the 1970s, when the interest in the 1950s first spiked, the Eisenhower decade, despite its own troubles, seemed to many to be the last clearly American decade. No matter how prosperous we have become we are constantly reminded that we live in a global economy, and the origins of the many products that fill our stores confirm it. In part the love of the fifties is fueled by a distaste for the current reality. As Lead East, one of the larger car events in the country, promotes itself in its 1999 program:

Lead East is NOT a car show, it's a party . . . a 50's PARTY! . . . to celebrate the best decade in American history. . . . One weekend a year we gather to escape the terrible music, lookalike automobiles, Johnny can't read (or dance) tabloid-slime TV media and no-religion-in-school 90's.

As Jean Baudrillard puts it, "When the real is no longer what it used to be, nostalgia assumes its full meaning" (in Denzin 1991, 31).

In this late capitalist/postindustrial/digital/information/global economy, the industrial machinery which so inspired the Futurists as the sign of a world constantly progressing, is itself passé, reduced to being just another source of nostalgia. Old factories and the remnants of industrial production have become like the ruined rural cottages and abandoned churches that inspired nineteenth-century Romantic poets, sad relics of a rapidly disappearing world. Factories have become living spaces. Metal pipes, gears, and stainless steel have become interior decoration. Gas station pumps have become collectibles. Modernist furniture and architecture, products of the most advanced design, that once seemed abstract, cold, and impersonal, today seem warm, witty, and quaint now that they have been historicized.

Nothing represents the once-dominant industrial might of America more than the American cars of the 1950s. Big, gaudy, gas guzzling, they ruled the land like the dinosaurs they were soon to become. One of the biggest of them all, the 1959 Cadillac El Dorado convertible, was a stretched-out 225 inches of chrome, giant fins, and bullet taillights, perhaps the gaudiest monument to American industrial arrogance or supremacy, depending on your point of view, since the Empire State Building. In the sixties this Cadillac represented everything that was wrong with America. Today, in movies, commercials, and music videos, where the '59 Caddy seems ubiquitous, it has come to represent sex appeal and individuality, fun and freedom, as well as a strong connection to a past that now seems much more appealing than the present.

Fifties cars continue to mean youth and youthful liberation, freedom and individuality to the fifties generation that has reached its fifties. These cars allow men to remain in touch with the dreams of their youth, and by merely possessing them, to remain young. Rods and customs mean even more. Owning one makes them feel that they are still in touch with the rebel, the maverick, the noncon-

formist that they were or wanted to be in 1958, no matter what their present circumstances are.

When contemporary customizers and street rodders declare that they are "Lost in the Fifties," it is not the fifties of Eisenhower and McCarthy, the Cold War, Red scares, sexual repression, and nuclear brinkmanship they remember. It's not the middle-class lifestyles depicted in *The Lonely Crowd* (1950), *The Man in the Gray Flannel Suit* (1955), and *The Organization Man* (1956) that fuels their nostalgia, but the teen fifties of drive-ins, dances, cruising, DAs, leather jackets, drag racing, and rock 'n' roll—the car culture. One of the striking things about this decade is how age-dependent conceptions of it are. Unlike the twenties which have become simply the Roaring Twenties, the thirties which are inseparable from the Great Depression, and the forties which can't be conceived of without the war at the center, or even the sixties which have been condensed, whether one celebrates or condemns the era, into a montage of protest, happenings, and combat helicopters, with a soundtrack from Buffalo Springfield, the fifties offer a range of completely differentiated experiences that hardly ever intersect.

For historians Douglas T. Miller and Marion Nowak (1975), "It was more an era of fear than fun." What stands out for them is the pervasiveness of stifling restraints and frightening threats. From their vantage point, the fifties can be defined as the decade of Nuclear Anxiety or of Sexual Anxiety or of Social Anxiety or can be seen simply as "The Age of Anxiety" as W. H. Auden did.

It is remembered by others as an idyllic era, the innocent decade of "Father Knows Best" and the values of Ozzie and Harriet, a decade typified by the ideal of the family living in the suburbs consisting of a father who knew best, a mother who did all the housework in a dress and high heels, and the children who were all, like those in Lake Wobegon, "above average." This is a world free of anxiety and stress. It is a television world, the world of the recent film *Pleasantville,* another interesting back to the future exercise, where everything is perfect and sex doesn't exist. Here are no gangs, no rods, nothing cool. Politeness and boredom rule. It is literally a colorless Eden that needs visitors from the real world of the present to bring it color, literally, through passion, art, rebellion and, of course, sex as they engineer its fall from grace.

This conception of the fifties as boring and repressed isn't just a distorted televised memory. These are much the same 1950s described as the "placid" decade in a book published in 1961. At about the same time the poet Robert Lowell called them the "tranquilized '50's." For David Halberstam, "The '50's appear to be an orderly era, one with a minimum of social dissent."

Thomas Hine says that he wrote *Populuxe,* his study of the flamboyant, "soaring, jet-propelled elaboration of private life," partly to answer critics who said the 1950s "were an ugly time, . . . a period of dull conformity" (Hine 1999, foreword).

But, from almost the very beginning, the idea that the fifties were indeed a conformist decade was being promoted by the print media. As early as November 5, 1951, *Time* magazine painted the portrait of a "younger generation" which, more than anything else, wanted "a good job with a big firm, and with it, a kind of suburban idyll." By 1955 the image, if anything, had gotten worse. According to "All the Sad Young Men," in *Commonweal,* "They might be the dullest generation in a long time."

In 1957 the *Nation* analyzed the current generation and came to the conclusion that they should be called "The Careful Young Men."

Even those who were teens in the fifties have very different views, depending on when they became teens. Those who were "old" teens (seventeen or eighteen) in the mid-fifties, for example, often didn't *get* rock 'n' roll. They were often as confused as adults as to what was happening to their younger brothers and sisters. As Richard R. Lingeman, who was in college in the early fifties, wrote in 1973 to protest the revival of interest in the decade: "Leather jackets and souped up cars and Bill Haley and d. a. haircuts were as distant from me as the mating customs of Trobriand Islanders. . . . I thought Elvis was a thug. . . . Songs like 'Teenager in Love' made me reach for the Dramamine" (Lingeman 1973, 26). In the end Lingeman found nothing in the fifties to be nostalgic about.

Others looked back at the same period with a tinge of envy. Regretting his and Lingeman's generation's lack of distinctive qualities, Lingeman's contemporary, Frank Conroy, summed up his experiences in the midst of the generational struggles of 1968, "We had no leaders, no programs, no sense of our own power, and no culture exclusively our own." In contrast to Lingeman, he envies his younger brothers, the ones who created the first teen culture:

> We became teenagers when to be a teenager was nothing, the lowest of the low. Our heroes were not of our own age group. For the most part they were athletes—Jackie Robinson, Joe DiMaggio, Sugar Ray Robinson. Our music was Dixieland jazz (a revival was going on at the time), pop music, and, for some of us bebop. . . .
>
> In college we were named The Silent Generation.

The Apathetic Generation. There was no doubt about it. The sleepy Eisenhower years. America in a trance, drifting leisurely through a long golf game while the clouds gathered. Among the students it was hard to find a rebel, virtually impossible to find a Marxist, a mystic, a reformer, or indeed, anyone who felt very strongly about anything. (Conroy 1983, 116–18)

Even David Halberstam, who sees the fifties as a clearly important era that set the stage for major changes to come in business, politics, and race relations, has underestimated the importance of teenage culture. He devotes only one chapter of his 700-plus page book to the growth of teen culture, and it concentrates on the careers of Elvis, James Dean, and Marlon Brando. Only about a page concerns the teens who were listening to Elvis and watching Dean and Brando, and they are defined largely by their purchasing power. It is not surprising then that he concentrates on media and ignores the actual experiences of youth as a major source of nostalgia: "One reason that Americans as a people became nostalgic about the fifties more than twenty-five years later was not so much that life was better in the fifties (though in many ways it was) but because at the time it had been portrayed so idyllically on television" (Halberstam 1993, 514).

Morris Dickstein, in *Gates of Eden: Culture of the Sixties* (1977), dismisses teen culture as "banal, if energetic," while he concentrates on the political, artistic, and social developments that serve for him as a prologue to the sixties. What he fails to note from his high culture vantage point is that the sixties, a decade "less than an epoch more than an episode," that is "likely to remain a permanent point of refer-

ence for the way we think and behave" (272), was created to a large extent by the fifties teenagers he dismisses so quickly: in 1958 Bob Dylan was seventeen, John Lennon and Frank Zappa were eighteen, Jerry Garcia was sixteen, Janis Joplin was fifteen, Stokely Carmichael and Jesse Jackson were seventeen, and Angela Davis was fourteen. The supposed rupture between decades that took place in the 1960s is accurate only if the social and cultural revolutions of the sixties are measured against the gray flannel 1950s of Lingeman, Halberstam, and Conroy. In important ways the sixties simply represented a maturation of the original teen rebellion. The key difference is that the rebels had found their cause.

But the portraits of teenagers, brief as they are, presented in books like Halberstam's and Dickstein's are much rosier than the views expressed in grim examinations of fifties teen culture, written in the 1950s, such as Harrison Salisbury's *The Shook-Up Generation* (1958), which depicted the violent, dead-end world of teen-age gangs with names like the Bishops and the Viceroys and Paul Goodman's *Growing Up Absurd* (1960), which described a generation drifting in a sea of existential indifference or erupting in meaningless violence. Here are the gang jackets, the DAs and switchblades that became emblems of the decade, but they are found in a much more depressing and frightening place than Arnold's Drive-in on "Happy Days." Salisbury and Goodman are not engaged in celebration but hand wringing and pity. Theirs are cries of alarm. Borrowing the liberal sociology that was the current fashion, they describe a teen culture that is populated primarily by victims—victims of poverty and of prejudice—who suffer from parental neglect, largely ineffective institutions, and widespread societal ignorance. Their plight has been exploited by the wider culture which sells sex and violence through its media:

It can be no accident that the most vigorous and vicious revolt and the most spectacular of its manifestations are found precisely in those strata of the population where conflict abounds, where insecurity is rife, where uncertainty is commonplace and where the ordinary pillars of humanity, the family and the social community, are debased or shattered. (Salisbury 1958, 162)

It is hard to imagine being nostalgic about this youth culture, if this is what it was really like. While there are certainly hard truths in these portraits, what they miss is the sense of how truly new it felt to be a teen, even a bad one, in the beginning, even in what were called slums—the excitement of the first rock 'n' roll show, the thrill of seeing *Rebel without a Cause,* the danger of a drag race, the exhilarating fear of the challenge of a fight, the delight in seeing a truly fine rod or custom, the joy of learning the bass part to "I Want You to Be My Girl"—the sheer uniqueness of being a teenager creating something that had never been seen before. Even being bad had its good points, within limits. It allowed a generation a chance to identify with an outlaw image that allowed them to overcome, at least in fantasy, the limitations of a straight world populated by "lonely crowds." As the wife of the owner of a custom Merc said to me when I asked her why so many were content to be "lost in the fifties," "It was the last decade when it was fun to be young."

It is a high school world that has been memorialized and mythologized, not prep school or college. It is a world where the blue-collar culture of the "hood" signifies authenticity—a world with its own values, its own culture, and its own art forms that critics from above have had a hard time seeing and understanding— the world that has been mythologized in *Grease, Crybaby, The Wanderers,* and *Hairspray.* It is a world created by teenagers who were born from just before the war to the arrival of baby boomers in the mid-forties while its idols were born a little earlier. It is an era that lasted from 1948 at the earliest (Wynonie Harris's "Good Rockin' Tonight" and the formation of the NHRA) to 1963 at the end (the assassination of JFK and the British Invasion). This is the Golden Age.

But before this golden age was revived, the Kustom Kulture itself was almost lost in its own dark ages. It took longer to respond to the revival of interest in the 1950s than did the culture at large. The downturn of interest in traditional customizing that had begun in the 1960s with the appearance of muscle cars, dunebuggies, surfer woodies, and modified VWs continued into the seventies. While interest in rods remained relatively strong, especially in T-Buckets, customizing almost disappeared. The September 1973 issue of *Car Craft* features not a single custom. The focus is on building drag racers. The featured car, a Mustang II, of all things, is evaluated as a potential street rod. The not very surprising conclusion: "It is regrettably underpowered."

In the 1977 edition of *Rod & Custom,* no longer a monthly, but an annual published by *Hot Rod,* customs are almost completely absent. There is a '39 Zephyr, a '40 Ford, and a '36 Ford featured among dozens of rods, mostly Model T and Model A resto rods (rods with essentially stock bodies). It is certainly surprising that a book called *Rod & Custom* should contain virtually no customs, but what is truly remarkable is that there is not a single car built in the 1950s in the whole issue. Not one T-Bird, not one '55 Chevy, and not a single '51 Merc. In the mid-seventies it was the fifties that were being "lost."

This is not to say that there were no traditional customs being built. There were still a number of loyal customizers; they just were not very visible on the cars culture radar screen. When Pat Ganahl offered a special feature on '49 to '51 Mercs in the August 1977 issue of *Street Rodder,* his tone is both defensive and apologetic:

We think that most street rodders are interested in the chopped Merc and its history, so we are hopeful for this issue's success. . . . If for some reason, however, chopped Mercuries remind you of sow bugs (and you happen not to like the looks of sow bugs), then I would cautiously point out that this issue . . . contains approximately fifty pages devoted to other topics. (Ganahl 1977, 6)

Later he laments the disappearance of the typical fifties mild street custom, "Perhaps my taste is peculiar. But it really surprises me that this 'street custom' trend, which was going so strong right before the muscle cars hit the scene, has apparently faded into oblivion. Where did all those '58 and '59 Impalas go?"

Five years later traditional Kustom Kulture made up only a small part of the rodding world. In *The Best of Hot Rod Show World Annual* (1982) only a few traditional rods and customs are shown among the ninety-six cars profiled. At that time the rodding world included reworked vans, muscle cars, show cars like the "Hustler"—with a genuine billiard table sitting over its V-8 engine—as well as gassers, competition-styled Corvettes and Vegas, resto rods, new pickups, drag boats, a rodded Kenworth, dunebuggies, VWs, and custom bikes.

But over the following ten years there would be a radical change in the popularity of the Kustom Kulture. It would not only rise from the dead, but begin to thrive as never before. This new Kustom Kulture was no longer at the center of the youthful car culture. It positioned itself clearly in opposition not only to the world of contemporary cars, but to everything in the rodding world post 1963.

By 1988 *Rod & Custom* was revived; within two years *American Rodder* and *Custom Rodder* also appeared; and groups like the National Street Rod Association, Kustoms of America, Kustom Kemps of America, and the Goodguys were sponsoring shows across the country. "Lost in the Fifties" began to appear on plaques, T-shirts, and continental kits.

This revived Kustom Kulture was different from the original, yet, paradoxically, the same. No longer the product of a youth culture it was now the product of middle age—the generation that had grown up with and built the original rods and customs created the new Kustom Kulture. They had the money, the time, and a renewed interest to invest in finding and building the cars of their youth. Rejecting contemporary cars and contemporary styling they embraced the aesthetics of the classic era. Not only were the mild customs, the ones Pat Ganahl mourned the loss of, rediscovered but they were being built in even greater numbers than ever before. In addition whole new classes of more radical customs began to appear as the revival gained momentum. By the late eighties Kustom Kulture had truly become part of the culture of nostalgia.

The typical rod or custom owner today is a male in his fifties. He responds to his car not because it represents some complex of meanings communicated through the media in a postmodern version of nostalgia, but because he lived through the fifties and wants to recapture that experience. As Preston Lerner reports in "Rebels with a Checkbook": "Originally, a young man's game, played mostly on the cheap, street rodding hasn't come of age so much as it's now of an age. Look around here in Southern California or at any hot-rod gathering and you'll have trouble finding a car owner younger than 40" (Lerner 1993, 22).

At shows from Rhinebeck, New York, to Paso Robles, California, you are likely to find the fifty-two-year-old insurance salesman who feels comfortable hanging a metal plaque that reads "Outlaw" from the bumper of his lowered '56 Chevy, the fifty-seven-year-old lawyer who is willing to spend $100,000 to build his dream Deuce roadster, and the fifty-five-year-old businessman who wears leather jackets and combs his hair into a DA on weekends when he cruises in his chopped '51 Merc.

Bob Conte, a lawyer in his fifties, who owns a custom Merc, sums up his memories, filtered through the icons of the era, that are shared by many contemporary car builders:

I wasn't a hood. But I hung out with hoods. They wore pegged pants, ducktail haircuts. They wore their collars up. They rode motorcycles. My mother wouldn't let me dress like that and the priests at Trenton Catholic—if you wore pegged pants, they would rip them right up the leg. They would cut the duck tail right out of your hair. But I was like a Fonzie. I would get the girls. I danced on "American Bandstand." I was kind of a rebel, like James Dean, even a little arrogant. The whole thing was to be

cool. We had to work hard, but it was a great time. The music, the dances and the cars. (Conte 1994, interview)

But there is also a new type of rodder, in his twenties, thirties, and forties, who has appeared recently, as passionately devoted to the fifties as those who were there the first time around. Dedicated not only to the cars of the early years of rodding and customizing but to the values, lifestyle, and culture of the original Kustom Kulture, they have joined together in small clubs with appropriate fifties names—the Shifters, Lucky Devils, Choppers, the Lucky Sevens, the Road Zombies—that are intent on keeping rodding and customizing pure. Reacting against the perfect, expensive high-tech rods and customs that older builders can afford, these clubs want to return to a time when rodders built their own cars, drove them, and didn't worry if there was a scratch here or a ding there. As Craig "Hot Rod" Hahn, forty-three, a founder of the Road Zombies near Hayward, California, says: "In the fifties a rod was a car you drove everyday to school, to work and on dates. It wasn't just a show piece. If it broke, you fixed it. You had to. You didn't have a second car to drive while it was in the shop. And it is not just about the money. It's about building traditionally styled cars that are drivers. The way it used to be" (Hahn 1999, interview).

These clubs are totally dedicated to authenticity, wanting to recreate the original Kustom Kulture as it *really* was. They study books like Don Montgomery's histories of hot rodding and old magazines to see what cars really looked like. They build their own cars the way that kids did in 1951, scrounging around junkyards, getting help from friends, and using their own ingenuity. While some of their cars, especially the customs, are really finely done, their typical ride is in primer, not a boutique primer done in a dustfree spray booth, but an in-the-driveway-right-out-of-the-spray-can paint job. They build rods with painted steel wheels and straightened but not perfectly smooth bodies, often chopped and channeled, with flathead power, just like it was. Some of them are such sticklers for authenticity that they won't use parts from late-model cars, even preferring original generators to more reliable alternators. Their cars have been given the name "Rat Rods" (they prefer "nostalgia rods"), but theirs is as refined an aesthetic as a Watson's or a Winfield's (see figures 44 and 45). As Aaron Kahan, a charter member of The Choppers, puts it: "We're all art directors or designers so we critique and help each other to ensure our cars look right and make the proper aesthetic statement" (Sheffer 1999, 31). What they want is respect for the work they put into their cars. As Axle of the Shifters Hot Rod Club writes in a letter to the editor of *Rod & Custom:* "It seems that we younger rod and custom builders don't get the recognition we deserve. The magazines constantly call our pre-War cars 'rat rods,' when in fact, our cars are painstakingly built in our garages as true, bare bone, nostalgic hot rods! There is no such thing as a rat rod and no such person as a rat rodder" (Axle 2000, 8).

Beyond building the cars, these younger rodders live the fifties. They wear white T-shirts, jeans with cuffs turned up, black trousers, engineer boots, and just the right shades. Their hair is also just right. Their clubs have the right jackets with correct fifties-styled logos (they were called "emblems" then). Some are drawn to the outlaw image that rodders had in the fifties—to the hard-partying,

Figure 44.
Nostalgia rod. Primered highboy coupe that has much in common with the original unfinished rod shown in figure 6.

Figure 45.
Nostalgia rod. The channeled primered coupe was very typical of rods built on the East Coast in the early fifties. Because of the weather, coupes were much more prevalent than roadsters.

street-racing, street-fighting Gene Vincent, Eddie Cochran, early Elvis, James Dean rebels without a cause and, for the many women who are part of the rockabilly culture, to the seductive Bettie Page. Hahn, a mechanical engineer, is caught up in the whole decade. "I love the music, the furniture, everything because everything was so cool then. My dining room is a fifties diner. It was just better then. More stable. There were clear lines. I want my existence to be more like that" (Hahn 1999, interview).

They get together at "rockabilly weekends" like "Viva Las Vegas":

This ain't no "Let's get dressed up in our 50's clothes" weekend. The assembled already drive vintage cars, dress in vintage clothes, wear vintage hairstyles and chill their beer in vintage refrigerators. They worship early Elvis and Gene Vincent. . . . They come to dance the bop, the stroll and the jive. They come to show off their hot rods and their tattoos. They come to drink Cape Cod's and smoke Camels, and drink some more and party like it's 1959. . . . Whether it's pure 50's Americana or a mix of cowboy, punk and rock 'n' roll, the look is a perfect fusion of innocence and rebellion. (Eisner and Alonso 2000, 99–102)

Not everything these new traditionalists love is fifty years old. They are trying to create a living culture out of what they see as the most vital elements of the past. They have their own music, a rockabilly-drag-punk-surfer sound, influenced not only by the music of the fifties and sixties, but also the music of the seventies and eighties with groups like the MonoMen, Didgits, Trashwomen, Mummies, Drags, Satan's Pilgrims, Demonics, Gas Huffer, among dozens of others. They have their own artists: Coop, Von Franco, Art Chantry, The Pizz, and

Frank Kozik, who have been heavily influenced by Von Dutch, Big Daddy Roth, and the painter Robert Williams, who also edits *JuxtaPoz,* a magazine dedicated to art that is "maliciously resplendent." They are on the net with dozens of sites found under key words: Customs, Hot Rods, Greasers, White Walls, and Cool Cats. These rodders have their own magazines like *Speed Kills, Wipeout!* and *Gearhead,* as well as *Hot Rod Deluxe,* a recent offering from Petersen, which also publishes *Hot Rod* and *Rod & Custom. Hot Rod Deluxe* tries to separate itself from the white-haired world of older rodders by courting this new rodding culture in its first issue in the summer of 1999:

What is the real issue then? The difference between riding around in a megamoney air-conditioned trailer queen or throwing together a makeshift speedster in your driveway with spare change. Checking out the latest Guitar World record or sticking with that stanky ol' Jan & Dean comp. Watching the grass grow with a glass of root beer at the local fogey custom show or catching the Cramps or the Reverend Horton Heat at the Hootenanny.

This issue is also paying attention to all the other things that go along with hot rodding: the music, the artwork, the clothes, even how to pick up the classy chicks. You know, the *kulture* in kustom kulture. And speaking of chicks, we've thrown a few of them in here too. Not greased-up and bent over the hood of a roadster (sorry, boys) but working on their cars, creating cool art, and corunning successful car shows. (Pecorelli and Ryan 1999, 5)

The first issue is as much about painting and music as cars.

Despite the intentions of those who want to go "back to the fifties," and those who are "lost in the fifties," the past cannot be recaptured as it was, only as it is constructed in myths that have grown up about it. To paraphrase Yogi Berra, "The past ain't what it used to be." As David Lowenthal points out in *The Past Is a Foreign Country,* an important investigation of how we understand and misunderstand, use and misuse, historic relics, records, architecture, and monuments, the past is affected by the futures it generates:

> Every act of recognition alters survivals from the past. Simply to appreciate or protect a relic, let alone to embellish or imitate it, affects its form or our impressions. Just as selective recall skews memory and subjectivity shapes historical insight, so manipulating antiquities refashions their appearance and meaning. Interaction with a heritage continually alters its nature and context, whether by choice or by chance. . . . Surviving Georgian structures look different in 1985 than they did in 1885 not simply because they are now older and scarcer but because a further century has added to the scene a host of neo-Georgian structures. (Lowenthal 1985, 263–64)

Thus, in our "remembered" recreations of the fifties every middle-class house is full of Formica, pink sofas, and amoeba-shaped tables; every diner is a forest of neon; and everybody dresses like Natalie Wood and James Dean or the cast of *Grease.* This is close to history as parody. A trip back to the actual 1950s would likely prove to be disappointing. It just wouldn't seem fifties enough. It wouldn't seem real.

In a short story, "Pierre Menard, Author of Quixote," one of the seminal texts of postmodernism that anticipates much of Lowenthal's argument, Jorge Luis Borges describes the attempts of a nineteenth-century French poet, Pierre Menard, to create Cervantes's *Don Quixote.* His intention is not to imitate it, or recreate it, but actually to "write" it. He devotes himself to years of elaborate preparation to accomplish this seemingly impossible, and absurd, task. Before his death he produces two chapters and a fragment.

On the page Menard's text is identical to the one written by Cervantes, but Borges suggests that they are, in fact, quite different. Surprisingly, Menard's text is richer, much more sophisticated than the text of Cervantes, which the narrator sees as simple and naive, thus turning the traditional value of original/copy on its head. After all, Menard's was written by a nineteenth-century French symbolist who knew much more than the unsophisticated Cervantes. And we know much more as well. We see Menard's effort in the context of a sophisticated nineteenth-century culture not the cruder seventeenth-century culture of Cervantes. The point of Borges's fable is that any use of the past is colored by all the intervening history as well as influenced by contemporary ways of understanding the past.

Consequently, no matter how accurate a 1951 custom Mercury might be in every detail, it is not a fifties custom if it was created in 2000. No matter how much research goes into the creation of a late forties rod today, it is not a forties rod. But in many ways it is more interesting. Rick Dore's '36 Ford "Tangerine Dream," for example, is an homage to the Westergard style. This model Ford is as archetypal for early customs as the '32 Ford is for rods. All of its major modifications look back to Westergard. Its main features—the vertical Packard grille, the teardrop skirts, the padded Carson top, the sunken headlight buckets, and lowered stance—would have made the "Tangerine Dream" look right at home in 1941.

The addition of Lincoln Zephyr rear fenders, for example, create a curved line that would have pleased the most devoted thirties streamliner. But the non-Westergard color (candy tangerine/murano pearl), and little touches like the aluminum spears on the hood, as well as the interior, suspension, and the engine turn what might have been a mere historical recreation into a postmodernist essay on the past that would have made this car stand out on the street in 1941 like the orange roses in black and white Pleasantville (see plate 33).

The meaning of these new cars is affected by everything that has happened in between the original Kustom Kulture and now—from the end of the Korean War to Vietnam, from the civil rights movement to the rise of feminism, from the arrival of the Beetle to the Toyota Camry, from the arrival of the Beatles to hip-hop. Today rods and customs are statements of reaction and rejection as much as they are statements of identification. In the 1950s to create such a car was to participate in a growing subculture that was about tackling contemporary automotive designs with youthful energy and imagination; in the 1990s to create a custom is as much an act of separating yourself from contemporary society, rejecting the history that places you at the millennium while still identifying with an idea of youth. Customizing is no longer a contemporary act but a historicized one. We cannot escape our experience, individual or cultural. We can no longer recapture the original Memphis Elvis without considering, comparing, and evaluating the Las Vegas or, even, the Andy Kaufman Elvis. Any attempt to recreate the past, despite the best intentions of the nostalgia rodders, must result in fakes, but fakes so convincing, so strange, so perfect,

and so transcendent that they are often preferable to the originals. They can become what Umberto Eco calls "hyperreal" in a book that considers America's love of weirdly "exact" and false historical recreations:

> There is, then, an America of furious hyperreality, which is not that of Pop art, of Mickey Mouse, or of Hollywood movies. There is another, more secret America (or rather, just as public, but snubbed by the European visitor and also by the American intellectual); and it creates somehow a network of references and influences that finally spread also to the products of high culture and the entertainment industry. It has to be discovered. (Eco 1986, 7)

Historicizing rodding and customizing results in an art that has evolved in a curious way: it is clearly an art which is obsessed with its past but it continues to celebrate innovation. Because the contemporary customizer lives in a closed car world that is no longer strictly contemporary, he is constantly being drawn back to the past because being innovative in the nineties still has to do with transforming cars that were built in the thirties, forties, and fifties so that history is an inevitable, inescapable, part of the meaning of current customs. These cars no longer express the rebellion of an emerging generation. Today, as products of that same generation in its maturity, they have come to represent resisting time, honoring history, and living a dream.

Hundreds of car shows, large and small, across the country help graying rodders remain "lost in the fifties," by offering a theme park virtual time travel experience replete with cruises, doo-wop contests, dances, T-shirts, pinstripers, muffler rapping contests, flea markets of memorabilia and old auto parts, flame-out contests to see who can shoot out the longest flames from their exhaust pipes, and fifties music continually blasting through bad speaker systems.

The most important time-bending elements are, of course, the cars themselves—dozens of '49 to '51 Mercs, high school cruisers, full radical luxo-customs, high-tech Deuce coupes next to authentic forties roadsters, clones, restorations, and reproductions—side-by-side, each marking a very specific moment in time. But they are to be understood as much by what is excluded as by what is included. In order to recapture that lost golden era it is necessary to banish, at least for a time, other forms of the car culture from different eras, even those associated with rodding. As Pat Ganahl announced in the premiere issue of the revived *Rod & Custom* in 1988: "What won't you see in *R&C*? You certainly won't see any new car tests, contemporary dragsters, Pro Street machines, muscle cars, stockers, Mustangs, Chevelles, Novas—*and no Camaros!*" (Ganahl 1988, 4).

The interest in the fifties and its cars is almost obsessive. Very few post-fifties cars are customized even as late as the nineties. Many of the shows prohibit cars later than a certain model year. The National Street Rod Association does not allow cars made after 1948 in its shows. The Kustom Kemps of America allow cars only up to 1963 models. The Goodguys allow cars up to 1964 at some shows. Even though brand-new cars were driven straight from the showroom into the bodyshop to be customized back in 1957 and 1958, most contemporary customizers want nothing to do with contemporary cars. No matter how fast

they might be—a 2000 Honda V-6 would destroy just about any production V-8 from the fifties in a drag race—new cars mean only dullness, uniformity, and giving in and giving up. The very essence of what rodding and customizing mean is now tied up with visions of the fifties, the Golden Age. Where the original rodder was fueled by his love of cars and the desire to improve them, the contemporary rodder is motivated as much by his contempt for contemporary cars (and culture) as by his love for his favorite models. Kustom Kulture is no longer a modern art, but something different, more complex, and surprising, something postmodern.

Seemingly time-bound contemporary customs, paradoxically, also exist in a world where time is free floating, subject to reinterpretation and invention, freed from the restrictions of a narrowly defined history of the sort that operates in the world of classic cars where the fetishes involve accuracy and exactness, where owners lose points if even screw thread sizes are incorrect for a particular model. Sometimes what results in the contemporary Kustom Kulture is an incoherent mélange of styles, but more often the freedom that customizers have to choose from the variety of historical options, to play with their history, produces genuinely new ways of using the past, what Lowenthal calls "creative anachronisms," and what postmodern theorists call "pastiche."

Richard Zocchi's striking design for his '39 Dodge, for example, which, like Tangerine Dream, looks very early forties in its basic body modifications and its stance. But it also employs late fifties canted quad Lincoln headlights and chromed reversed wheels. The fact that the original was a business coupe and the custom is a club coupe, providing rear seating, a change that was very difficult to perform and not very noticeable to the uninitiated, makes it contemporary (see the discussion of phantoms below). But it is the two-tone coral and cream paint job, beautifully done by Bill Reasoner with understated scallops and striping by Art Himsl, that truly separates this custom from the past. Like a number of Zocchi's cars it shares a pastel palette of cream, peach, yellow, pink, and lavender—not the candies one might expect—that allows his cars to transcend their influences. The fact that it is a '39 Dodge, a car rarely, if ever, customized like this in the forties or fifties, is the most subversive element of all, changing our way of imagining how cars looked in the past and thus creating an alternative history (see plates 34 and 35).

His 1957 Dodge, another unpopular choice for customizing in the fifties, is an equally disruptive exercise in reinventing the history of the custom (see plate 36). While respecting the basic shape of the car, Zocchi cleans up the lines by removing trim, lowering the car, and slightly chopping the top. The most effective restyling involves the simplification of the original busy front end. By adding a massive front bumper and grille from a 1958 Cadillac and by smoothing the lines of the hooded headlights, he gives the front end the weight and focus that the original never had. The rear similarly benefits from the addition of '54 Packard taillights that extend the line of fins whereas the stubby bullet lights on the original worked against the fins. With its exquisite Winfield blend paint job, this could have been a late fifties custom if such cars were customized (refer back to plate 12).

Zocchi began by building Mercs in what he calls the "Barris style." But for the last fifteen to twenty years he has been at the forefront of the custom revival by deliberately seeking cars that were ignored, even despised, by customizers of the original Kustom Kulture. At the same time he is very respectful of the past:

I look for oddball cars that I can add something of my own to that makes them look better. I grew up admiring the work of men like Barris and Winfield. I always have it in my mind that I want to build something that they would like and admire. When Barris presented me with the Barris award for the '56 Dodge, he said, "How could he take something so ugly and make it so beautiful," that was a great thrill. (Zocchi 2000, interview) (see plate 37).

What we find here are cars that honor the history of customizing in their styling, but that stand out from the past because they violate that very history. Here is another example of a kind of "back to the future" exercise where customizers can go back and ask, "What if we look at an old Rambler or Nash or Studebaker as if it were new and we had no prejudices?" Thus, just by the choice of car they can reinvent the past. A particularly nice example of an unusual car modified in the classic forties style is Billy Hayes's '48 Nash (see figure 46). In recent years DeSotos, Hudsons, late forties Pontiacs, early fifties Plymouths and Dodges, Grahams, and even Rambler station wagons have received much more attention than they ever did in the fifties (see figure 47). The "Frankenstude," designed by Thom Taylor, one of the least popular and most unlikely models to be customized in the 1950s, looks positively advanced when it is customized in the 1990s. Based on an assortment of Studebaker parts from 1947 to 1951 (thus the name) the smoothed-out final version, built by Greg Fleury for Steve Anderson, takes one of Raymond Loewy's odder designs (the joke question

Figure 46.
Billy Hayes's 1948 Nash.

at the time was, "Which way is it going?") and gives it the charm we now find in one of Flash Gordon's art deco spaceships—something that once looked like the future, but now looks like a particular past's vision of a future that, for us, is deeply embedded in the past (see plate 38).

Because customizers know what was done to particular models in the past and which particular cars were usually modified, seeing an extensively modified car like Frankenstude, or Zocchi's '57 Dodge is likely to produce a shock of recognition that is no longer possible with a similarly modified '51 Mercury just because so many have been done. In fact, for many car buffs, one of the ironies is that customized '49 to '51 Mercurys have become as numerous and ordinary at car shows as stock Mercurys were on the streets in 1953. Modifying untraditional cars, either in traditional ways or through a contemporary approach that em-

Figure 47.
Monochrome 1948 Hudson. Owned and built by Jerry Hobgood. Features a combination of contemporary and nostalgic styling.

phasizes the original lines, keeps the practice alive through a postmodern version of stylistic dynamism.

The contemporary custom is no longer measured only against stock models, the standard when customizing was beginning. At that

Figure 48.
Resto rod. '34 Ford.

In the 1970s and 1980s a new class of car that reflected a changing attitude toward the past began to appear—the resto rod. These were stock-bodied cars, Model A's, Deuces, '39 Fords, and so on, that had been meticulously restored. What made them rods was their running gear. They had modern V-8's, modern suspensions, and modern brakes. Even though the bodies looked very stock, they were treated to the lowered stance of the classic rod and custom to make sure that you knew they weren't. They often featured chromed wire wheels and high-performance black-walled tires that helped differentiate them from simply restored classic cars. What would have seemed tame and without much imagination in the fifties seemed fresh in the seventies and eighties (see figures 48 and 49).

In today's Kustom Kulture the old categories of mild, semi, and radical customs have a much different meaning than they did in the fifties. They are now historical references, not measures of complexity or value. Some of the most important customs of recent years would have hardly qualified as a mild custom in 1959.

Because the contemporary car builder is so knowledgeable about his art's history, he now measures his cars against the examples of exceptional cars built in the past as well as against what Detroit originally produced. Anyone who chops a '54 Chevy today calls to mind the "Moonglow." Any '51 two-toned Merc with Buick side trim built in 1999 is making allusions to the Hirohata Merc regardless of the intentions of the builder. No T-Bucket can exist outside the shadow of Norm Grabowski. Postmodern art is an art of quotation.

Much of postmodernist theory is concerned with how the art of the past impinges on the present with its specific codes that underlay genres, styles, and forms and how the present

time there were thousands of stock Chevys, Fords, and Mercurys on the streets that the customizer had to differentiate his car from in order to stand out and show his identification with the Kulture—the more different the better. To drive a forty-, fifty-, or sixty-year-old car in 2000 is in itself a radical act that sets one apart from ordinary drivers. Even a completely stock 1953 Chevrolet will attract attention today in ways that never would have occurred in 1957. Rods and customs no longer challenge current designs offered in the latest Detroit models since those designs are largely irrelevant to today's builders. The models customizers favor from the thirties, forties, and fifties have themselves become part of history and nostalgia and, consequently, look different than they used to. Stock models are no longer just raw material for customizers but a tangible connection to the era they prefer to the present. So these models receive much more affection in stock form than they did in the fifties when "stock" was only a term of contempt.

undermines the solidity of that past. Thus, contemporary customizing becomes an art form consistent with the postmodern practices found in film in the works of directors such as Quentin Tarantino, David Lynch, Brian De Palma, and Steven Spielberg, in the work of postmodern architects like Michael Graves, Robert Stern, and Robert Venturi, in the music of groups like De la Soul, Enigma, and Kronos Quartet, and in the works of artists like Sherrie Levine, Cindy Sherman, and Victor Burgin. These artists construct contemporary work by altering, borrowing, copying, quoting, manipulating, imitating, appropriating, and sampling what has been done before, often with a strong sense of irony. Their work problematizes previously held modernist notions of originality—the imperative to "make it new"—which fueled the various early modernist revolutions where creating unprecedented new work, liberated from the chains of history, was the goal. Marinetti confidently asked, "Why look back?" But the modernist's heroic breaks with the past have been supplanted by contemporary art's immersion in history, art in the rearview mirror. Postmodernism is about difference, not invention. Originality itself is now a suspect term since, according to postmodernist theory, it is impossible to escape history and the history of art which provides precursors for everything.

In other words, to borrow another term from postmodern theory, customizing has become more "intertextual." Intersexuality has to do with references works make to other works so that art imitates art and, ultimately, art refers to art, not reality—the way that ads are as much about other ads as they are about a product or the way movies are more about other movies than any life that exists outside of film (*Scream* and *The Freshman*, for exam-

Figure 49.
Resto rod. Model T.

ple). The term also applies to music, art, and literature.

When contemporary customs routinely quote from classic cars such as the Hirohata Merc, the Larry Ernst Chevy, or the Watson T-Bird they are assembled into re-versions of the past. But contemporary cars are defined as much by what they don't refer to as to what they do. This absence becomes a "presence" in postmodern terms. The current resurgence in interest in authentically styled nostalgia rods is as much a reaction against the high-tech and high-cost rods of the eighties and nineties as it is an expression of longing for the good old days. To choose to build a car with vintage parts in 1999 is both to call to mind and reject the billet aluminum, digital dashboards, and tweed interiors that became synonymous with rodding in the 1980s and to assert the importance of the root meanings of rodding and customizing—authenticity, simplicity, ingenuity—that are found through faithful replication. One's take on the practice is measured against what was done five years ago as much as against what was done fifty years ago.

As rodders and customizers looked back at their origins with rekindled interest and a better sense of history, they recognized how many early masterpieces had been neglected and abandoned, often stored in boxes in the back of old garages. Many others had been destroyed. They soon realized there was a danger that a good portion of history would be lost. Like scholar detectives, builders, collectors, and those with a particular mission to find the car of their dreams often spent years tracking cars to see if they could be found and restored to their previous glory. By turning their attention to these important cars they have written the history of customizing in steel, chrome, and lacquer. They have created a rolling museum. Dozens of cars thought lost have been brought back to life. The Sam Barris Buick, the Larry Ernst Chevy, George Barris's "Ala Kart," Ed Roth's "Road Agent," Tommy Ivo's T, George Barris's "Aztec," Ron Courtney's "X51," and "The Dream Truck" are just a few of the most famous cars resurrected in recent years (see plate 39).

Jim McNiel's recent restoration of the original Hirohata Merc is a telling example of how careful contemporary restorers are, rivaling those of any museum. When McNiel and his wife, Susan, discovered the original colors under nine layers of paint, they had it analyzed under the most sophisticated instruments they could find. PPG agreed to match it exactly. But because the old magazines often published washed-out color photos the restored Hirohata Merc doesn't look the way many people who never saw it in person remember it. McNiel insists that the color is "right on"—another example of how history can be misleading.

When he dismantled the dashboard during the restoration, McNiel discovered business cards from Barris and Hirohata. As the car was being reassembled, the cards were put back where he found them. "I didn't want to change anything" (McNiel 2000, interview).

When important cars disappear or are known to have been destroyed, builders have turned to a second way of bringing back these influential classics by replicating or "cloning" them down to the smallest detail after extensive and often exhausting research (magazine articles were often not very detailed, for example). Similar to the practice of contemporary artists like Sherrie Levine, who makes "pirated prints" by photographing the photographs of other, earlier, artists like Edward Weston and Eliot Porter, contemporary customizers reproduce exact copies of original cars that are nonetheless different from the originals just as Levine's works are not Westons or Porters, but occasions for a complex and complicated dialogue with a past that keeps leaking into the present.

Some car cloners improve on the original and create what might be called "near clones," further complicating the relation the cars and their builders have with the past. While still others use famous cars as their inspiration rather than their blueprints, adding their own individuality to masterpieces. Among the most prominent clones are many versions of the Matranga Merc; the Hirohata Merc (created by Jack Walker before the original was rebuilt by Jim McNiel after being stored for more than three decades); "Blue Danube," also by Jack Walker; "Moonglow"; and a number of Larry Watson–influenced '50 Chevys (see plate 40).

Contemporary customizing plays with the

same elements of reality/representation that so intrigue theorists of postmodernism, particularly those having to do with issues of original/copy. As Simon During points out, in a postmodern world: "It is no longer possible securely to separate the 'real' from the 'copy,' or the 'natural' from the 'artificial,' in a historical situation where technologies (including technologies which produce and disseminate information) have so much reach and control" (During 1993, 170).

The appearance of clones has produced some interesting paradoxes of the sort that are favorites in science fiction movies when a time traveler meets a younger or older self, like Marty McFly's meeting a version of himself in the sequel to *Back to the Future*. When two clones of Larry Watson's '50 Chevy were recently photographed next to each other, with Watson himself in the middle, Watson faced the same paradox since the clones were of different versions of the original: Manuel Arteche's middle version in purple and lavender and Randy Rhoades's scalloped pink-coral metallic recreation of the last iteration of the Chevy. Seeing them all sharing the same space is to experience a kind of cultural vertigo—like hearing a dead Nat King Cole sing a duet with his living daughter.

Copying is no longer seen as being derivative or unimaginative. In a postmodern culture it has become a key element in the creative process. This is not to suggest that copying wasn't done in the fifties. Innovative art is always imitated, but in the fifties the imitators were trying to keep up with the latest contemporary styles. There is a big difference between Joseph Stella's borrowing from the cubists in order to paint the Brooklyn Bridge in 1917 and David Hockney's recreation of Stella's painting

Figure 50.
Early forties style custom. 1936 Ford Convertible. It has the right touches: the ribbed bumper, the La Salle grille, the molded headlights, and the spinner hubcaps, and it is painted an appropriate solid dark color.

via a cubist construction made out of photographs more than sixty years later. Just as there is a world of difference between the original Matranga Merc's borrowings from Westergard and Terry Cook's recent '39 Zephyr ("Scrape"), a hyperreal celebration of the original Westergard style (see plate 41) that goes far beyond Bill Abate's copy of the Matranga Merc.

Other builders are not so much interested in copying a specific car as they are in evoking a specific historical style. Although not always completely accurate, there have been a number of homages to Westergard and Bertolucci's early Fords and Mercs, thousands of early fifties deuce highboys, dozens of T-Buckets, and a number of East Coast–styled customs, even on the West Coast, completed in the last fifteen years. Thousands of imitations of early

Figure 51.
Late forties style rod. Deuce Highboy that would be
right at home in Don Montgomery's *Hot Rods in the
Forties* (which probably influenced its design). See
figure 8 for a comparison.

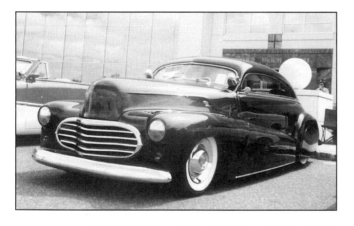

Figure 52.
Early fifties style custom. This 1948 Chevy has the
look and the details of the forties Chevys and Fords
that Barris built in the early fifties, especially the ones
he built for movies like *High School Confidential*.

'49 to '51 Barris-influenced Mercs, the most
popular body for customizers, pack shows from
coast to coast. Early fifties customs and rods
continue to be the most popular styles (see
figures 50, 51, and 52).

In recent years there has been growing interest in the customs of the late fifties and early
sixties, but it is not highly sculpted customs like
"Jade Idol" or "Aztec" (although there is considerable interest in restoring cars like these) or
handmade show cars like Roth's "Rotar" or
Cushenberry's "Silhouette" that have fueled
the new interest, but cars like Larry Watson's T-
Bird, Joe Wilhelm's Inman Chrysler, and Bailon's
candy '57 Buick which honored the stock lines
of the originals. Rick Dore's T-Bird is a prime
example. Although extensively modified, including a hand-formed billet grille (which only
looks like it could have come from a Caddy), it
is clearly a 1963 Thunderbird (see plate 42).

Even the more modestly styled cars of the
fifties, the mild customs Pat Ganahl was so interested in reviving, have become increasingly
popular. Interest in this class of reenvisioned
high school cruisers is another reflection of the
"back to the future" phenomenon that is so
pervasive in contemporary Kustom Kulture. The
fantasy is not so much to create a masterpiece
but to answer a question—What car would I
actually have driven back then if I had a little
money and more sense?

The truly new dimension in these cars is
found in the running gear. In Ken "Posies"
Fenical's '51 Ford a basically stock body is
mounted on a 1985 Monte Carlo front and
rear, basically changing the '51 into a modern
unibody configuration (which entailed a great
deal of work). All of the running gear is modern. So what looks stock is in fact not so. These
cars run, sit, and stop better than any typical

high school cruiser in the fifties. Back then many customs, often to save money, retained stock engines, stock brakes, and suspensions (except for the mandatory lowering which often played havoc with the handling) while the bodies were extensively modified. Today, because of the affection contemporary customizers have for stock forms, that original tactic is often reversed, creating another type of simulated experience—it looks old, it rides new (see plate 43).

In many ways the history of rods and customs is the history of paint—from the early Bertolucci's maroons to Jeffries's curly flames to Bailon's candy apple and Watson's panels— the paint treatment alone will put a car into a place in history. This is especially true of mild customs. But even here that history is played with and revised. There has been, for example, a big revival of flame jobs. Almost every year and style of rod and custom is flamed today regardless of what might have been done in the 1950s. For example, of the eleven '49 to '51 Mercs identified by Pat Ganahl as the most important "original radical" Mercs, built between 1950 and 1956 by the Barris brothers, the Ayalas, and Frank Sonzogni, not a single one is flamed. Today it seems that every third one has some sort of flame job. Some of the cars take advantage of new paint technology and create flames that change color depending on the light. Others employ "ghost" flames, scarcely visible outlines of flames in barely contrasting colors (see plates 44, 45, and 46).

Because the contemporary Kustom Kulture is so willing to reconfigure its history, because it accepts both traditionalists and revisionists, and because it is interested in both creation and recreation, it has been able to keep the

historical play vital and avoid becoming trapped in the past like a Dixieland band or a doo-wop group.

While historically accurate restorations, clones, and imitations allow us to understand more clearly what was done in the past, they can never, as Lowenthal emphasizes, be seen as they originally were. But there are a number of distinctly contemporary approaches to rodding and customizing that work through more complex combinations of difference and recapitulation. The result is a proliferation of styles that reexamine and reconfigure original practices. The pluralism that results is decidedly postmodern.

A variation on the traditional custom, at about the same time as the resto rod, appeared in the 1980s, and which is still very popular, involves reworking fat-fendered late thirties and forties Chevys, Fords, and Mercurys, primarily—cars largely ignored in the glory days. Often dropped very low, influenced to some extent by lowriders, they are frequently painted in sherbet colors: raspberry, lime, grape, orange, and strawberry, which evoke the technicolor fifties without being historically accurate. Although there were candy pinks and purples on cars in the fifties, they were nothing like these brilliant nonmetallic tints. On the sides and hoods and trunks, customizers often employ a contemporary take on striping and scallops by including bold, often witty, at times silly, graphic designs in contrasting colors (see plates 47 and 48).

Another new element that distinguishes these cars from those of the past is their favoring a completely monochromatic color scheme that involves painting the grilles, side trim, and even the bumpers the same color as the body, thus resembling similarly styled Maximas, Ac-

Figure 53.
 A Sam Barris near clone. Herbert Segrist's fine 1950 Buick has frenched headlights, while the original had '54 Buick headlights. Segrist retains the portholes, while Barris filled his in. These are just two of the kind of small details that separate a near clone from the original.

Figure 54.
Monochrome 1948 Buick. This sleek custom breaks from fifties style in its clean lines, its monochromatic color scheme, the absence of any polished metal except on its contemporary billet wheels. Built on the West Coast, it is owned by Ralph Naylor.

cords, and Camrys, whose style originates, at least in part, in late fifties customs—another example of time looping back on itself. Some of the more extreme "low-fats" favor a high-tech look which has been influenced by after-market companies, who made their reputation reworking Mercedes Benzes. They rely heavily on billet aluminum not only for large diameter wheels, but also for steering wheels, pedals and other accessories, elimination of all chrome, digital instruments on the dash, painted engine compartments, and extremely smooth lines as well as an overall monochromatic color scheme. These cars are hybrids of historical and contemporary styles. Like so much in postmodern culture, the contemporary customizer straddles eras—borrowing from the past as he displaces it (see figures 53 and 54 for a comparison of the competing aesthetics operating in a near clone of the Sam Barris Buick, one of the original fifties customs, and a monochromatic Buick of the same vintage done in a more contemporary style).

Innovation in the contemporary Kustom Kulture often occurs with unexpected twists. Two recently customized postwar Fords, known as "shoe boxes" because of the shape of the stock body, are especially rich in contradictory meanings. Both refer explicitly to the high school cruisers, those very mildly modified cars driven by thousands of teens who could not afford the exotic full radical customs that set the trends. These two, however, are not simple recreations of mild customs. They take the resurgence of interest in recreating these cruisers to unexpected levels of sophistication and complexity. Their sense of play is exquisite.

What makes these two cars unusual and innovative is the way that they are, in fact, highly modified despite their initial appearance. Designed by Steve Stanford and built for Billy Gibbons of ZZTop by Pete Chapouris, the "Kopperhed," for example, is an exact replica of a model that never existed—a three-window business coupe. To create this new model the original sedan's top was chopped, the rear side windows removed, and doors ten inches wider than the originals were installed. The amount of work required to produce this car rivals that of any traditional radical custom. But the overall appearance is deceptively stock: the original grille, headlights, and even the door handles are retained. The hood ornament is replaced by a simple bull nose strip. The wheels appear stock; they're not (see figure 55).

The "Fantom," a '49-looking Ford sedan (the original body is a 1951) built by Sam Foose and based on a Harry Bentley Bradley design, is similarly *trompe l'oeil.* Bradley's design is smoother than Stanford's, but it also retains the original grille configuration (the grille only looks stock; it is itself highly modified with a much smaller center bullet from a '51 grille), wheels, and side trim to give the appearance that it might be a production car. There is even a hand-crafted miniature hood ornament to counter the almost automatic nosing of the hood, typically the first modification of a backyard customizer in the fifties. In addition to the chopped top, the body is sectioned in an unusual way that results in a narrowed trunk and grille. The final effect is of a sleeker, lower, more flowing body that still looks a lot like the stock form, unless it is sitting next to a truly stock Ford.

Both cars are painted conservatively: "Kop-

Figure 55.
Kopperhed. Built by Pete Chapouris for Billy Gibbons. Courtesy of Petersen Publishing.

perhed," a basic black, and "Fantom," a very dark Mercedes green, which, except for the perfect finish, could have been factory colors (see figure 56). As Sam Foose, who has been building cars for more than four decades, sees the challenge facing contemporary customizers:

Too many customizers can't get out of the '50's. This is the millenium. You can't build cars today the way that George Barris did in 1950 or 1960. And customs don't have to be gaudy and in poor taste. Today's best customs are high-tech customs with good designs—elegant and clean. They drive easily. They ride decent. They look right. Even if it costs fifty or a hundred thousand, you should drive it. People drive Ferraris. As I say, "If you can't drive it, you can't afford it." (Foose 2000, interview)

Yet the car he uses to demonstrate this new aesthetic is still an early fifties shoe-box Ford. The "Fantom" and the "Kopperhed" mark a significant shift in direction for Kustom Kulture. On the street both could easily be mistaken for

Figure 56.
Fantom Ford. Built by Sam Foose. Courtesy of Sam Foose.

basic stockers by the general public, especially since sources of comparison, the original '49 and '50 Fords, are so rare today. They won't stop traffic the way that Watson candy paint jobs did in the late fifties or the way the Hirohata Merc did a few years earlier. Like Jasper Johns's "Ballantine Ale Cans," they are sculpted pieces in the form of ordinary found objects.

These shoe boxes function like virtual history. Playing a "what if" kind of game, Foose says he wanted to build a car "that could have been introduced by Ford at the Detroit Autorama" (Foose 2000, interview). This new breed of custom is actually called "phantom." They are imitations of something for which there is no original. With efficient modern running gear, new Ford overhead V-8's, and elegant Spartan interiors, they also exist as some exaggerated and transformed ideal of the high school cruiser. Customizers, however, know Fords and recognize how radically different

these cars are from those built in the factory. This degree of subtlety in radically modified cars is very new in the world of customs.

Another shift in practice from the past is the collaborative effort involved in the creation of these two cars. Builders are no longer the designers of the most innovative cars. Designer/artists like Thom Taylor, Steve Stanford, Harry Bentley Bradley, Larry Erickson, and Chip Foose, among others, have assumed a much more prominent place in the world of contemporary customizing than they ever had in the past when builders like Bailon, Barris, Winfield, and Cushenberry, like the early modernist masters, were the "heroic" creators of the designs that determined the directions the art would follow. This is not to say there weren't teams involved in the creation of early customs. Barris had a number of skilled craftsmen, like "Junior" Conway and Frank Sonzogni, working for him. But designer/builders such as Rick Dore, Richard Zocchi, and John D'Agostino, functioning more like architects than masons, tend to supervise the project as it moves from shop to shop—from initial sketch through the final paint job. These illustrators and designer/builders have helped Kustom Kulture avoid becoming involved in mere historical conservancy by offering contemporary interpretations of classic models like Deuce roadsters and '51 Mercs and by opening up the possibilties for customizing previously neglected marques like Hudsons and Ramblers and ignored models like Pontiac Safaris. Thom Taylor, who was "born the summer that Watson started striping cars for his pals after high school," brings a different perspective to models from the past: "I don't understand why mid-fifties Dodges and Plymouths were ignored. They look good to me. A '56 Plymouth is every bit as good looking as a Ford. I want to go back and rethink how those cars look. That's what I was doing with Frankenstude" (Taylor 2000, interview).

Although there are exceptions, contemporary builders are likely to be skilled fabricators working from the designs of others rather than creative artists in their own right. This displacement of the individual artist from the center of interest is another postmodern element in contemporary customizing.

Another new direction in customizing, one which has strong connections with the creation of phantom high school cruisers, has been led by Richard Zocchi and John D'Agostino of northern California and Rick Dore of Arizona. They have created a new class of luxo-customs by applying customizing techniques to luxury models of the fifties and early sixties—the Cadillacs, Chryslers, Imperials, and Lincolns that were rarely customized in the fifties partly because they were so expensive. (One of the ironies of today's market is that, because of the power of fifties nostalgia, '55 to '57 Chevys are worth much more than comparable Lincolns and Cadillacs.) As with the "Kopperhed" and the "Fantom," the goal is less to transform the original into something completely distinct from the original (as Winfield had done with "Jade Idol") than to epitomize fifties notions of luxury through a highly refined and sophisticated reworking of the original that suggests what these cars might have looked like if they had been designed by customizers rather than in Detroit studios. The key for Rick Dore "is taking a basically well designed car, the best from Ford and GM, and adding my own sense of design. I want to clean up the lines and bring out the form that is already there. Too

many oddball cars are being done today just because the old coupes have been done to death" (Dore 2000, interview).

It is not that these luxo-customs are unprecedented. They have created their own precursors. D'Agostino's, Zocchi's, and Dore's Caddys and Lincolns produce a new history where basically stock-bodied customs like Watson's '59 Caddy become much more significant now than they were in the late fifties and early sixties when extensively sculpted show cars were the essence of the art (see plate 49).

The trend toward more understated modifications—cutting as little as two inches from the top, for example—that respect the original lines of the car, sets up a more sophisticated and intricate play of subtle differences for the viewer to dissect than the clearly radically altered cars of the fifties ever did. Dore's chopped "Majestic," like "Kopperhed" and "Fantom," has the feel of a mildly modified custom, that would rarely have been a high school cruiser back in 1953, but which today creates a fantasy of such a ride (see plate 50).

Built for Don and Flo Makofske, Dore's 1956 Lincoln Continental Mark II, one of the most expensive cars of the fifties, originally costing almost $10,000 compared to about $2,200 for a comparable top-of-the-line Chevy, is a refined example of improving the original lines of an already striking car. The amount of work that has gone into producing such subtle variations in the original is remarkable. Just to point to some of the more important modifications: the top is chopped three inches and leaned slightly rearward. The hood is extended into the reworked grille shell. The front bumper has been widened and recessed. The rear bumper matches the front. The original faux "continental" bulge on the rear deck lid has been cut three inches and leaned slightly forward. In addition the body is dechromed, tasteful scoops added, and the wheel wells reworked. An air suspension system handles the lowering. The paint is a custom-mixed pearl blue. A comparison between the original Continental and Dore's reveals how subtle and how significant these changes are. Dore's is so much more fluid in its lines, especially with the addition of a stepped-up line that runs along the sides, contouring the body. The original Continental, a striking car in its time, seems crudely built next to it (see plates 51 and 52).

In 1998 D'Agostino introduced a '53 Cadillac, painted in an appropriate blonde blend, named "Marilyn," which celebrates the excesses of the fifties from cars to movie stars. The original lines of the Cadillac, despite a number of subtle modifications, are retained, as well as the chrome trim, taillights, and headlights. It is not even nosed and decked. It does not look much different from a stock Caddy. The fact that "Marilyn" won a first place award in the Radical Custom Convertible class at the Grand National Roadster Show demonstrates how much the criteria for judging customs have changed since the Golden Age.

Today rod builders' options parallel those in the custom world. Significant rods have been restored and cloned. Rodders have meticulously reproduced rods that fit a particular era, going as far as using no part that would not have been available to a builder at that time. But rod builders also feel free to create their own mix of styles, building an authentic-looking forties-styled rod, then painting it candy apple, for example, or using large-diameter billet wheels on a chopped and channeled fifties-styled Deuce coupe. Today early Plymouths, Chevys, and Dodges are as likely to be rodded as classic Fords.

As interest in rodding picked up in the early seventies after a decline in the sixties, dedicated rodders began sponsoring rod runs, mass versions of Hirohata's journey east to attract interest in rodding, and to comfort one another in those dark days. *Rod & Custom* sponsored the first national meet for rods in Peoria, Illinois, in 1970 and drew about 600 cars, the largest gathering of rods to that date. (In contrast, the twenty-fifth anniversary 1994 Street Rod Nationals drew more than 14,000 pre-1949 cars to Louisville, Kentucky.) The event and its fall-out weren't enough to keep *Rod & Custom* from suspending publication in 1974. It wouldn't resume publication until 1988 when the renaissance was in full swing.

Interest in rodding also got strong boosts from the appearance of John Milner's Deuce coupe in *American Graffiti;* Pete Chapouris's "The California Kid," a flamed full-fendered '34 Ford coupe (see plate 53) in the 1974 movie of the same name; and ZZTop's "Eliminator," a bright red '33 Ford coupe, in their music videos in the early eighties. Builders like Pete Chapouris, Andy and Roy Brizio, John Buttera, Bob Alloway, and Ken "Posies" Fenical continued to turn out beautiful rods in the seventies and into the eighties, but in the early eighties rods built by Boyd Coddington's shop, Hot Rods by Boyds, in Stanton, California, began to offer a sleek high-tech look that seemed perfect for the time.

Coddington is very much the Barris of the eighties and nineties, as much a master of promotion and of attracting talent as a skilled metalman. Following the lead of builders like

John Buttera, Coddington took trends that were beginning to emerge and refined them to the point that they became his signature. He was also an effective ambassador of rodding who was able to interest the *New York Times* and the *Smithsonian* in his work, and not just car magazines like *Hot Rod*.

Approaching finely crafted European cars like Ferraris in quality, a point Coddington reinforced with his favorite combination of bright red paint and natural leather interiors, his high-priced rods are among the most successful and influential in rodding history. Employing a team of skilled technicians and the work of designers like Chip Foose (Sam's son) and Thom Taylor, he perfected a style of rod that evoked the past at the same time it was right at home in the new high-tech computer-driven economy. These rods came to be known as "smoothies." And they were smooth—Coddington eliminated all decoration, anything that would detract from the basic lines of the car, including windshield wipers. Taillights were hidden in little slits of metal. There were no bumpers or nerf bars. Side mirrors were minimalist. The engines were not exposed but encased in a smooth-sided jewel box of an engine compartment as spotless as an operating room. Even engine wires were hidden. Employing Coddington's favorite metal, billet aluminum, for the wheels, steering wheels, gear shifts, and mirrors, the cars looked high tech and their running gear lived up to the look. With the most advanced suspension and braking systems as well as the latest in performance engines, these cars handled like sports cars and were as reliable as Hondas. They cost from $50,000 to as much as $500,000. These are amounts that strike some original rodders as obscene, but for his clien-

tele, rock stars and business executives who might also be potential purchasers of a Ferrari or a Bentley, they were right in the ballpark.

The first truly significant car Rods by Boyds built was the extremely smooth chopped and channeled Vern Luce '33 Ford three-window coupe designed by Thom Taylor that appeared in 1981. It recalls the many chopped and channeled coupes of the early fifties, but, at the same time, it looks thoroughly contemporary because of its extremely fine metalwork: the bobbed rear is lifted an inch, the wheelbase is lengthened 3 inches, the top chopped 3 inches in front and 2.75 inches in the rear to alter the lines just enough to make a difference. One of the most striking touches is having the bottom of the body run parallel with the frame rails—a very difficult job. The effect is to emphasize the rake of the grille, roof, and rear, resulting in a sweeping line that is organic to the design and not simply a product of jacking up the rear. But it is not the lines of the car that are so striking, it is the surface. This design is about skin, the way the original streamline was about surfaces, and nothing breaks the skin here—nothing. Like minimalist sculptures that consist of flat pieces of perfected, polished metal, this car announces its surface as its subject. It's a shame to call a rod as sophisticated as this a "smoothie." It makes it seem like an ice cream confection (see plate 54).

The following year Coddington won the first of his many AMBR awards with Jamie Mussleman's '33 roadster based on very similar design to the Vern Luce coupe. Both look back to the classic era of hot rodding in their stance and in the basic modifications, but the extremely clean design, the attention to every detail, including placement of screws, and the overall excellence of the build quality bring them comfortably into the high-tech eighties and nineties. Over the next decade and a half Boyd built dozens of rods, full fendered and open wheeled, highboy and channeled, that bore his signature. Even among exceptional cars with exquisite paint jobs, a Coddington car stands out because of its finish (see plate 55).

Not all rods and customs demonstrate the complex subtlety and seeming conservatism of phantoms and luxo customs with their apparently stock bodies and tasteful leather or tweed interiors. There is still room for the outrageous and even the bizarre. Rods by Boyds was responsible for a number of the most unusual customs of the eighties and nineties. In fact his best customs are more imaginative than his rods, which take craftsmanship and attention to detail to a new level, but don't add very much to our conceptions of what a hot rod might look like. "CheZoom," for example, is a hand-formed fantasy of one of the fifties most desired cars, the 1957 Chevy. Boyd's version, designed by Thom Taylor, could have come from a Tex Avery cartoon. It is stretched, dropped, expanded, and widened. It looks nothing like any customized Chevy done in 1957 or 1958. Where "Fantom" and "Kopperhed" offer us virtual reality, "CheZoom" is a dream image that condenses memory and fantasy. Everything about its re-conception of the original, of which, according to Coddington, only "part of the front fenders and part of the trunk were from a real '57 Chevy" (Wolkomir 1993, 51), is exaggerated—from its stance to the fins, yet it never loses sight of the original stock form—even the side trim refers to the original in a hyperreal way. In some way this smooth teal creation represents everything, including the excess and distortion, that the

fifties had come to mean in the nineties. Like "Kopperhed" and "Fantom" it also reconfigures the customizing vocabulary (see plate 56).

But the most radical car that came from Coddington's studios was the CadZZilla, designed by Larry Erickson and fabricated by Craig Naff. Based on a very clean 1948 Cadillac Sedanette, it was built in 1989 for Billy Gibbons, who wanted a car that looked forward to the nineties at the same time it connected to the past. He also wanted a custom that would not be embarrassed to run at Bonneville. Finally, it had to be a car that fit the image of the band.

The resulting car is sleek and sinister, low and fast. As the most celebrated custom of the last ten years (*Hot Rod* devoted ten pages to its debut), it has had an impact on the nineties reminiscent of the effect the Hirohata Merc had more than three decades earlier (see plates 57 and 58).

CadZZilla acknowledges its heritage without copying what a Barris or Winfield did in the fifties. It is not a clone nor is it an homage exactly. Even though it is a Cadillac it is no luxocustom or phantom either, rather it is a radical reexamination of the original intention of the customizer—making a car look very different from the original model and more advanced. Because it was built in 1989 this reexamination is tied up in a complicated relationship with the past. This Cadillac was fifty years old when Naff put the torch to it; the Hirohata Merc was less than a year old when it was chopped by Sam Barris. Customizing was relatively new when Barris customized the Mercury. Customizing now has an involved history. What is so impressive about this car is how Erickson incorporates so much history into CadZZilla without the car's design collapsing under the weight of that history.

The front end is a mixture of fifties customizing and sixties rodding styles to meet the goals that Gibbons had for the car. The hood is nosed, although there is a channel in the center of the hood for a new ornament, and the headlights are frenched, just like a Barris custom. The front end is collaged in the early fifties style from various cars: the bumper is from a '55 Chevy, the bumper guards are built into the bumper rather than merely attached, the top grille is from a '49 Caddy, the rearview mirrors are made from Caddy bumper bullets. But the hood is seamlessly joined to the fenders in a single unit so that the whole front end tilts up like a sixties Gasser, a drag-racing style, and to emphasize the racing potential of the 500ci Caddy engine under that hood, a polished Moon tank is mounted in the middle of the grille, also more typical of rods of the fifties and sixties than customs. The rear of the car is almost completely hand formed. Extending the fenders into a smooth flowing line, Erickson has molded the rear in late fifties style eliminating a conventional bumper. The hand-formed built-in taillights also allude to that era. On the other hand, the curved window guide

is a direct quotation of the earlier Hirohata Merc as are the teardrop knobs on the dashboard. The dark eggplant color that turns almost black refers back to the dark colors of Westergard/ Bertolucci customs in the late forties.

There are many nineties touches as well: the hand-formed discs that seem to imitate stock Cadillac hubcaps; the attention to detail; the natural leather interior; the paint, as opposed to the color, a candy eggplant over gray that changes tint depending on the light; the hand-formed frame; the overall functionality of the car; and, most tellingly, the fact that it is a Cadillac and not a Mercury. And yet, it all comes together. It is a creation of impressive coherence.

Even though the car has strong connections to the forties, fifties, sixties, and nineties, the ways the lines flow, the sense of movement it has even standing still, and its flowing rearward tilt finally, and surprisingly, have a lot to do with the designs of the thirties, those art deco masterpieces from Lagonda, Bentley, and Dubonnet that inspired the humble beginnings of customizing in the first place. Pulling it all together CadZZilla, both a custom and a rod, is the postmodern masterpiece of the customizer's art.

AFTERWORD

In terms of sheer numbers the state of Kustom Kulture has never been healthier. More new cars are being created today than ever were built in the fifties. A recent marketing survey estimates that there are "350,000 rods and customs registered in the United States," with an additional "50,000 under construction" (Gobetti 2000, 4). Masterpieces continue to be rediscovered and to be restored, thus expanding the history of the practice. Shows keep getting bigger and more numerous. Performance parts, suspensions, customs wheels, classic bodies, and crated engines are available from dozens of suppliers. There are first-rate shops all over the country that are known locally for quality work but aren't yet national names. And a remarkable number of cars are still built by one man in one garage, Gobetti estimates perhaps as much as 90 percent of the 50,000 currently being built.

The second and third generations of great car artists, the ones who emerged in the late fifties to the early seventies are more active than ever—Sam Foose, Pete Chapouris, Art Himsl, Dick Dean, Posies, John Buttera, Troy Trepanier, and Bob Alloway are producing some of the most important cars of their careers. Amazingly some of the first-generation customizers are still active: Joe Bailon continues to work, more slowly than before, but he is still working. Bill Hines is still working. Gene Winfield hasn't slowed down a bit. Putting in fourteen-hour days, he continues to paint and build. When I visited his shop in 1998 he had three projects going. His luxo-custom, a 1961 Cadillac called "Maybellene," debuted in 1999 (see plate 59). It was picked as one of the ten best new customs of the year by *Custom Rodder* magazine. Dean Jeffries has recently restored his "Manta Ray." George Barris and Larry Watson continue to act as ambassadors of customizing, appearing at shows and awarding prizes.

Recognizing the growth of interest in the world of rodding and customizing, Detroit has gotten back in the act as well. In 1993 Chrysler introduced a Plymouth V-6 factory-built street rod, the Prowler, that bears a striking resemblance to Chip Foose designs. They also offer a retro-styled surfer wagon (the PT Cruiser) that bears a strong resemblance to the late thirties and early forties Ford woodies that became synonymous with surfing in the sixties. Wildly popular on its introduction, even though it is underpowered, the PT Cruiser marks the first real threat to the dominance of the SUV as an American family car. Ford has plans to release a retro-styled Thunderbird that revives the original look of the '55 to '57 two-seaters. Its latest concept car, called the "Forty Nine," is based on a shoebox Ford. Whether Detroit's attention will increase interest in true hot rods and customs or help speed the decline of the art as it did in the sixties is not clear.

A larger question is, what is the future of an art form whose primary appeal is to men in their fifties and sixties? How long can it continue? What is in store for an art form that is so caught up with a particular decade that it often guards itself against anything that threatens its narrow conception of what is a real custom or rod? If Kustom Kulture is now defined historically as well as stylistically, can it remain vital once the current resurgence of interest by fifty-somethings passes? Or will it lose too much of its uniqueness if it is no longer "lost in the fifties"?

There is a cultural battle going on, and the contested territory is the fifties and who has the right to claim the decade—those who remember it or those who live it. One of the ironies is that the older generation, the white-hairs, seem to be much more open to innovation and change than the young Turks. They are the new traditionalists who have truly gone back to the future—living a kind of virtual reality. They have energy, ingenuity, and attitude, but not a lot of creativity with their cars, at least not yet.

The battles that are being fought over the direction of Kustom Kulture: oddball cars versus traditional models, high-tech smoothies versus nostalgia rods, smooth contemporary styling versus traditional collage approaches, show cars versus drivers, big money versus backyard customizing, and so forth suggest to me that the Kustom Kulture is still vital. Without passionately held opinions on opposed sides, art forms collapse into entropy.

At one of Marinetti's Futurist performances the audience had come prepared with rotten vegetables. He was furious. Not because he had been pelted, but because the response was so mindless. He stood before them as they continued to throw and yelled, "Throw ideas, not tomatoes!" Ideas are being thrown around the Kustom Kulture, along with a few tomatoes.

How it will turn out is hard to say. Will rockabilly rodders remain a vibrant fringe movement or become just a passing fad like swing dancing or lounge music, or will they move to a dominant position as older rodders fade away? Will rodding and customizing continue to mirror the art culture as it moves into post-postmodernism? Will the creativity that has recently spawned "phantoms" and luxury cruisers and that has helped the Kustom Kulture to flourish despite the restrictions it places on itself continue to keep the practice fresh, or will it sink into mere sentimental nostalgia? The signs are mixed. I think Richard Zocchi captured the paradox of contemporary Kustom Kulture when he told me, "I keep saying it's got to come to an end, but it keeps getting bigger. And better."

Sources

Alland, Alexander, Jr. 1977. *The Artistic Animal: An Inquiry into the Biological Roots of Art.* Garden City, N.Y.: Anchor Press/Doubleday.

Apollonio, Umbro. 1970. *The Documents of Twentieth-Century Art: Futurist Manifestos.* New York: Viking Press.

Asimov, Eric. 1994. "A Bluesman's Songs of Joy." *New York Times,* October 6: C1, 4.

Axle. 2000. "Shifters Fight Back." *Rod & Custom* (November): 8.

Bailon, Joe. 1991. "Mr. Candy Apple Red." Interview with Tim Guymon. *Custom Rodder* (summer): 64–67.

Banham, Reyner. 1960. *Theory and Design in the First Machine Age.* New York: Praeger Publishers.

Barris, George. 1997. *Barris Kustom Techniques of the 50's.* Vol. 4. Sebastopol, Calif.: Thaxton Press.

———. 1998. Interview with the author.

Barris, George, and David Fetherston. 1994. *Barris Kustoms of the 1950s.* Osceola, Wisc.: Motorbooks International.

Batchelor, Dean. 1989. "L.A. Streets in the 40's." *Rod & Custom* (December): 70–74.

Bell, Clive. 1914. "The Aesthetic Hypothesis." In Feagin and Maynard, eds. (1997), *Aesthetics.* New York: Oxford University Press.

Bernard, Jessie. 1961. "Teen-Age Culture: An Overview."

Annals of the American Academy of Politics and Social Science (November): 1–12.

Bernstein, Jonathan. 1997. *Pretty in Pink: The Golden Age of Teenage Movies.* New York: St. Martin's Press.

Boccioni, Umberto. 1912. "The Technical Manifesto of Futurist Sculpture." In Chipp (1968): 298–304.

Bordua, David J. 1961. "Delinquent Subcultures: Sociological Interpretations of Gang Delinquency." *Annals of the American Academy of Politics and Social Science* (November): 119–35.

Borges, Jorge Luis. 1964. *Labyrinths and Other Stories.* New York: New Directions.

Braque, Georges. 1908–1909. "Statement." In Chipp (1968): 259–60.

Breeding, Michael. 1998. "Brian Setzer's Switchblade 327." *Rod & Custom* (August): 25–27.

Breton, André. 1934. "What Is Surrealism?" In Chipp (1968): 410–17.

Browne, Ray B. 1970. "Popular Culture: Notes toward a Definition." In Ray B. Browne (1973), *Popular Culture and the Expanding Consciousness.* New York: John Wiley & Sons, 14–22.

Cheney, Sheldon, and Martha Candler Cheney. 1936. *Art and the Machine: An Account of Industrial Design in*

Twentieth-Century America. New York: Whittlesey House.

Chipp, Herschel B., ed. 1968. *Theories of Modern Art: A Source Book for Artists and Critics.* Berkeley and Los Angeles: University of California Press.

Conroy, Frank. 1968. "America in a Trance." *Esquire.* Reprinted in *Esquire* (June 1983): 115–22.

Conte, Bob. 1994. Interview with the author.

Denzin, Norman K. 1991. *Images of Postmodern Society: Social Theory and Contemporary Cinema.* London: Sage Publications.

Desmarais, Charles. 1993. "Preface." *Kustom Kulture.* Laguna, Calif.: Laguna Art Museum.

Dickstein, Morris. 1977. *Gates of Eden: American Culture in the Sixties.* New York: Basic Books.

Dobrin, Michael, and Philip Linhares, co-curators. 1996. *Hot Rods and Customs: The Men and Machines of California's Car Culture.* Oakland: Oakland Museum of California.

Dore, Rick. 2000. Interview with the author.

Drake, Albert. 1982. *Street Was Fun in '51.* Okemos, Mich.: Flat Out Press.

Dunning, William V. 1995. *The Roots of Postmodernism.* Englewood Cliffs, N.J.: Prentice Hall.

During, Simon, ed. 1993. *The Cultural Studies Reader.* London: Routledge.

Eco, Umberto. 1986. *Travels in Hyperreality.* New York: Harcourt Brace Jovanovitch.

Editors of *Motor Trend.* 1952. *Restyle Your Car.* Hollywood: Trend Books.

Ehrenreich, Barbara. 1983. *The Hearts of Men: American Dreams and the Flight from Commitment.* New York: Anchor Books/Doubleday.

Eisner, Lisa, and Román Alonzo. 2000. "Cherry Bombs." *New York Times Magazine,* Part 2, August 20: 98–106.

Erikson, Eric. 1968. *Identity: Youth and Crisis.* New York: W. W. Norton.

Fass, Paula S. 1977. *The Damned and the Beautiful: American Youth in the 1920s.* New York: Oxford University Press.

Feldman, Edmund B. 1995. *The Artist: A Social History.* 2nd ed. Englewood Cliffs, N.J.: Prentice Hall.

Felsen, Henry Gregor. 1950. *Hot Rod.* New York: E. P. Dutton.

Fetherston, David. 1992. *Heroes of Hot Rodding.* Osceola, Wisc.: Motorbooks International.

———. 1995. "Barris Kustoms of the '50s." *Rod & Custom* (April): 49–55.

Fish, Stanley. 1993. "The Unbearable Ugliness of Volvos." In Susan Gubar and Jonathan Kamholtz, eds., *English Inside and Out: The Places of Literary Criticism.* New York: Routledge.

Fiske, John. 1989a. *Reading the Popular.* Boston: Unwin Hyman.

———. 1989b. *Understanding Popular Culture.* Boston: Unwin Hyman.

Flink, James J. 1990. *The Automobile Age.* Cambridge, Mass.: MIT Press.

Foose, Sam. 2000. Interview with the author.

Fuller, R. Buckminster. 1963. *Nine Chains to the Moon.* Carbondale: Southern Illinois University Press.

Ganahl, Pat. 1977. "Mild Customs." *Street Rodder* (August): 6–7.

———. 1988. "Upfront." *Rod & Custom* (December): 4.

———. 1989. "The Bertolucci Story." *Rod & Custom* (October): 67–71.

———. 1993. "Direct Descent: Von Dutch to Robert Williams." In *Kustom Kulture.* Laguna, Calif.: Laguna Art Museum, 8–9.

———. 1995. "The Candy Man: The Life and Times of Customizer Joe Bailon." *Rod & Custom* (July): 81–88.

———. 1995b. *Hot Rods and Cool Customs.* New York: Artabras.

———. 1996. "The California Hot Rod." In Dobrin and Linhares (1996): 20–25.

———. 1998. "The Emergence of the Hot Rod." *Hot Rod* (January): 130–35.

———. 1999. "The Illustrated History of the Custom Car, Part One: The Early Years." *Rodder's Journal* 12 (fall): 98–112.

———. 2000. "The Illustrated History of the Custom Car, Part Two: The Later Years, the Chopped Merc Era." *Rodder's Journal* 13 (spring): 58–73.

Glassie, Henry. 1982. "Folk Art." In Thomas J. Schlerth, ed., *Material Culture Studies in America.* Nashville, Tenn.: American Association for State and Local History, 124–40.

———. 1999. *Material Culture.* Bloomington: Indiana University Press.

Gobetti, John. 2000. "Lowdown." *Goodguys Goodtimes Gazette* (August): 4.

Goodman, Paul. 1960. *Growing Up Absurd.* New York: Random House.

Gribin, Anthony J., and Matthew M. Schiff. 1992. *Doo-Wop: The Forgotten Third of Rock 'n' Roll.* Iola, Wisc.: Krause Publications.

Halberstam, David. 1993. *The Fifties.* New York: Villard Books.

Hahn, Craig. 1999. Interview with the author.

Hebdige, Dick. 1979. *Subculture: The Meaning of Style.* London: Methuen.

Himes, Joseph S. 1961. "Negro Teen-Age Culture." *Annals of the American Academy of Politics and Social Science* (November): 91–101.

Hine, Thomas. 1999a. "The Rise and Decline of the Teenager." *American Heritage* (September): 70–82.

———. 1999b. "Teen Century." *Inquirer Magazine,* August 22: 24–27, 30–32.

———. 1999c. "Foreword." *Populuxe.* New York: MJF Books. Original publication in 1986.

Hinton, S. E. 1967. *The Outsiders.* New York: Dell Publishing.

Hirth, Bill. 1999. Interview with the author.

Jackson, John Brinckerhoff. 1994. *A Sense of Time, A Sense of Place.* New Haven, Conn.: Yale University Press.

Jeffries, Dean. 1998. Interview with the author.

Jencks, Charles. 1992. "The Postmodern Agenda." In Charles Jencks, ed., *The Post-Modern Reader.* New York: St. Martin's Press.

Jones, Michael Owen. 1997. "Art, Folk." In Thomas A. Green, ed., *Folklore: An Encyclopedia of Beliefs, Customs, Tales, Music, and Art.* Vol. I. Santa Barbara, Calif.: ABC-CLIO, 56–61.

Kannapell, Andrea. 1999. "Car Artists Make Every Trip a Traveling Show." *New York Times,* October 20: 18.

Kaplan, Abraham. 1967. "The Aesthetics of the Popular Arts." In Deer and Deer, eds., *The Popular Arts: A Critical Reader.* New York: Charles Scribner's Sons, 314–43.

Kellner, Douglas. 1995. *Media Culture: Cultural Studies, Identity and Politics between the Modern and the Postmodern.* New York and London: Routledge.

Kett, Joseph F. 1977. *Rites of Passage: Adolescence in America, 1790 to the Present.* New York: Basic Books.

Key, Mike, and Tony Thacker. 1990. *Dream Cars of the Fifties: The Chrome, the Culture, the Charisma.* Secaucus, N.J.: Chartwell Books.

Kouwenhoven, John A. 1948. *The Arts in Modern American Civilization.* New York: W. W. Norton.

Kramer, Temma. 1993. "Rites of Passage—Customized." In *Kustom Kulture.* Laguna: Laguna Art Museum, 44–45.

Léger, Fernand. 1924. "The Aesthetic of the Machine." In Chipp (1968): 277–79.

Lerner, Preston. 1993. "Rebels with a Checkbook." *New York Times Magazine,* May 30: 20–23.

Lewis, David L., and Laurence Goldstein, eds. 1983. *The Automobile and American Culture.* Ann Arbor: University of Michigan Press.

Lingeman, Richard R. 1973. "There Was Another Fifties." *New York Times Magazine,* June 17: 26–32, 39–40.

Lipsitz, George. 1990. *Time Passages: Collective Memory and American Popular Culture.* Minneapolis: University of Minnesota Press.

Lowenthal, David. 1985. *The Past Is a Foreign Country.* Cambridge: Cambridge University Press.

Macdonald, Dwight. 1953. "A Theory of Mass Culture." In Rosenberg and White (1957): 59–73.

McLuhan, Marshall. 1964. *Understanding Media: The Extensions of Man.* New York: McGraw Hill.

McNiel, Jim. 2000. Interview with the author.

McShane, Frank. 1994. Interview with the author.

Majors, Richard, Richard Tyler, Blaine Pedan, and Ron Hall. 1994. "Cool Pose: A Symbolic Mechanism for Masculine Role Enactment and Coping by Black Males." In Richard G. Majors and Jacob U. Gordon, eds., *The American Black Male.* Chicago: Nelson-Hall Publishers, 245–59.

Margolis, Joseph. 1960. "Juvenile Delinquents: The Latter-Day Knights." *American Scholar* (spring): 211–19.

Marinetti, F. T. 1909. "The Foundation and Manifesto of Futurism." In Chipp (1968): 284–89.

Matza, David. 1961. "Subterranean Traditions of Youth." *Annals of the American Academy of Politics and Social Science* (November): 102–18.

May, Rollo. 1973. *The Courage to Create.* New York: Bantam Books.

Medley, Tom. 1990. *Tex Smith's Hot Rod History. Book One: The Beginnings.* Osceola, Wisc.: Motorbooks International.

Metcalf, Eugene, Jr., and Claudine Weatherford. 1988. "Modernism, Edith Halpert, Holger Cahill and the Fine Art Meaning of American Folk Art." In Jane S. Becker and Barabar Franco, eds., *Folk Roots, New Roots: Folklore in American Life.* Lexington, Ky.: Museum of Our National Heritage, 141–66.

Miller, Douglas T., and Marion Nowak. 1975. *The Fifties: The Way We Really Were.* Garden City, NY: Doubleday.

Mondrian, Piet. 1943. "Statement." In Chipp (1968): 362–64.

Montgomery, Don. 1987. *Hot Rods of the Forties.* Fallbrook, Calif.: self-published.

Motherwell, Robert. 1951. "What Art Means to Me: A Symposium." In Chipp (1968): 556–64.

Nye, David E. 1994. *American Technological Sublime.* Cambridge, Mass.: MIT Press.

Nye, Russel. 1970. "The Popular Arts and the Popular Audience." In William Hammel (1977), *The Popular Arts in America*. 2nd ed. New York: Harcourt Brace Jovanovich.

Palladino, Grace. 1996. *Teenagers: An American History*. New York: Basic Books.

Peckham, Morse. 1965. *Man's Rage for Chaos: Biology, Behavior and the Arts*. New York: Schocken Books.

Pecorelli, John. 1999. "Social Distortion's Mike Ness." *Hot Rod Deluxe* 1: 46–51.

———, and Christine Ryan. 1999. "The Wrong Side of the Road." *Hot Rod Deluxe* 1: 5.

Perloff, Marjorie. 1986. *The Futurist Moment: Avant-Garde, Avant-Guerre, and the Language of Rupture*. Chicago: University of Chicago Press.

Post, Robert C. 1994. *High Performance: The Culture and Technology of Drag Racing 1950–1990*. Baltimore: Johns Hopkins University Press.

Pound, Ezra. 1929. "How to Read." In *Literary Essays of Ezra Pound*. rpt. 1968. New York: New Directions.

Rae, John B. 1965. *The American Automobile: A Brief History*. Chicago: University of Chicago Press.

Reiss, Ira L. 1961. "Sexual Codes in Teen-Age Culture." *Annals of the American Academy of Politics and Social Science* (November): 53–62.

Remus, Timothy. 1990. *Custom Cars and Lead Sleds*. Osceoloa, Wisc.: Motorbooks International.

Rice, Anne. 1985. *The Vampire Lestat*. New York: Alfred Knopff.

Riesman, David. 1956. "The Found Generation." *American Scholar* (autumn): 421–36.

Robert, Henry Flood, Jr. 1984a. "Go or Show." In Silk (1984): 179–80.

———. 1984b. "In Pursuit of Speed." In Silk (1984): 181–88.

———. 1984c. "Customs:Wild or Mild." In Silk (1984): 189–99.

Rosenberg, Bernard, and David Mannng White. 1957. *Mass Culture: The Popular Arts in America*. New York: Free Press.

Rubin, William S. 1968. *Dada, Surrealism, and Their Heritage*. New York: Museum of Modern Art.

Russolo, Luigi. 1913. "The Art of Noises." In Apollonio (1970): 74–88.

Sales, Grover. 1992. *Jazz: America's Classical Music*. New York: DaCapo Press.

Salisbury, Harrison. 1958. *The Shook-Up Generation*. New York: Fawcett World Library.

Satin, Joesph, ed. 1960. *The 1950s: America's Placid Decade*. Boston: Houghton Mifflin.

Schwitters, Kurt. 1921. "from Merz." In Chipp (1968): 382–84.

Seitz, William C. 1961. *The Art of Assemblage*. New York: Museum of Modern Art.

Sharp, Greg. 1977. "Kustom Is Spelled with a 'K.'" *Street Rodder* (August): 48–52.

Silk, Gerald. 1984. "Proliferation and Assimilation." In Gerald Silk, ed., *Automobiles and Culture*. New York: Henry Abrams, 57–95.

Soff, Ray. 1997. Interview with the author.

Southard, Andy, and Tony Thacker. 1993. *Custom Cars of the 1950's*. Osceola, Wisc.: Motorbooks International.

Stecyk, C. R. 1993. "Origins of a Sub-Species." In *Kustom Kulture*. Laguna, Calif.: Laguna Art Museum, 10–43.

Taylor, Thom. 1996. "Watson: The Crazy Paint King." *Rod & Custom* (June): 32–42.

———. 2000. Interview with the author.

van den Haag, Ernest. 1957. "Of Happiness and of Despair We Have No Measure." In Rosenberg and White (1957): 504–36

Van Laar, Timothy, and Leonard Diepeveen. 1998. *Active Sights: Art as Social Interaction*. Mountain View, Calif.: Mayfield Publishing Co.

Venturi, Robert et al. 1977. rev. ed. *Learning from Las Vegas*. Cambridge, Mass.: MIT Press.

Watson, Larry. 1998. Interview with the author.

Weschler, Lawrence. 1982. *Seeing Is Forgetting the Name of the Thing One Sees: A Life of Contemporary Artist Robert Irwin*. Berkeley and Los Angeles: University of California Press.

Whitford, Frank. 1984. *Bauhaus*. London: Thames and Hudson.

Williams, Raymond. 1988. *Culture*. London: Fontana.

Williams, William Carlos. 1986. *The Collected Poems of William Carlos Williams*. Vol. 1. New York: New Directions.

Wilson, Richard Guy, ed. 1986. *The Machine Age in America: 1918–1941*. New York: Harry N. Abrams.

Winfield, Gene. 1998. Interview with the author.

Witzel, Michael Karl, and Kent Bash. 1997. *Cruisin': Car Culture in America*. Osceola, Wisc.: Motorbooks International.

Wolfe, Tom. 1963. *The Kandy*Kolored*Tangerine*Flake Streamline Baby*. New York: Farrar, Straus and Giroux.

Wolkomir, Richard. 1993. "Big Boys, Big Toys and the Perfect Hot Rod." *Smithsonian* 4: 50–58.

Woodham, Jonathan M. 1997. *Twentieth-Century Design*. New York: Oxford University Press.

Zocchi, Richard. 2000. Interview with the author.

INDEX

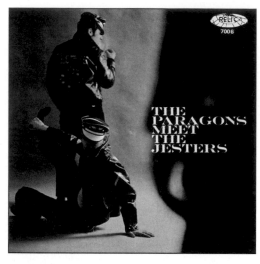

Plate 1.
Album cover. *The Paragons Meet the Jesters.*

Plate 2.
DeBore Pontiac. One of Larry Watson's most complex panel paint jobs. Courtesy of Jim Potter Collection.

Plate 3.
Kandy Kane. Painted by Larry Watson for D. A.
McCutcheon about 1960. Courtesy of Larry Watson.

Plate 4.
Futurist painting. *The Dynamism of an Automobile* by Luigi Russolo in 1911. Bears a striking resemblance to some graphics on contemporary customs. Musee National d'Art Moderne, Centre de Pompidou, Paris.

Plate 5.

Hirohata Merc. Restored by Jim McNiel to its original
condition. The original colors were recreated by PPG
after an incredibly thorough investigation. In a won-
derful conclusion to the story, the new paint was applied by "Junior" Conway, the man who had originally
sprayed the car at the Barris shop in 1952. Courtesy of
Susan McNiel.

Plate 6.
Hirohata Merc. Side view. Courtesy of Susan McNiel.

Plate 7.
Hirohata Merc. Detail of the rear fender scoops and side trim. Barris added grille teeth from a 1952 Chevy to emphasize the scoop. But it is the rhyming of the curves of side trim and scoop (as well as rear window and roof line, which can't be seen here) that makes this design element work so well. Courtesy of Susan McNiel.

Plate 8.
Le Suze. Pablo Picasso, *Glass and Bottle of Suze,*
1912. Pasted papers, gouache, and charcoal, 25 3/4
x 19 3/4 inches. Washington University Gallery of
Art, St. Louis. University Purchase, Kende Sale Fund,
1946. © 2001 Estate of Pablo Picasso/Artists Rights
Society (ARS), New York.

Plate 9.
Larry Ernst Chevy. This is a picture of the second version of the Chevy. The major difference is color. The original was painted in two-tone purple and orchid. Photo by George Barris.

Plate 10.
Grabowski T-Bucket. Shown almost weekly on "77 Sunset Strip," Grabowski's car signaled a new direction in rodding. The uniquely configured body, the big Caddy engine, the shortened bed, and the upright driving position resulted in a whole new type of hot rod which still produces hundreds of imitations.

Plate 11.
Ala Kart. Built by George Barris this Ford Model A truck also marked a new direction—customizing cars that had been previously only rodded. The truck also led the shift away from the collage styles of the early fifties toward more sculptural treatments. Photo by George Barris.

Plate 12.
Stock '57 Dodge fins.

Plate 13.
Winfield Chevy. Lanny Erickson's 1956 Chevy named the "Violet Fantasy," was built by Gene Winfield in 1957–1958 and featured a four-inch chopped top, '57 Chevy front bumper, a '57 Chevy grille bar with '54 Chevy teeth, DeSoto side trim, lakes pipes, a signature Winfield violet fade paint job, an even lowered stance without skirts, reversed wheels with bullets (note the upholstered wheel wells), and Lincoln taillights. Very much a West Coast custom of the mid to late fifties that maintains strong connections to the earlier collage style. Courtesy of Gene Winfield.

Plate 14.
East Coast style. A 1956 Chevy with the same basic modifications as Winfield's, but the paint is a conventional two-tone and the car is lowered more in the rear than in the front. The car also has modified Dodge Lancer hubcaps in the front and bubble skirts in the rear, and there is the almost obligatory continental kit mounted on the back, just the way it was done in the East.

Plate 15.
Custom reversed wheel.

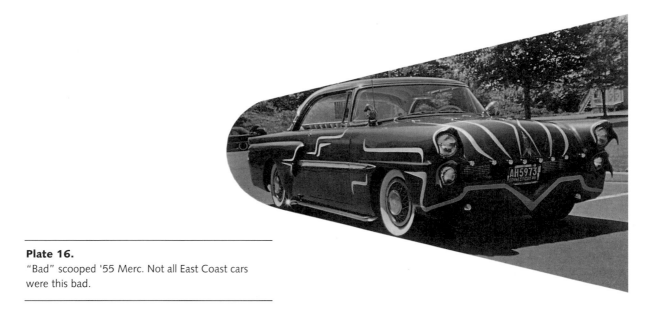

Plate 16.
"Bad" scooped '55 Merc. Not all East Coast cars
were this bad.

Plate 17.
Modern Grecian. A 1948 Studebaker built by George
Barris in 1960–1961. It was featured on the cover of
a number of books and magazines. It is a reworking
of a simpler car, the Grecian. Photo by George Barris.

Plate 18.
Wild interiors. This 1961 cover of *Car Craft* reveals just how bizarre custom interiors became in the late fifties and early sixties, especially in show cars. This is one aspect of the original Kustom Kulture that hasn't been revived. Today's customs favor tweed and/or leather or classic rolled and pleated naugahyde. Courtesy of Petersen Publishing.

Plate 19.
Dutched Hirohata dash. Courtesy of Susan McNiel.

Plate 20.
Dutched flamed Mercedes. Courtesy of Jim Potter
Collection.

Plate 21.
Seaweed flames. Jack James's Buick is in the foreground in a grouping of Watson-painted cars. This breakthrough paint job changed not only the way that flames were painted, but also how the surface of the car was thought about in terms of paint. Courtesy of Jim Potter Collection.

Plate 22.

Grapevine. The price that Watson paid for getting his car so close to the ground was considerable. In a very short time he received hundreds of citations for violating the minimum height laws in California. It reached the point where his license was "revoked for life," and he had to petition the state to get the license so that he could work. This photo was taken by Lowell Helms. Courtesy of Larry Watson.

Plate 23.

Scalloped Grapevine. Watson added particularly elegant scallops on the final version of the Grapevine, more flowing and organic than many of his scallop jobs which were often geometric and confined to hood and front fenders as in the cars next to the Jack James Buick in plate 21. The original Gravevine was destroyed after being sold several times. But its memory has resulted in a number of clones, near clones, and dozens of Grapevine-influenced Chevies. Courtesy of Jim Potter Collection.

Plate 24.
Paneled '58 T-Bird. Another innovation from Watson. The fairly simple technique of outlining body lines in contrasting colors eventually led to exuberant experiments with multileveled bandings of contrasting colors that created the illusion of contours in the body. Courtesy of Larry Watson.

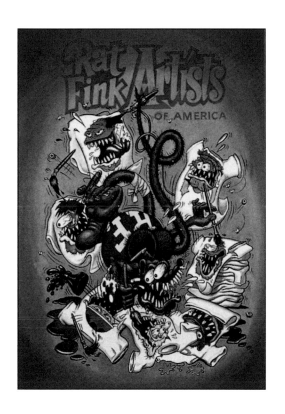

Plate 25.
Roth Trading Cards. Roth's famous figure of the Rat Fink has become a Kustom Kulture icon. His "hot rod art" began a new genre that has been extended by painters like Robert Williams and Coop. Courtesy of Ed Roth. © Ed Roth 1999.

Plate 26.

Blue Collar Bravado. Painting by Robert Williams, one of the most successful and admired artists who have emerged from Kustom Kulture. His work often explores the mythic world behind the Kustom Kulture. His shows sell out years in advance. Courtesy of Robert Williams, fine arts artist.

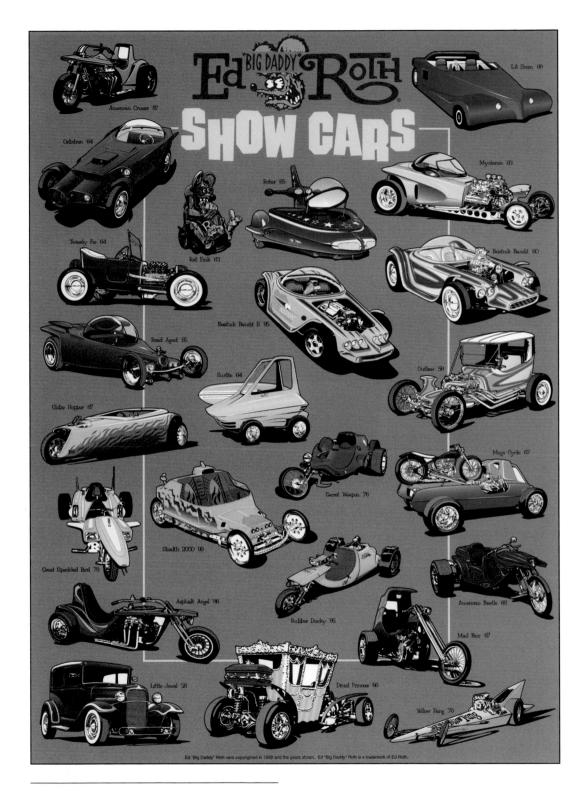

Plate 27.
Roth show cars (poster). Roth was prolific. His cars range from the clearly Kustom Kulture "Outlaw," "Little Jewel," and "Tweedy Pie" to the futuristic "Rotar," "Mysterion," and "Orbitron." Courtesy of Ed Roth. © Ed Roth 1999.

Plate 28.
Scoopy (3/4 rear). Despite all of the excess in this car—the scoops, the pipes, and the bars—somehow it does pull together the way that complicated style cars do not. Courtesy of the *Rodder's Journal*.

PICKS UP SPEED ON 30% GRADES. The Big M took the steepest, roughest grades in Colorado with no strain, no hesitation.

We took THE BIG M up the steepest mountains
...so you can sail up any hill with ease

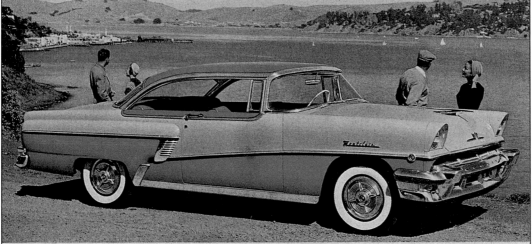

NEW SAFETY-SURGE V-8 ENGINE. Gives you the thrill, ease, and safety of the highest horsepower, compression, and torque in Mercury history.

We went all out to pre-prove The Big M. We proved it on the toughest mountains in America. Again and again these cars were put to power-killing grades, up to altitudes of 9,000 feet or more. And always there was power to spare.

This is power you can *use*. It's *Reflex-action* power, quick as an athlete's reflexes in response to your every command, to every demand of the road.

We made similar exhaustive tests to prove every one of Mercury's *dividend features*. From the road-hugging steadiness of ball-joint front suspension to the extra security of our new impact-absorbing safety steering wheel. (Both are Mercury exclusives in its field.)

So make your own test—your own comparison. Get an eyeful of that young-minded *Big M beauty*. Get the facts-and-figures story of the Big M's *provable value*—at your Mercury dealer's showroom today.

MERCURY DIVISION · FORD MOTOR COMPANY

For 1956 — the big move is to
THE BIG MERCURY
A MAGNIFICENT VALUE IN THE FORD FAMILY OF FINE CARS

Plate 29.
1956 Mercury ad. Despite the claims of performance, the appeal of this car is solidly middle class as the ad shows. This is not a factory hot rod.

Plate 30.

The Jade Idol. Built by Gene Winfield for Le Roy Kemmerer in 1960. The first article about it compared it to designs by Pininfarina. Courtesy of Gene Winfield.

Plate 31.

Predicta. Based on a 1956 Thunderbird wreck (very little was left) this product of Darryl Starbird's imagination debuted in 1960 and won the Oakland Roadster Show "Car of the Future" award. It's hard to find the original T-Bird under the four-inch channel job, the bubble top, the fusion of space ship/bedroom in its cockpit complete with a television, headrests, and "stick" steering. Courtesy of Petersen Publishing.

Plate 32.
Mossimo ad. Courtesy of Mossimo.

Plate 33.
Rick Dore's Tangerine Dream. Courtesy of Rick Dore, designer-builder.

Plate 34.
Richard Zocchi's 1939 Dodge (front). Courtesy of
Rich and Cherie Zocchi.

Plate 35.
Zocchi's 1939 Dodge (rear). Courtesy of Rich and
Cherie Zocchi.

Plate 36.
Richard Zocchi's 1957 Dodge. Courtesy of Rich and
Cherie Zocchi.

Plate 37.
Richard Zocchi's 1956 Dodge. Courtesy of Rich and
Cherie Zocchi.

Plate 38.
Frankenstude. Designed by Thom Taylor. Courtesy of
Thom Taylor Collection.

Plate 39.

Restored Karcher Ford. Restored by Ray Soff. Like many restorers, he had to decide which version of the car he wanted to bring back to life—the original one with bumpers, the Titian red version with molded front and rear ends, the green version, or the gold? There is no consensus as to what constitutes the true form of a custom.

Plate 40.
Matranga Merc clone. Owned by Bill Abate, a connoisseur of customs and custom history. One of a number of versions of this car that have been built in the last few years.

Plate 41.
Scrape. Built for Terry Cook, the promoter of Lead East, by Ramsey Mosher of Dover, Delaware. What makes this car so hyperreal is that it concentrates on lowering the roof line, lowering the stance, and smoothing surfaces like early Westergard designs, but it does so in such an exaggerated way that it goes beyond what seems even possible.

Plate 42.
Rick Dore's custom T-Bird. Courtesy of Rick Dore,
designer-builder.

Plate 43.
Posies's seemingly stock '51 Ford high school cruiser.

Plate 44.
Traditional flames on a 1950 Merc.

Plate 45.
Contemporary flames. The flames on this Merc change color at different angles because of a new technology that incorporates mica chips in the paint. This paint job also employs a variation of Jeffries's flames within flames. Appropriately named "Illusion" by its owner/builder Bob Duzak.

Plate 46.
Flamed fifties style rod. Built by Tom Otis, this highboy is a beautifully rendered mid-fifties rod. The wheels are right, the flames are right, the stance is right.

Plate 47.
Fat-fender monochrome Ford.

Plate 48.
Graphic. This is not a typical graphic which usually in-volves bold bands of color or murals of drive-ins, but I was struck by the wit of this one—playing a visual game with the customizers obsession with perfect surfaces—very postmodern.

Plate 49.
Watson 1959 Caddy. Courtesy of Jim Potter Collection.

Plate 50.
Majestic. Bill Reasoner did the bodywork for Dore
and the brilliant orange to pearl fade paint.

Plate 51.
Stock Continental MK II. Courtesy of Ford Motor Co.

Plate 52.
Rick Dore's Continental. Courtesy of Rick Dore,
designer-builder.

Plate 53.
California Kid. The real star of the 1974 movie of the same name which also starred Martin Sheen. Built by Peter Chapouris at the nadir of interest in traditional rodding. It helped spawn the revival as well as hundreds of imitators. Courtesy of Tony Thacker Collection.

Plate 54.
Vern Luce coupe. Courtesy of Thom Taylor Collection.

Plate 55.
Flamed Boyd coupe.

Plate 56.
CheZoom. Courtesy of Thom Taylor Collection.

Plate 57.
CadZZilla. Courtesy of Tony Thacker Collection.

Plate 58.
CadZZilla (detail). Picture gives some sense of how the paints react to light, shifting from black to purple. Courtesy of Tony Thacker Collection.

Plate 59.

Maybellene. A 1961 Coupe De Ville built in 1999 by
Gene Winfield. Like many contemporary customs,
what looks stock turns out not to be so. The flat roof,
for example, is from a 1960 four-door hardtop resulting in something that appears, from a distance of
four decades, to be an original Cadillac model, but
not a Coupe DeVille. Subtle changes accumulate: the
upper fins were raised a mere inch, extended three-
fourths of an inch forward and about three inches
back to slightly alter the proportions. The list goes
on. It's fitting that one of the masters of the original
Kustom Kulture reaches the millennium at the top of
the curve. Courtesy of Gene Winfield.

Plate 60a.
Early fifties style. Owes much to the original chopped bathtub 1949 Merc built by Sam Barris in 1950.

Plate 60b.
Mid-fifties style. Incorporating newer parts, candy paints, and finer finish. Note rounded hood corners, tasteful hood scoops, and frenched parking lights.

Plate 60c.
Late fifties style. At this time cars often emphasized new painting techniques like scallops and panels over innovative bodywork. The modifications on this Merc are standard: chopped top, bar grille with '53 Chevy teeth, '54 Buick headlights. It is the paint that marks its era.

Plate 60d.
Early sixties style. Built in the early sixties by Barris, it is relatively conservative for that era, but, nevertheless reveals usual touches, particularly the completely molded front end.

Plate 60e.
1980s style. All-over monochromatic paint scheme, including bumpers, grille, and trim, with barely visible "ghost flames," marks this as an eighties styled car.

Plate 60f.
1990s style. This mixture of high-tech (smoothie) elements and traditional customizing techniques from various eras marks this as a contemporary custom.